Prize
Country
Quilts

Prize
Country
Quilts

DESIGNS ❧ PATTERNS ❧ PROJECTS

Mary Elizabeth Johnson

Oxmoor House, Inc.
BIRMINGHAM

ISBN: 0-8487-0444-4
Library of Congress Catalog Card Number: 76–40858
Printed in the United States of America
Copyright © 1977 by Oxmoor House, Inc.
P.O. Box 2463, Birmingham, Alabama 35202
All rights reserved
Third Printing, 1979

Oxmoor House, Inc., is the Book Division of
The Progressive Farmer Company:

Eugene Butler   *Chairman of the Board*
Emory Cunningham   *President and Publisher*
Vernon Owens, Jr.   *Senior Executive Vice President*
Roger McGuire   *Executive Vice President*

Conceived, edited and published by Oxmoor House, Inc.,
under the direction of:

John Logue   *Editor-in-Chief*
Mary Johnson   *Senior Editor, Crafts and Sewing*
Ann H. Harvey   *Managing Editor*
Robert L. Nance   *Production Manager*

Prize Country Quilts

Design: Robert L. Nance; Barbara Exum
Photography: Tim Olive, pp. ii, vi, ix, x, 7, 17, 48, 57, 64, 70;
      Steve Logan, pp. 12, 21, 73–87; Joe Wilkinson, p. 31;
      Glea Adams, p. 22
      Assistants: David Matthews; Chuck Pittman
Pattern illustrations: June Taylor Shrum
Technique illustrations: John Anderson; Mary Cobb Martin
Editorial Director, *Progressive Farmer*: C. G. Scruggs
Family Living Editor, *Progressive Farmer*: Felicia Butsch

Grateful acknowledgment is made by the author to the following people who
made invaluable contributions to this book:

Technical consultants: Mary Sherrill; Amy Laird; Margaret Whaley; Lu Cruce;
      Candace Franklin
Loan of Quilts: John Meigs, *Cigar Ribbon Quilt*; Nova Lee, *Memory Quilt*;
      Mrs. Jewell N. Shores, *George Washington's Cherry Tree*; Mrs. Stella Davis,
      The Courthouse Square; Mrs. A. S. Dorminy, *Kathy's Quilt*
Construction of projects: Margaret Richmond; Martha Roberts;
      Jane Joyner; Lynda Bagwell; Betty Moon; Jane May Battaglia
Locations: Dr. & Mrs. J. W. Johnson; Mr. & Mrs. J. J. Rutherford; Mr. A. DuPont;
      Karen Penick; The Great American Cover-Up, Dallas, Texas;
      Murrow Bros. Watkinsville Bonded Warehouse, Watkinsville, Georgia;
      Botanical Gardens, Birmingham, Alabama

Contents

Introduction

This is a very special quilt book. It comes from the hearts and minds of hundreds and hundreds of quilting enthusiasts. The people who entered *Progressive Farmer* magazine's "Joys of Country Living" Heritage Quilt Block Contest provided the essence and inspiration for this book of brand-new quilt designs. Each contestant submitted an original design, drawn from her personal heritage of country living. The contest created great joy for the editors, not only because so many people responded, but also because their original designs said so much about the stature of quilting as an art form today.

The objective of this book is to share with you the pleasure that all of us at *Progressive Farmer, Southern Living, Decorating & Craft Ideas,* and Oxmoor House experienced at seeing and working with the quilt blocks. All the entries were on display in The Progressive Farmer Company's headquarters building while the judging was taking place, and staff and visitors alike were fascinated by and delighted with the wealth of original talent represented in the quilt blocks. The photographers, artists, and seamstresses who later worked with the various projects in the book were, to a person, overwhelmed by the originality and striking beauty of the designs. Everybody had a favorite quilt block, and everybody's favorite was different! Surely, if these quilt blocks are not representative of the state of art and the pulse of the people at this time in our history, what is?

The most outstanding impression to be gained from seeing the field of entries is that there are many, many creative people involved with quilting, a means of expression that is equal in beauty and style to any other art form. The reason for this involvement is perhaps explained by the fact that fabric is the medium rather than brushes and paint. There is something comforting about working with fabric. We know it so well— what it will do, what it will not do. Even though there are occasional "mystery guests" in our scrap baskets, we still know the basic nature of the material—its flexibility and softness, its need to be treated gently, ironed carefully, and cut precisely so that the pieces fit together. Most of us began this intimate relationship with fabric in early childhood. Now when we turn to it as the medium we wish to use for creative expression, we find an old friend that best helps us interpret our personal visions of shape and color harmony.

The major portion of this book is devoted to a selection of the designs submitted to the contest. The most difficult decision we had to make was choosing which of the patterns would be included. We have selected a range of geometrics, florals, scenics, and abstracts with an eye to including those which may stimulate your own creativity. In addition, because the contest closely paralleled the time of this nation's Bicentennial, there were many patriotic designs. These personal tributes become a well-loved part of our folk heritage and, in addition to providing pleasure now, will someday become family heirlooms—and, who knows, maybe even prized museum pieces!

Some of the quilt blocks in this book will have a familiar look about them, although each of these patterns is original as far as we know and as far as the individual designer knows. This familiarity is to be expected; there are a limited number of shapes with which to work. Variety comes with the placement of these shapes within the block and the way the colors are arranged.

It occurred to the editors as we studied the entries that designing a quilt block is not so easy as it first appears. While we marveled at the overall success of the designs, we realized in some cases that if the contestant had only known to change one little thing, her quilt block could have been spectacular rather than good. So, we have included a brief chapter on how to design a quilt block. We hope that you will find it useful and stimulating, not only in choosing colors and fabrics for the designs we have included in the book, but for starting from scratch on your very own designs. Designing your own quilt is not difficult, but more than that, it is an extremely personal and rewarding experience.

We should also like to think that you will use your design knowledge and instinct to create quilted items other than bed coverings. If the quilt block *designs* are a reflection of the 20th century, so should be the *end uses* of the quilting. Take off from the ideas we've shown you in our photographs. Quilting is a contemporary craft and, to fit into our life-styles, should be mobile and quickly done. With proper planning, such as using an embroidery hoop and the apartment quilting technique, you can take it with you. Think of quilting in terms other than a months-long commitment to produce a lovely bedspread, although that is an admirable undertaking. Think in terms of "quickies": a pillow top, machine quilted; a banner using the trapunto technique; a spiffy work shirt featuring a patchwork block of a hundred pieces. (Well, if you make only one block, it can't be so bad!) Why not make your own luggage, satchels, or bags out of quilted corduroy or imitation leather? Use relief appliqué to construct a smashing design for the back and seat of a director's chair. A friend is making a quilted guitar "cozy" to protect the guitar from scratches and dust. Speaking of musical instruments, quilt a guitar or banjo strap for your favorite musician. If you can make a strap, you can also make a belt, suspenders, luggage rack strips, handles for bags, etc. Outline-quilt a favorite print fabric to add dimension and interest to upholstery or garments. Make your own quilted kitchen gift sets of mitts, potholders, and appliance covers. Quilt a bedside caddy for reading glasses and magazines.

So come with us now, and learn how to put together your very own quilt design, and share with us the lovely patterns for award-winning quilt blocks. Who knows, next time it could be *your* design that's featured in a book!

The peaceful reassurance of tradition is skillfully captured in this quilt block rendering of an old country church. The simplicity and purity of the design strike a responsive chord, for who among us has never seen this church? Pattern: Old Country Church.

Designing: Inspiration Plus Interpretation

An inner drive exists in most of us to somehow express our personal sense of beauty. Indeed, this compulsion is what led to the development of quilting as we know it today. Because the women who made the first quilt tops did not have time, in what was often a survival situation, to pursue purely aesthetic interests, they combined the joy of producing something beautiful with the practical task of making warm bed coverings. The result, executed in fabric, was some of the most stunning graphic designs in our folk heritage.

The desire of our foremothers to express themselves creatively is something we all share. The primary difference between them and us is the source of inspiration for a design. And the best source for anyone, no matter what her life-style, is what she sees every day and the feelings these daily observations create inside her. Therefore, not surprisingly, the early quilt designs reflect an influence not only of the hardships suffered in carving new communities out of an alien setting but also of the wondrous beauties of an unspoiled natural environment. Imagine the glories to be seen all across this country

before civilization and its attendant congestion altered the landscape! These influences are reflected in the names of the early quilt patterns as well as in their actual designs. Traditional patterns such as *Delectable Mountains, Milky Way,* and *Stars and Stirrups* (see page 2) reflect a way of looking at the world that was determined by the experiences of the individual designer.

Other sources of influence have been political and current events, religious beliefs, commercial products, a nostalgia for some time, place, or emotion, and superstition or folktales. A fascinating example of the influence of commercial products is the *Cigar Ribbon Quilt* on the adjoining page. This

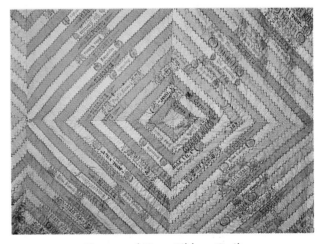

Closeup of Cigar Ribbon Quilt

A rare antique cigar ribbon quilt, one of the finest of the few in existence, is a unique example of how a common household item of the time, a silk cigar ribbon, inspired a work of beauty. From the collection of John Meigs.

Delectable
Mountains

Stars and Stirrups

Milky Way

quilt is made up of hundreds of ribbons at one time found in cigar boxes. Each ribbon was placed in a box underneath the cigars so that when the ends of the ribbon were grasped, all the cigars could be lifted from the box at once. The woman who made the quilt collected the ribbons, then sewed them together with a catchstitch (sometimes called a briar stitch). She carefully planned alternating light and dark bands and set them together in such a way as to produce converging squares. The closeup photograph (preceding page) shows some of the names printed on the ribbons as well as the stitch used to join the ribbons. (This quilt was loosely tufted, as it was probably intended more as a showpiece than as a utilitarian bed covering.)

What Are You Going to Quilt?

The best way to start a design is to determine exactly what item you want to make, whether bed cover, jacket, potholder, or pillow. Then plan your design to complement the shape and end use of the item. Obviously, a place mat will have a different shape entirely from that of a garment. The shape of the finished item gives you the total area within which you will be working. Since quilt block designs are usually based on a square (even a round design is placed on a background square) or sometimes on a rectangle, you will want to plan the size of the block to be easily repeated on the finished item. Consider at this time whether you will want to set the blocks next to one another or to separate them with strips of fabric, because these strips will take up much of the space needed for the project. (See pages 16–19 for more discussion of how to set the blocks together.)

Also, think of what happens when you quilt. By stitching through the layers that make up a quilt, you add softness, warmth, puffiness, and a dimension of highlights and shadows. Be aware of how these qualities will enhance the usefulness and the beauty of the finished piece. Additional warmth is welcomed not only in clothing and bedcovers, but also in "cozies," which are used to keep the contents of tea and coffee pots at the right serving temperature. Softness is desirable for anything a baby plays on or with—a quilted playpen pad, for example. Also, pillows, cushions, mats, and snuggly throws gain a luxurious extra softness when quilted. The puffiness that accompanies a quilted item is welcome when a fragile item must be protected; thus, a quilted jewelry roll makes good sense. Quilting also adds dimension: when used purely as a decorative device on the lapels and cuffs of a jacket, it creates a beautiful pattern that does not overwhelm the design of the garment.

In addition to considering the shape of the finished item and the qualities to be gained in quilting it, you should also think about how your finished project will be used. If the object is to be functional, rather than merely decorative, it should be planned to best fulfill its intended purpose. Consider the differences between a purse, which is functional, and a wall hanging, which is decorative. The purse will need a durable fabric and colors that do not easily show soiled areas. The stitching will need to be close and strong. A wall hanging, however, will not carry a burden of hard wear, so the fabric and construction of such a piece can be more fragile.

When planning any quilted project consider the following guidelines:

- ➤ Relate the size of the design to the size of the finished item. A large coverlet may utilize large, bold design that would be inappropriate for a small, delicate pocket on a garment.
- ➤ Consider the qualities of warmth, softness, puffiness, and dimension that will result from your quilting and how these can be used to strengthen the purpose of your project.
- ➤ Some items will receive more wear than others and will therefore require stronger fabrics and construction. Consider carefully the fiber content of the fabrics you choose, particularly if the item is to be laundered often or will receive rough treatment.

Choosing a Theme and a Preliminary Design

Choosing a subject for your design is an important decision. You alone know the things which have a special meaning for you. If you find it hard to get started, look around at your world. What do you see every day that has become a part of you? Do you have a special hobby that intrigues you—bird-watching, sports, collecting something? Consider interpreting your surroundings as a city or country dweller or what you remember about growing up. Examine those doodles you make as you talk on the telephone; they could be the beginning of a fantastic design.

Nature provides us with a world of intrigue, beauty, and inspiration. Consider the earth in its different seasons. Have you noticed the yellow-green of April as compared to the dark green of September, or that weeds provide us with some of the prettiest of flowers? Study the plants that grow in your home or yard. Look at the beautiful curves of sand dunes on the desert or beach.

There is also a wealth of animal life to portray. Animals of the jungle or farm or a favorite pet are interesting subjects for a quilt design.

Do not overlook special events and/or dates that could be recorded in a quilt. The lovely album and heritage quilts that have become a part of the historical records of this country illustrate events and dates that made an impact on the designers. A birthday of a family member or a friend or of a nation, as happened in 1976, can inspire lovely commemorative quilt designs. Or, you may want to make a statement about your views on our national elections, political parties, current social or political issues, or national leaders.

The important thing is to look about you with hungry eyes. Open yourself up to the design inspiration all around you. Take a fresh look at things that are a part of your life.

A very perceptive grandmother created a very special heirloom in *Kathy's Quilt* on page vi. The grandmother saved her granddaughter's earliest drawings and writings and later rendered each one with fabric and thread, making enough individual blocks for a whole quilt. After putting the blocks together to make the quilt top, she added a puffy filler and a lovely red gingham backing, creating a priceless work of love that her grandchild will treasure forever and will most likely hand down to future generations.

Because subject matter is a springboard for design ideas, it is important to remember that your designs will be more compelling and have more meaning if they have involved you personally through observation, knowledge, or experience. (A spectacular example is the lovely *Memory Quilt* on page 21.) Be honest with yourself as you choose your subject and the manner in which you will depict it. Try not to use photographs or paintings done by someone else. Make your heirloom design a part of your own observation and life. Even if the design is less than perfect according to art school standards, its value will still be greater as an original design than as a copy of something . That is why we have not given patterns for some of the quilt blocks based on very personal recollections; you should make up your own designs from your own memories.

Sometimes more than one look is needed to capture the essence of what is before you. Here is what the designer of the first prize winner in the *Progressive Farmer* Heritage Quilt Block Contest has to say about one aspect of her design:

> Since Cheaha Mountain was in the background of the land where I was raised and lived until I married, I had to have mountains in my quilt block and I colored them purple. Recently we drove from Anniston to Lineville over the Cheaha Mountain range and to my surprise the mountains were a dark blue, so I had to go home and change the color in my pattern.

Rural Background

Once you have chosen your subject matter, the next step is to get a preliminary design. If you are working directly from a design source, rather than from memory, try one of the following methods.

VIEWFINDER METHOD: Use a sheet of paper or cardboard which has approximately the same proportions as you plan for your quilt block. Cut out the center section of the paper or cardboard, leaving a frame of 1" to 1½" (2.5 cm to 3.8 cm) all around. Hold this frame away from you, and look at your subject through the center hole to "compose" your design. By changing the distance from your eye, you can change the area of view available in the viewfinder. The farther away you hold it, the smaller the field of vision contained in the viewfinder becomes. This helps to get extraneous objects visually out of range so that you may compose more easily. Move the viewfinder around until you find a grouping that pleases you. Remember that you are the artist and can change, rearrange, add to, or leave out segments of the subject on your design. Make a rough sketch of your viewfinder selection, including as much detail as you wish at this stage.

PROJECTION METHOD: This method requires either a slide projector or an opaque projector, and it is an extremely accurate way to work. Take a photograph of your chosen subject, and project it on a hard surface. Select the portion you wish to use as your design; then place paper on the surface where the slide is projected, and outline the desired design. Move the projector closer to the surface to reduce the size of the design, farther away to enlarge it.

DIRECT METHOD: If you are lucky enough to have some skill at drawing or sketching, you can copy the source of your design directly; then work from your sketch to come up with your final design. It is a good idea to use paper of the same proportions as the quilt block so the design will correctly fit the allotted space.

CONSTRUCTION PAPER METHOD: If you plan to work with geometric shapes, use construction paper cut-outs in the desired shapes, assigning a different color to each shape. This will help you visualize an effective arrangement.

If you are working from memory, or if you are trying to capture an event or time, start by making a sketch of something that is most representative of what you want to portray. Let your imagination and creative juices run wild at this stage, and put in as much as you can think of. Research the subject, if possible, to get additional ideas.

Refining Your Design

Having chosen your subject matter and made a preliminary design, you must now decide how to render it for a final design. This step generally involves simplifying the subject matter to the essentials that make it beautiful and meaningful. There are two different and equally valid methods to use in this simplifying: one is to interpret the design realistically, and the other is to portray it in abstract terms. If you are new at designing, you will probably find that your first inclination is to try to render your design as nearly like the original source as possible. Sometimes, however, you will see that the statement you wish to make becomes stronger if you choose an abstract interpretation.

In a realistic interpretation, the design appears very much as the actual subject appears. You might change the colors or somewhat alter the shapes, but the subject is still easily recognizable to others. A realistic translation is especially good if you have a cherished memory or scene that you wish to permanently capture for others to enjoy. *Our Heritage, The Church* (see right) eloquently pictures a memory and requires no further explanation from the designer.

Another instance when realistic interpretation works well is when the source of the design is so breathtakingly beautiful that we long to reproduce it exactly to preserve it for future enjoyment. An example of this is the design of *Southern Dogwood*, shown on page 7 in its white version and on the frontispiece in pink. The designer went so far as to make the petals three-dimensional so that they would curve upward on the ends like real dogwood blossoms.

An abstract interpretation of a design source reduces the source to the basic geometric shapes which make up the design. These geometric shapes can be arranged realistically as in *Proud Pine* (see right), or they can be used to convey a feeling, as in *Old Rail Fence* (see right). An important point to consider is that both of these designs work because the shapes effectively tell the story of the original source. Many of our treasured traditional patterns are abstracts.

No matter which interpretation you use, remember that most designs for quilting should be fairly simple—especially if you plan to repeat the basic design many times on your project. Therefore, look for the simplest shapes in your preliminary sketch. Disregard small, unnecessary details for the present. Simplify all the objects to their purest shapes. If your subject is too busy, consider doing only a small part of it.

Our Heritage, The Church

Proud Pine

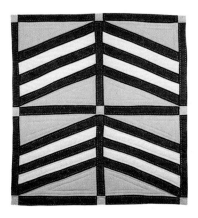

Old Rail Fence

A good example of simplifying a subject to create a more interesting design is *Peach Tree*. In illustration A, a large portion of a peach tree is shown. In illustration B, we have simplified the design by taking a close-up of a single peach and a few leaves. The design is bolder, better arranged, and would be easier to construct in fabric.

Additionally, a point of interest has been created. A point of interest is that spot in a design which captures the eye immediately. Although it may be created in one of several ways, all designs should have this focal point. In the case of the peach tree design, it is the round shape of the peach, along with the fact that it is set near the center of the design, which creates the point of interest. Another way to create a center of interest is to make the shape you wish to emphasize a light color and place it on a dark background, or put a dark shape on a light background. Another way is to make the point of interest a different size from anything else in the design. A point of interest also can be strengthened by using detailing, especially on a plain background. *Jack-in-the-Pulpit* (see page 9) is an example of this last principle: the lavish stitching on the flower helps direct attention to the center of interest, which is the pink inside the blossom.

A

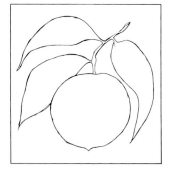

B

Adding Color

Up to this point, we have been primarily concerned with the shapes and spaces within your design. Now is the time to begin to think of the colors you want to use to carry out the theme you have established.

You have learned that you may interpret the shapes in your design in either a realistic or an abstract manner. The same is true of the colors you choose. If you are working with a scenic design, such as a landscape, building, or garden, you may want to keep your colors realistic, as you did your shapes. However, a lovely fantasy feeling can be obtained by using colors other than those found in nature even when you have realistic shapes.

By the same token, if you have come up with an abstract design, you can select a color scheme based either on the colors which were in the basic inspiration for the design, or you can let your imagination lead you to totally fanciful color arrangements. Of course, you might want your color scheme to match or complement a specific room setting, garment, or dinnerware.

The important thing about the colors you choose is that they should make you feel good when you look at them and they should work together to produce a pleasing design. We are not going to try to give you a lot of color theory because you are probably not in a position to mix the exact color fabric dye you want—your colors are determined by the colors of the fabrics available to you. However, here are some basic pointers on the qualities of color which may make the selection for your design easier.

Colors differ in visibility and "attention getting ability." Yellow is the brightest color and can be more sharply focused than any other color. Red-orange is first in getting attention. Reds, oranges, and yellow-greens are all outstanding colors with high visibility.

Colors can also make a shape appear larger or smaller, nearer or farther away. Light or pale colors

Glistening white juxtaposed against a dark background in this quilt block effectively recalls the dogwood in early spring. Realistic details abound from the turned-up petals to the embroidered dark spots on the tips of the petals. Design: Southern Dogwood.

tend to make a shape look larger, especially when placed on a darker background. Darker colors give the general impression of making an area smaller. *Warm colors*—red, yellow, orange, yellow-green—seem to advance. *Cool colors*—greens, blues, violets—seem to recede. These are principles that we have all been aware of in choosing our clothing, particularly when we wanted to increase or decrease our apparent size.

Color also has the quality of creating a very definite mood. Warm colors generally give a bright, sunny, active impression. Cool colors lead to a relaxed, peaceful feeling. In addition, there are traditional qualities linked with color which form very powerful associations in our minds. For example, dark, rich colors tend to make us think of fall and winter; yellows, pinks, and other light, bright colors are associated with spring and summer. Black is associated with sophistication and/or somberness, red with fun and/or danger, yellow with sunniness and/or cowardice, purple with royalty, pink with baby girls, blue with baby boys. Dull, faded colors give an impression of age, while bright, vibrant colors seem new and contemporary and are perfect for many modern room settings. These psychological associations can be important when you want to make a special statement, especially of a rather abstract idea.

Color harmony is perhaps the most important thing you need to consider in your quilt design. The colors you choose must work well with one another in order for the total effect to be pleasing. A safe rule to follow in planning your colors is that one color should be dominant, while other colors should harmonize with and accent that color. In some cases, your major color will be only slightly stronger than the other colors, but the overall effect should be one of harmony. Be careful, though, to work variety into your color plan. A design with all pale colors can easily appear washed out, and one with all dark colors can appear dull.

There are traditional color combinations, or schemes, as they are often called, which have proven through time to be harmonious. In order to explain these combinations, we have included a diagram of a color wheel which shows you how colors are positioned in *relation to one another**. (Color schemes can be explained only in terms of how the colors relate to one another on the color wheel.)

A complementary color scheme is one which uses colors opposite one another on the color wheel.

---

* To obtain a free color wheel chart with 12 colors and a diagrammed explanation of color theory write to The American Crayon Company, Sandusky, Ohio 44870

Diagram of a color wheel

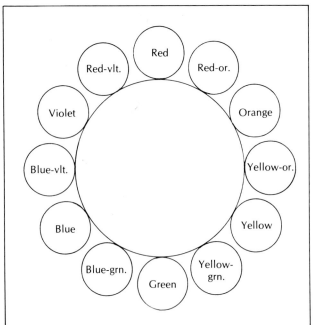

Complementary color scheme

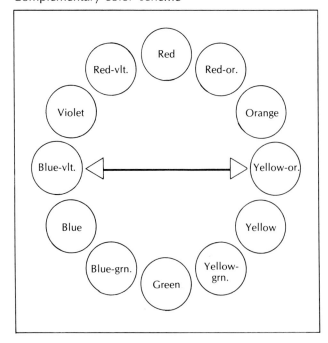

Examples of complementary color schemes are red and green, yellow and violet, orange and blue. These can be the most exciting color schemes, but they are easier to live with full-time if you make at least one of the colors lighter or darker than full strength. If the pure colors are used side by side, they tend to vibrate, or move back and forth on the design in relation to one another. *Jack-in-the-Pulpit* utilizes a complementary color scheme, but instead of pure red, the designer chose a pink (which is, of course, red with white added to it). In addition, instead of a pure green, she used a green that had been darkened with gray. The result is far more harmonious than the pure colors used together would have been. Even in *Christmas Poinsettia* the designer used a green which had been "toned down" to go with the pure red. Again, the effect is most pleasing.

A *triadic color scheme* is based on any three colors which are the same distance apart on the color wheel. Examples are red, yellow, and blue; orange, green, and violet; yellow-green, red-orange, and blue-violet. (Be aware that there are additional colors between the ones we have shown on the color wheel, which makes the possibilities for interesting triadic combinations numerous.) *Aunt Fanny's Flower Basket* is a good example of a triadic color scheme, artfully interpreted with red, yellow, and blue.

Triadic color scheme

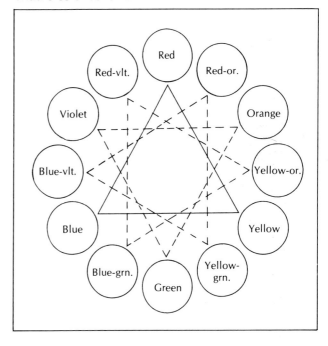

Jack-in-the-Pulpit

Christmas Poinsettia

Aunt Fanny's Flower Basket

A *related color scheme* is one that utilizes colors next to one another on the color wheel. In this scheme, each color must contain the same base color. A good example is yellow-green, green, and blue-green. Again it is wise to vary the lights and darks of the colors to prevent the scheme from becoming monotonous.

Summer Leaves

Related color scheme

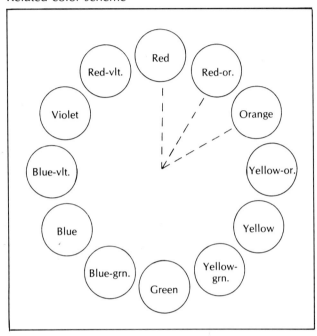

schemes. For every one we've mentioned, there are a dozen others for you to discover. Remember, too, that you are bound to be happy with a color scheme based on your own favorite color.

Experiment with color. Start with crayons and paper and try different color arrangements to see how your design pleases you. Collect swatches of a number of fabrics in lights and darks of the colors you select and swap them around in different combinations until you find the one most pleasing to you; do not stop experimenting until you are satisfied. Remember, you are going to put a good deal of effort into this project, and it should totally please you. If you are having difficulty getting your colors to work out to suit you, color a few different combinations, then leave them alone for a day or so. Chances are that when you look at the whole group with a fresh eye, the best scheme will show up immediately, or you will be able to see what needs to be done to perfect one of them.

A *monochromatic color scheme* is one which is based on a single color. This one color is used in its different light and dark variations to produce variety within the scheme. *Summer Leaves* (see upper right) is a good example of this idea: a deep yellow-green has been used for half the leaves, and a medium-toned yellow-green has been used for the other half. The effect is sophisticated and soothing.

An accented neutral color scheme begins with one of the neutrals—white, gray, black (and sometimes brown, beige, or navy) and is completed with splashes of at least one other color. White and red form an accented neutral scheme; so do black and yellow.

There are many other recognized color schemes, but the ones described here are basic and should give you a starting point. Do not feel limited by these

Hints on Prints

Now, what about the print fabrics we all love so much? Those pretty calicoes, florals, batiks, and geometrics are quite tempting and should be used in your quilt block design.

Indeed, it is often the challenge and excitement of combining fabric patterns that attract us to quilting in the first place. Here are some guidelines to help you achieve a successful mix of prints and solids.

- A print can be used just about anywhere you would use a solid. In combining several prints in one design, however, remember that there must be a unifying element running through all the prints. In most cases, this unifying element is color—the colors in one print will be the starting point for a whole color scheme. However, the *theme* of the print can be the unifying element, as illustrated in our batik projects (see page 12).

- If a print or pattern is placed on a colored background, the strength of that background color is somewhat reduced. If the print is dark colored, it will have the effect of darkening the background color; if the print is light colored, the background will appear lighter because of the print.

- The overall impression of the color of the printed fabric is taken from the color which is most dominant in the print. If a fabric with a white background has a great many green ferns and just a few yellow and pink butterflies in it, the overall impression of the color of the fabric will be green. Also, a small, dense print will appear darker than a large, open print.

- Recognize that you will be using only a part of the overall design of the fabric, unless you choose a very small print. The reason calicoes and tiny geometrics show up so often in special quilts is that the total design can be captured in just a snippet of fabric. If you use a large print, the impression will be of the colors used in the print, rather than the shapes in the print. Be aware that these colors can change across the width of the fabric, making it hard to believe that three 2" (5 cm) squares came from the same fabric. Make yourself a gauge for evaluating print fabrics for quilting: draw a triangle with 3" (7.6 cm) legs onto clear plastic or acetate, and cut it out. Move the triangle around on any print

Triangle Gauge for prints

fabric that you are considering for a portion of your design to see how the fabric will look in small sections. You will get a pretty good idea of the final appearance from the portion you are able to see underneath the triangle.

- Sometimes it will prove interesting to use only a selected part of a print. In our batik patchwork on page 12, we worked with a blue and rust geometric print that had "bull's-eyes" laid out in regular intervals. We cut out the bull's-eye portions for the small squares in the *Oklahoma Fields and Trails* floor pillow. The bull's-eyes filled up the squares and provided a colorful unity that would have been completely lost had we just cut the squares at random from the fabric. (The same fabric can be seen in a larger piece in the other floor pillow.)

A Word to the Wise

Once you have made your fabric selections, it is imperative that you test them for colorfastness. Cut a square of each chosen fabric and baste it to a slightly larger piece of white fabric, one square per piece. Wash the basted square with the method, detergent, and the water temperature you expect to use with the final quilted item. When the fabric is dry, examine it to see if any color has leaked from the square onto the white piece, or if the color of the square itself has changed appreciably. If either has occurred, you can do one of the following: delete that particular fabric from your design; or wash the square repeatedly (each time on a new white piece) until it shows no color change; then wash the fabric for your project the same number of times before using it. Either choice means you will have to alter your plans somewhat, but it is worth it to avoid heartbreak over color changes when you launder your finished item.

What If Your Design Doesn't Work?

Sometimes, in spite of careful planning, you may come up with a design that simply doesn't look quite right. This is when it is good to know a little of the theory of design that all successful artists apply to their work.

BALANCE, FORMAL OR INFORMAL: Every design has a centerpoint (different from the center of interest). Divide a square or a rectangle in half both horizontally and vertically; it is where the two lines cross each other that the actual center of the design occurs. To be pleasing to the eye, the weight of the design should be evenly distributed around this centerpoint. The easiest way to accomplish this is to make each side of the motif the same. When a design is the same on both sides of the center line, it is said to be in formal balance. *Holly Haven* and *Cotton Boll* are examples of formal balance.

Holly Haven

Quilt designs and batik-patterned fabrics work together to create a comfortable contemporary setting.
Flower Bed, a pattern that repeats well in a long strip, wraps around bolster pillows. Also on the loveseat are two pillows done in one design, Wild Flower, *but with the solid and patterned areas reversed. A tiny accent pillow sports an outline-quilted butterfly, as does the footstool. The floor cushion in the foreground begins with a quilt block,* Oklahoma Trails and Fields, *which is enlarged with the addition of several borders. The other floor cushion features a quilt block,* Wheels, *that was geometrically enlarged to the desired size. A screen covered with quilted fabric acts as a mini-gallery for quilt blocks.*

Cotton Boll

Formal balance is relatively easy if you are working with geometric shapes. However, if you have decided to re-create a landscape or a similar realistic subject, you might find formal balance too stiff. Many designs can be made more exciting by moving the main shape away from the center and adding other shapes to the opposite side to rebalance the design. An illustration of this is shown in the following drawings. In example A the design is the same on both sides of an imaginary center line; it appears very static and rigid. In illustration B the main object is away from the center and rebalanced by an object of the same visual weight at the right side. When one views the second arrangement, the eye tends to travel all around the design; more excitement and interest are created in this manner.

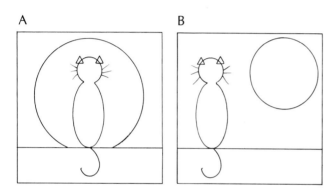

Sometimes the placement of a single shape will make a design well balanced or poorly balanced. Notice the difference in these two examples; even the small shape of the moon can make this design off-balance. In illustration C everything is on the left side, making the design too heavy on that side. In illustration D the moon is on the right and helps achieve a well-balanced design.

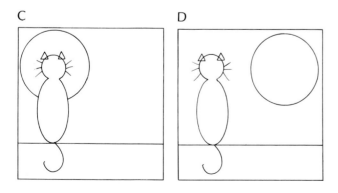

In many cases, the balance of a design is determined not only by the arrangement of the objects but the distribution of color. Certain colors weigh more, or have more impact on the eye, than others. A small amount of bright yellow is about three times as heavy as the same amount of violet. It is good to keep this in mind when deciding the color arrangement of your design. Knowing that a small bright shape can equal a large dull one, you can take steps to distribute colors in a design so it doesn't appear lopsided and off-balance.

RELATIVE SPACES: Consider the relationships of the shapes within your design space. Make sure the sizes of the individual shapes are in proportion to the surrounding space. If the shapes are too large, the design will appear crowded. If the shapes are too small, the surrounding area will overwhelm the design.

Shapes that are placed too high on the design appear to be flying or floating off the top. However, care should also be taken not to place the shapes too low, where they would appear to be sinking, or falling through the bottom of the design.

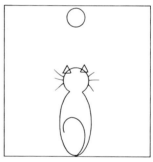

Poorly placed elements

There is an additional phenomenon that occurs in designing: the shapes within a contained space direct the movement of the eye either into or out of the space. If an object is only partially shown inside the boundaries of the design, there will be some question as to what is going on in the part that cannot be seen. Unless you have a specific reason for not doing so, place all objects within the design boundaries. This will prevent the feeling that the background block was cut too small.

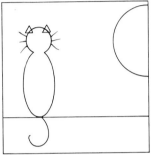 

Eye directed out of design   Eye directed into design

POSITIVE AND NEGATIVE SPACES: The shapes within your design are important, but the spaces around the shapes are equally important. These are called *negative spaces*. It is a mistake to ignore the significance of negative spaces, particularly if your quilt blocks are going to be placed next to one another with no separating bands of fabric. In some cases, the negative spaces can become more powerful than the planned shapes.

Julia Campbell, noted fabric designer, is very aware of the importance of recognizing this phenomenon and tells how she deals with it: "I can see a similarity between quiltmaking and silk-screening fabrics. When I'm designing a silk screen, I often think in terms of one set of colors—such as red and yellow. In order to keep myself from getting in a rut with a design, I will stop and force myself to use a different set of colors—such as blue and green. This way, I can better see what shapes are occurring and can envision the total piece of fabric, which is made up of these smaller units."

You might want to use the same idea of temporarily changing colors to force your eye to spot the negative shapes in your design.

For another idea of how positive and negative shapes relate to each other, take two sheets of white paper and one sheet of colored paper, all the same size. Fold the colored paper in half and tear or cut any random shape from the center. Now place the colored shape on one piece of white paper and the leftover portion on the other white sheet. You now have identical designs with the positive and negative shapes reversed. This idea can be used to make exciting designs, especially when the designs are repeated in alternating colors.

Another way to judge the effect of negative space on your design is to make a mirror image of it, or "flop" it, in the adjoining quilt block. To see how this will look, hold the quilt block next to a mirror. Often, it will show that fascinating negative shapes are created. One of the exciting facets of *Courthouse Square* (see page 70) was this potential for interesting negative shapes.

MOVEMENT: Movement is created when the eye is carried to all parts of the design. This is achieved by planning spaces and shapes so that actual or imaginary lines flow from one shape to the next. When movement is created, the design is unified. *Abundance* (see below) is an excellent example of movement.

HARMONY: If everything about your design is right, you should have achieved harmony. If it does not seem right to you yet, try limiting the number of

Abundance

colors and shapes you used. Check also to see that the colors are placed in such a way as to pull the design together, as in *Windmill*. The use of blue in the blades and vane and again in the water trough creates harmony between the upper and lower portions of the design. Harmony can also be developed if shapes are repeated several times in a design. Notice in *East Tennessee Farm* the skillful use of horizontal lines, triangles, and circles to create a very harmonious design.

Windmill

East
Tennessee
Farm

Taking the Design through the Final Steps

Having perfected the design of one individual quilt block, it is now time for you to think about three things: how to execute the design in fabric, how to set the blocks together, and how to quilt the design.

Specifics on how to sew your design are given in the "Portfolio of Quilting Techniques." However, you should now decide which of the many methods—appliqué, patchwork, embroidery, trapunto—or combination of methods—you wish. It may be that your design will come to life even more after you decide to raise one area of it with padding, make the background out of patchwork, and embroider the details. Or the design may need modifying if you have already decided you would rather appliqué than do patchwork. Consider carefully the construction requirements of the design; be aware of the exciting results to be achieved by using an unusual technique. A geometric that looks at first to be patchwork could really be a surprise when it turns out to be reverse appliqué instead!

The technique you choose to execute the design could influence how you draw the actual pattern pieces for your design. First, read the description of the technique in the "Portfolio"; then turn to the section on "Patterns and Templates."

You will need to consider how to set the blocks together and how to finish the edges of the project, no matter what you are making—a garment or a bed-size quilt. Borders, bindings, and sashing (those strips between blocks, also called lattice strips) are very important components of your design. They provide a frame for the quilt block. On many of the items photographed for this book, we have shown ruffles, eyelet and lace edgings, cording, tassels, different bandings and borders in order to stimulate your own creativity. Remember that if the design is going to work as a unit, all parts should be planned in advance. A rough sketch or diagram is an invaluable aid, both for seeing how the design works when it is repeated, including color distribution, and for estimating fabric yardage requirements.

A study in masterful composition, this quilt succeeds with a distinctive plan for setting the blocks together. Note especially the way the design is filled in at the corners and sides of the quilt. A vibrant color scheme is accentuated by the subtle use of the lighter green in the sashing. Pattern: George Washington's Cherry Tree.

When planning how to set your blocks together, it helps to make up four of the blocks and experiment with different arrangements. Do they look better placed side by side, or do they really need sashing to complete the design? Would corner squares add a nice finishing touch? Look at the totally different designs that result from using four identical quilt blocks next to each other without sashing, then with solid-color sashing, then with sashing that has a strong design that complements the quilt block.

Remember that sashing will add to the overall size of your project. It is an inexpensive and easy way to enlarge a bed covering. Borders and bindings also increase the size of the piece, as well as contributing immeasurably to the beauty. Another trick for increasing the size of a quilted piece is to alternate plain blocks with fancy ones. The plain ones can be a display area for stitched designs you make either by hand or by machine. Plain blocks are also a perfect place for trapunto designs.

With solid-color sashing

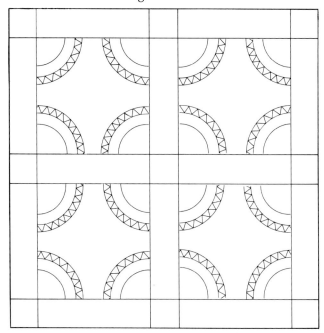

Without sashing

With sashing in strong design

In designing borders and sashing, there are several qualities you will want to consider: color, width, and intricacy of design. See the "Portfolio of Quilting Techniques" for how to sew sashing (found in "Setting the Quilt Together") and attach borders and bindings.

Repeat colors or pattern motifs found in the quilt blocks. Use harmonizing bands of solid colors, perhaps mixing more than one color in the strips. Try a continuous appliqué or patchwork design. The outstanding beauty of *George Washington's Cherry Tree* (see page 17) is due in great part to the sashing and the way the blocks are set on the diagonal.

Decide on sashing width carefully. A too narrow border can appear skimpy. Yet a border that is too wide can overpower and detract from the overall design. If your quilt top is sashed, use a border similar in design to the lattice strips, if you use a border at all. Plain fabric borders are usually made 2" to 5" (5 cm to 12.7cm) wide. A beautiful, traditional quilt style known as a medallion quilt has a single central motif, usually in appliqué and embroidery, and anywhere from three to ten different borders. There are no definitive rules for using borders or sashing, just so long as the width of the borders and sashing is in balance with the rest of the design.

The quilting plan itself is an important part of the overall design of your project. Outline quilting, the most popular type of quilting, is done by stitching around the outstanding shapes in the design. On appliqué or patchwork shapes, the stitching is generally done outside a seamline. Outline quilting gives a nice effect because the quilting makes the shape puff up while holding the background flat.

Scenic quilting uses quilting stitches to make a picture. Examine the nursery scene on page 31, and you will see a barn quilted onto the baby pillow in the cradle. Favorite subjects for scenic quilting are buildings, clouds, suns, rain, flowers, birds, and trees.

Fill-in quilting is done across big open sections of a design, and this is where the traditional diagonals, diamonds, shell shapes, feathers, and so on are displayed to such lovely benefit. You may want to pick a shape from your design and repeat it for your quilting pattern. Or think of a shape related to your design subject—for example a *Sunbonnet Girl* quilt with little footprints stitched into the sashing.

Just One More Thing . . .

In designing your own quilt block, there are many things you need to remember at one time. This may seem to be overwhelming at first, but after a while it will become more natural to you. Keep in mind the following points basic to designing your own award winning quilt:

- ➤ The feeling you want to convey with the design
- ➤ The purpose to which your quilted item will be put
- ➤ The method you are going to use to translate your design into fabric
- ➤ How you are going to set your quilt blocks together to achieve a unified effect
- ➤ How you are going to quilt the piece.

You may want to make several trial quilt blocks before you get started on the major project you have in mind. Most quilting authorities agree that it is good to try out your design first to see if you enjoy working with it and if it pleases you aesthetically. Save your trial blocks and use them in a gallery setting, as we did in the screen on page 12, or turn them into pillows, pictures, potholder, pockets—whatever you dream up.

Oh, and one more thing: be sure you sign and date your quilted projects. You don't want posterity to become frustrated trying to figure out when the heirloom was created!

My Memory Quilt

This unique album quilt incorporates patchwork, appliqué, embroidery, and special three-dimensional effects to create a series of extraordinary fabric paintings. The individual stories accompanying each block give an idea of how the designer sorted out the memories most precious to her and how she chose in each case the object most illustrative of that memory.

First Row (top to bottom):

DUCKS ON POND—*When I was quite young, I became ill, and the doctor recommended that my parents get something for me to do that would more or less occupy my time and take my mind off my illness. They bought me a pair of ducks, and from them I raised many more. Everyday I followed them to a little pond below the small grain barn and watched them swim.*

CHINABERRY TREE—*A large chinaberry tree stood just outside my bedroom window. Sometimes at night in the springtime I would sit by the open window and enjoy the fragrance of the blossoms as it rode the soft breeze while I listened to the call of the faraway whippoorwill.*

WASH DAY—*Monday was usually wash day on the farm. My mother boiled the clothes in a large iron kettle. They were then hung on the clothesline to dry in the fresh country breeze.*

RURAL MAILBOX—*In springtime many wild flowers dotted the area around the old mailbox. Every day some member of the family went after the mail— seed catalogs, mail-order books, the weekly newspaper, and letters from faraway relatives.*

AUTUMN—*Autumn was my favorite season. I looked forward to the gathering of the crops, fruits, and vegetables. I loved to see the fodder in the shocks and the golden pumpkins waiting to be hauled in and stored in the barn for winter's use. Come the holidays they would be cooked for pie baking.*

Second Row:

RABBIT IN THE CARROT PATCH—*On many moonlight nights in spring a wild rabbit would slip into my mother's carrot patch and help himself to fresh carrots. Next morning, when my mother saw the tops in a heap, her remark was, "Well, after all, what are a few missing carrots?"*

MY CHILDHOOD HOME—*In spring the honeysuckle vine was the home of the mocking bird, and the cardinal built its nest in the lilac bush. Fresh fruit and vegetables were always on the table, and spring showers cooled the air. Summer meant picnics in the woods, watermelons eaten under the big oak tree, fishing in the streams and wading in cool water.*

TEDDY BEAR—*What security when Teddy sleeps on your pillow in a darkened room after the old kerosene lamp is out! He doesn't have to be right off the Christmas tree to be appreciated. He may be old, worn, and faded, but it's his presence that makes the difference.*

SNOWMAN—*We watched with eager eyes for the first snowfall. Then as soon as it covered the ground, we dashed out and built a snowman. He was a real person to us, so we found a woolen scarf and old worn hat in the attic to protect him from the falling snow.*

Third Row:

CHINA ANNIE—*This doll was not received at Christmas. It was a gift after I recovered from a long illness. She was a delicate china doll with her own purse, hat, fan, and parasol.*

MY FIRST RAG DOLL—*This doll was not as pretty as the china doll but I adored her, especially because my sister made her for me. When she was not with me, she occupied a place on my bed which was covered with the patchwork quilt.*

CHRISTMAS TREE—*Our Christmas trees were always very large. My father went into the woods and chopped down a special tree for us. It took up one corner of the room and was decorated with strung popcorn, paper chains, candy canes, cookies and nuts. Colorful twisted candles in metal holders were fastened to the branches.*

STOCKINGS HUNG BY THE MANTEL—*Every Christmas Eve we hung our stockings under the mantel. We knew Santa would fill them with the candy, nuts, and perhaps a small gift in addition to leaving our larger gifts under the tree. We were never disappointed when on Christmas morning we ran to our stockings first.*

BARN IN WINTER—*The old barn was a playground in spring and summer. Off-limits in the winter, it was still a lovely sight. When the snow fell deep outside, we loved to watch the birds hop along on the white drift to search for a small grain or other tidbit that might have fallen when hay was tossed out for the cattle.*

Quilt and text by Nova Lee of Brownwood, Texas.

Portfolio of Quilting Techniques

Most of the sewing techniques that come into use with a quilted item are very familiar if you've done any sewing at all. It is the application of these familiar techniques to new uses that makes quilting a challenge.

While a tradition of precision needlework accompanies the craft of quilting, the excellence of the needlework in itself is no longer the point. The point today is to create something you love, something that is an expression of yourself. This doesn't mean you should throw workmanship to the winds, because the quality of the workmanship is going to determine to a great degree the beauty and performance of the finished piece. What it does mean is that you should not let a lack of experience stop you from enjoying this versatile needlecraft. Your skills will grow as you work; the more projects you do, the more you will learn.

Experiment with different techniques. The stitching of a piece should be as much fun as the planning, preparation, and use of the piece. You may find that one of the techniques suits you so well that you will want to dream up special designs to utilize the unique qualities of that particular technique. Trapunto is one technique which has recently stimulated the imagination of several artist-craftsmen. Some fascinating pieces have been done with all-white fabric, stitched and stuffed to form interesting shapes—even faces! Whole scenes can be interpreted in trapunto.

Read current magazines for ideas, not only for projects, but for techniques. You may not care for a particular design, but the method used to put it together might be a terrific inspiration for you. One new technique in quiltmaking uses fabric paint to make the design; another technique incorporates photography as part of the design. Ideas like this might just lead you to a fantastic creation!

Quilts on the bed, on the wall, the bookcase, the trunk, even the ceiling! Plain, fancy, floral, abstract, geometric . . . pieced, appliquéd, embroidered, stitched, tufted . . . every style of quilt and technique known to quilting is represented. Quilt shops such as these often rival museums in that their collections contain many lovely, old, and sometimes rare pieces. From the Great American Cover-Up, Dallas, Texas.

Order of Work

The four methods most usually associated with the preparation of the quilt top are patchwork, appliqué, reverse appliqué, and embroidery. *Patchwork* is the sewing together of many small pieces of fabric into a design; *appliqué* involves sewing shaped pieces of fabric onto a larger background piece; *reverse appliqué* is a method in which layers of fabric are stacked together, then cut and stitched in such a way as to expose portions of the different layers so that a certain design emerges; with *embroidery*, the decorative design is formed with fancy stitches and special threads. Each of these methods may be used alone to make the decorative design of the quilt top, but often two or more are used together for interest and excitement.

The decorative qualities of the piece are further enhanced by the manner in which the top is secured to the filler and backing—or how the piece is *quilted*. This may be done in one of three ways. In the most generally used method, the backing, filler, and quilt top are laid carefully on top of one another and stitched together, either by hand or by machine. In the second method, called *trapunto quilting*, the top and backing are first stitched together in a predetermined pattern, and the filler is then inserted in one of several ways. A third way of fastening the three layers together is by *tufting* (also called tying), which involves taking stitches through the three layers at selected intervals. These stitches are usually made with yarn or decorative thread, and the thread ends are cut to make little tufts.

With almost any of these methods, you can choose whether you want to work by hand or machine. The easy rhythm of hand stitching is soothing and rewarding to many people, and it has the advantage of making your quilted project portable. You can make each of your quilt blocks, then use the apartment quilting method to quilt them, and finally set the blocks together. Only the last few steps of assembly have to be done on a flat surface. One industrious quilter organizes the materials for individual quilt blocks into separate plastic bags and happily appliqués or sews patchwork as she rides the commuter train every day from Connecticut to Manhattan! Another advantage of hand sewing is that it makes it easier to ease one piece to another, at tricky corners and points especially.

Machine stitching, however, can be a real time-saver, particularly in sewing patchwork. It is often stronger than hand stitching especially for someone who has not sewed much by hand. Machine stitching is also more durable for items that will be frequently washed. Machine embroidery can be used with appliqué (at last—a chance to use all those fancy stitches on your machine!), and the straight stitch is perfect for outlining a design on printed fabric. Quilting can be done by machine, but it is generally recommended for small pieces, as it is difficult on large pieces to prevent the layers of filling and lining from shifting as you guide them under the needle. It is also sometimes a major tactical maneuver to figure out how to position a piece under the needle so that you are stitching through only the part you want.

Because we have no way of knowing the directions your imagination and enthusiasm may take when you begin to quilt, we have set up this technique chapter as an easy-reference dictionary. The techniques are arranged alphabetically so that you can choose a technique and go straight to it, rather than having to read through the whole birth of a quilt. Where applicable, we have given you both the hand and the machine method for the technique, and you can choose which method is best suited to your needs and abilities. We expect you to select what you need from the techniques and combine them as you wish. If you need help deciding when to do what, consult the following steps for the preferred working order.

1. Decide on the finished item you want to make and select the design.
2. Choose and prepare fabrics.
3. Draw the patterns and prepare templates.
4. Cut the pieces for each quilt block.
5. Sew all the quilt blocks needed for the project, using patchwork, appliqué, reverse appliqué, embroidery, or whatever method fits your scheme.
6. Set the blocks together in the arrangement required for the quilt top, either with or without separating bands of fabric (sashing). Adjustments in the working order must be made here for apartment quilting. (See page 62).
7. Put the quilt top together with the filler and backing, and quilt or tuft it. For trapunto, put the quilt top and backing together; then insert the filling.
8. Finish the quilted piece with a border or binding, cording, ruffle, or whatever it needs to become the bedspread, garment, pillow, etc. that you planned.

Anatomy of a Quilt

The identification of the different parts of a quilt can be cause for disagreement among quilt authorities. For the purposes of this book, we include a labeled diagram of a quilt top, along with a cross-section of a quilt.

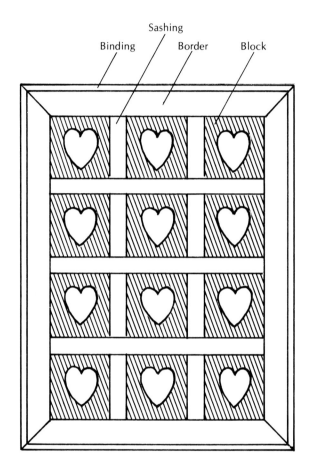

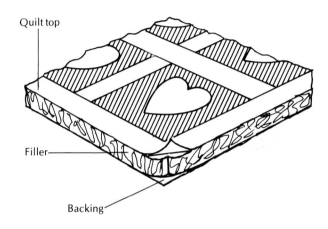

Appliqué

The word *appliqué* is from the French language and sounds very much like the word *applied,* which is what it means. And that is how this technique is accomplished. To appliqué, you *apply* a piece of material to a larger background of fabric. The traditional form of appliqué, which some ladies refer to as "laid-on work," is fabric on fabric, stitched in some way to be durable.

Actually, a variety of materials can be used for appliqué, and the method of application depends on the material. Beads, buttons, or small shells, for example, might be glued or tied onto a background fabric. Lace, ribbon, or antique fabrics of particular beauty or sentimental value might be tenderly embroidered. The materials and methods you use, of course, will depend on how you plan to use the finished work and on what appeals to you.

On the finished work, the applied piece of fabric should be as smooth and flat as possible, but it should not be stretched so tightly that it puckers. There will be times when you will pad a piece of appliqué to raise it above the surface of the background fabric and give more of a textured interest to the piece (known as relief appliqué), but the applied fabric should still have a smooth surface.

Cut out and prepare the shapes

Once you've decided on your design and prepared your templates (see "Patterns and Templates"), cut out the shapes you need. Add a ⅛" (3mm) to ¼" (6mm) seam allowance all around if your pattern has not allowed for it. Note that all the patterns in this book allow for ¼" (6mm) seam allowances. Keep the material straight, and in most cases, cut with the grain. Bias strips or packaged bias tape are often used for stems and connecting lines.

Fold under seam allowances to the wrong side along the seamline, and crease with your thumb and forefinger, or press.

To help with turning corners and keeping curves smooth, first stay-stitch along the seamline by machine. Then clip the seam allowance almost to the stitching: the sharper the curve, the closer together the clips should be. Also helpful is a finished-size template, placed on the wrong side of

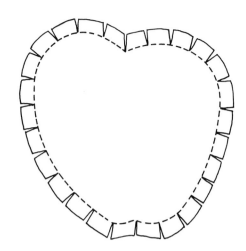

the shape, to use as a guide for pressing the seam allowances to the wrong side. Another aid is a piece of very lightweight fusible interfacing cut to the finished size of the shape and pressed in place on the wrong side of the fabric. With circular or oval shapes, turn under and baste the seam allowance in place all around, leaving the knot on the top side of the shape so that it can easily be pulled out later. Press the folded edges, avoiding the knot.

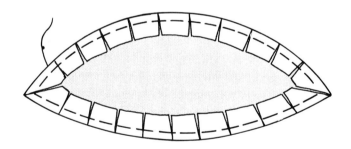

Prepare the background fabric

Make certain that your background fabric has been pre-shrunk, is on grain, and is wrinkle-free (see "Preparing fabrics for cutting"). The shape of the background fabric should be perfectly true; if it is a square, all four sides should be exactly the same length and the corners should be right angles.

Centering guidelines on the background fabric are invaluable for positioning the design. Fold the background block in half, lengthwise, then crosswise, and press lightly to make creases. If you expect to need more than four guidelines, press in more by further folding each quarter of the block.

Place a piece of tracing paper over the drawing of your quilt block design. Divide the design into as many parts as you did the background block by drawing on the tracing paper. Study the design through the tracing paper to see where the shapes are placed in relation to the centering guidelines, and place the shapes on the background fabric accordingly.

Assemble the design

Arrange the shapes on the background block according to your design, tucking smaller edges under larger ones wherever possible to minimize stitching. Hidden edges will not be stitched. To eliminate ridges, do not turn under seam allowances in those hidden areas; clip at the point where they become covered so they can lie flat. If you want to pad parts of the design for a raised effect, do it now. Put a same-shape piece of quilt batting under each piece you want raised. (Or wait until everything is stitched down, then use one of the trapunto techniques on page 66–67 to raise the desired part of the design.) Baste or pin-baste all the shapes in place before actually stitching any of the shapes.

Hand stitching

The traditional laid-on look utilizes a slipstitch, with stitches ⅛" to ¼" (3mm to 6mm) apart. However, a tiny overhand stitch may also be used. Choose the stitch most comfortable for you. Match the thread to the color of the shape to make stitches as invisible as possible. An alternative to either of these stitches is a suitable embroidery stitch, planned in advance as an integral part of the design.

Machine stitching

A short straight stitch (12-stitch length) close to the edge of the shape can look very neat and attractive. If your machine is so equipped, you may wish to use a narrow zigzag, a satin stitch, or a feather stitch, in which case you do not turn under the edge of the pieces, but simply cut each one without a seam allowance. Start with a full bobbin—it can be maddening to run out before you get all the way around a shape. To secure the stitching, draw the long top thread to the underside; then tie it to the bobbin thread. Do not backstitch or overlap stitching at the beginning and end—it will make an unsightly lump of stitching.

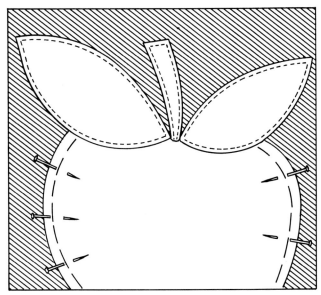

Reverse appliqué

Reverse appliqué means just what its name describes. In appliqué you cut out a shape and attach that shape to a background fabric. In reverse appliqué, it is the piece of fabric with the shapes cut out of it that becomes the top piece of your design. Each cutout hole is like a little "window" through which you see the next layer of fabric. The cutout areas are carefully sewed (around the inside edge) to the next layer of fabric. Some interesting effects can be achieved by combining reverse appliqué with regular appliqué. The shape that you cut out of the top layer can be applied to the third layer, with the second layer framing the appliquéd piece.

Reverse appliqué is particularly suited to quilting because as it is done, it develops a dimension which is similar to, and can be accentuated by, quilting. Even before a reverse appliqué piece is quilted, it has high and low areas, depending on how many layers were used in the design.

When planning your original design in reverse appliqué, there is one important rule to remember. Keep your cutting lines at least ¾" (1.9cm) apart. This will give you the ¼" (6mm) seam allowance you need for each cutout, and it will provide a ¼" (6mm) margin between the finished shapes. While you can have shapes within shapes, you cannot have shapes with sides touching each other.

Fabric

Since the top layer of fabric will, in essence, be the background of your design, you will want to choose that fabric as carefully as you would the background or main-emphasis fabric for any other work. Generally, the reverse appliqué technique in itself is so interesting in texture and finished appearance that you will probably find it desirable to use solid, contrasting colors rather than prints, especially in intricate designs. Decide which of the following two approaches to fabric you want to use with your reverse appliqué project:

MAKE ALL LAYERS OF FABRIC THE SAME SIZE: If your design is relatively small and simple, you can cut all the layers of fabric the same size, then pin or baste them together along all four sides.

SECTION THE LAYERS: You can use small separate pieces for the layers, so that on the second layer, for example, the left-hand section of your design could be red and the right-hand section could be yellow. This approach is really preferable to the first because it saves fabric, cuts down on the overall weight of the work, and allows you to use as many different fabrics as you like in your design. Each separate piece should be large enough to fit behind the "window" plus at least ¼" (6mm) extra. When you are working with separate pieces, add one piece at a time to the project. Baste it to the underside of the next layer, leaving yourself room to cut and stitch within the basting.

Marking the fabric

First, draw your entire design on paper in actual size. Start with your top piece of fabric, and using carbon paper and tracing wheel, trace onto the right side of the fabric those parts of the design that will be cut out of *that* piece of fabric. Mark both the cutting lines and the seamlines. Staystitch by machine with an 18 to 20-stitch length on all seamlines on each layer.

After you have cut the first layer and stitched the cutout shapes to the second layer as described below, you will be ready to mark the next part of your pattern on the second layer, again marking only the portion that will be cut out of that layer.

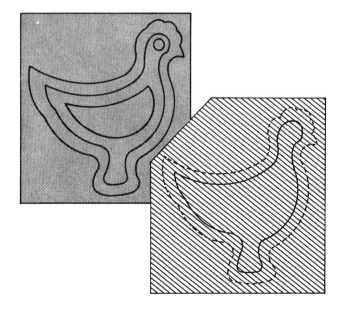

Cutting and stitching

Very carefully, with small, sharp-pointed scissors (embroidery scissors), cut the shape out of the top layer.

Clip curves and corners so that they will be easy to turn under. Clip inward curves all the way to the seamline (which has been staystitched). If seam allowances fold back on themselves when turned under, notch out the excess fabric.

Tuck the edge of each cut-out shape under with the tip of your needle as you sew. Make very tiny overcast stitches, and turn under so the seam line mark is just out of sight. An alternative choice is to choose a decorative machine stitch to sew the turned-under edges in place.

If your design is large or intricate, don't do all your cutting at one time. You should have your design well worked out and carefully marked. Cut just a little at a time, sewing as you go. This will save you the bother of trying to keep a lot of loose pieces in place.

If a shape is too small to cut away any of the fabric, make slits within the shape.

If corners present a problem, and if your fabric doesn't mind getting a bit wet, try putting a small drop of water in the corner to make the fabric do your bidding. Or try just the tiniest dot of glue.

Proceed through each layer

When you've finished sewing the top layer to the second, you're ready to mark the second part of your design on the second layer; then cut, tuck under, and stitch. Proceed through each layer in the same way: mark, cut, tuck under, stitch.

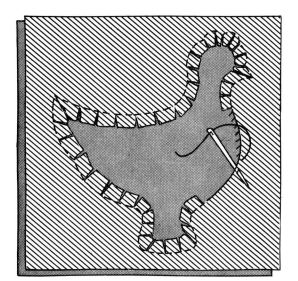

A nostalgic nursery for a boy or girl centers around charming farm themes done in bright primary colors. On the floor is a pre-playpen babysitting device, known as a crawler quilt. The dark border supposedly sets up an optical barrier, preventing the baby from crawling off the quilt. Patterns: Lily Garden for the crawler quilt; The Hay Wagon and Red Barn on chair cushions; Mrs. Feathersome on crib quilt; free-form appliqué and quilting on baby pillow.

Borders and Bindings

A border is a wide frame of fabric used around the outside of a quilt top to enhance the design; it may also function as a finish for the raw edge of the quilt. A binding is a narrow edging used to finish off the raw edges of the quilt and although not primarily intended to be decorative, it may be when done in a color that contrasts sharply with the quilt design.

Making a border

To make a plain, embroidered, or appliquéd border, cut fabric strips as wide as you want the finished border on top *plus* the width you want on the back *plus* an extra ½" (1.3cm) for two ¼" (6mm) seams, one on front, one on back. Cut each strip somewhat longer than the length of the side or top of the quilt to allow for finishing the corners. Appliqué or embroider the border strips as desired. Press in the seam allowances.

A patchwork border would need to meet the same length and width requirements as above. In addition, it must be attached very carefully if you wish to make the patterns come out even at the corners. No matter how hard they try, though, even the very best quilters are sometimes off ¼" (6mm) or so in matching corner patterns. To make such an error less noticeable, put a plain or contrasting square in the corners of the border.

If you need to put seams in a border that is not patchwork, be sure to put seams in corresponding positions on the opposite sides of the quilt.

Piecing borders

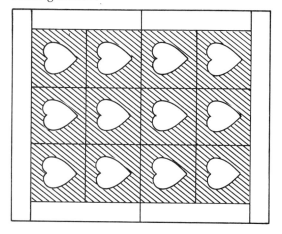

The border may be attached directly to the quilt top before quilting, or it can become the binding for the quilt. Remember in either case to cut the filler and the backing large enough to extend into the border for quilting.

Another border possibility is to start with enough extra backing fabric all around to form the border of that fabric. This may be decorated with appliqué, embroidery, or quilt-stitching when it is folded over and hemmed on top.

Making a binding

To bind with the backing fabric, first trim the backing on all sides to ¾" (1.9cm) larger than the quilt top. Turn under a ¼" (6mm) seam allowance, fold the extra backing fabric over the raw edge of the quilt, and sew to the quilt top with a slipstitch. You should use this method only if you have quite a bit of close quilting, because the binding does not serve to anchor the filling.

Plain binding may be done with commercial bias tape: the best binding for a smooth finish and long wear is double-fold bias tape. A scalloped edge on a quilt must be bound with bias for smoothly finished curves.

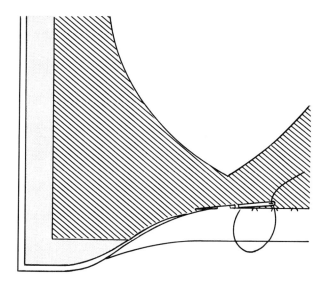

Corners

If you have planned a separate border or binding—one that is not made as part of the backing—you must make a choice about finishing the corners. Straight corners are easier, but mitered ones are very handsome and add a touch of quality.

To make straight corners, cut the lengthwise border strips the same length as the quilt top plus seam allowances at each end; then attach one to each side of the quilt. Stitch the first seam on the back of the quilt through all layers (this helps anchor the filler and may be done by machine); then fold the border over to the front and slipstitch it to the quilt top, making sure the stitching line from the first seam is covered. Leave the seam allowances extended at the top and bottom of the quilt. Then add borders across the top and bottom of the quilt, as shown here.

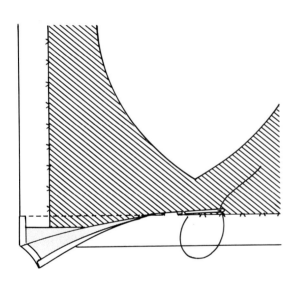

Mitering

For mitering a corner, the border strips should all be long enough to extend beyond the corners of the quilt by at least the width of the border. In other words, if your border is to be 3" (7.6cm) *wide*, you'll need 3" (7.6cm) of extra material at *each end* of *every* border strip.

Pin-baste each border strip to the back of the quilt, right sides together, first making sure all edges of the quilt top, filler, and backing are even. Stitch ¼" (6mm) from the edge through all layers, stitching only to a point ¼" (6mm) from each end of the quilt—*not* all the way to the edge.

Holding the right sides of the border strips flat against the back of the quilt, fold each border extension back until the two form a 45° angle.

Stitch the diagonal fold lines together by hand; trim off excess border fabric.

When all four corners are mitered in the same manner, fold the border over the edge and hem neatly onto the quilt top with a ¼" (6mm) turn-under.

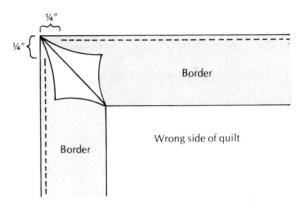

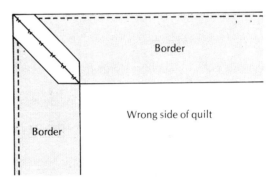

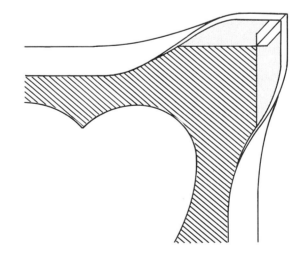

Embroidery

Although embroidery can be the single technique employed to create a design for a quilt block, it is often used with appliqué and patchwork to highlight and emphasize portions of the design. Basically a means of creating a personal fabric design with needle and thread, embroidery also has a functional aspect in that it is used to hold pieces of fabric in place and to finish cut edges.

The stitches traditional to hand embroidery can be closely simulated with sewing machine stitches. The choice of hand or machine method depends on your own personal preferences. Hand embroidery can move with your activities and can be stitched as you travel, watch television, or whatever. Machine embroidery is faster. Weigh the factors and decide which method suits you better. However, if you have never tried machine embroidery, you should; you will probably find it very enjoyable. There are three types of machine embroidery: crewel, which is accomplished with wool yarns and clear nylon thread and can be done with a straight stitch machine; free-motion, which employs a very small zigzag stitch and requires that you hand-guide the material under the needle; and decorative stitching, which utilizes automatic stitches either built into the machine or available with special attachments.

Transferring the design to the fabric (for hand or machine work)

Commercial embroidery designs are applied to the fabric with a hot iron. Check the instructions that come with the design. To transfer your original embroidery design from paper to fabric, use one of the following methods:

- Place dressmaker's carbon paper face down on the right side of fabric; position the design over the carbon paper, and draw over all the lines of the design with a pencil or tracing wheel.
- If you are using a transparent fabric, as you might in trapunto work, simply place the fabric directly onto the design and trace the lines with a soft pencil.
- Perforate the lines of the design with a pin, tracing wheel, or unthreaded sewing machine. Place the pattern over the right side of the fabric, and rub stamping powder or charcoal through the perforations.

- Place the design directly on the fabric, wrong side of design to right side of fabric, and baste through the paper and fabric around all the lines of the design. Tear the pattern off the fabric, leaving the basted design on the fabric. Remove basting after embroidery is completed.

Hand embroidery

THREADS: Six-strand embroidery floss is a most popular hand embroidery thread. It is made of cotton and comes in many lustrous colors. Six strands may be used at one time, or the strands can be separated into groups of two, three, or four, depending on the effect you desire. Pearl cotton is a smooth corded thread, easy to work with, as are *coton à broder* and *retors à broder*, two other tightly twisted, non-divisible cotton threads. Tapestry wool or any firm, tightly twisted wool yarn can be used and even washed if the label guarantees it.

NEEDLES: Crewel and chenille needles are used for most stitches; round point tapestry needles are required for working a second thread through a first stitching.

SCISSORS: Choose sharp scissors with pointed blades. They should be small enough so that they do not obstruct your vision as you snip fabric and thread ends.

THIMBLES: A must for your middle finger as you push the needle through the fabric, your thimble should fit well and should be made of metal or plastic.

FRAMES: It is strongly recommended that your embroidery work be done on a frame to prevent the possibility of puckering. Choose a ring (hoop) style which has a screw adjustment to fit different thicknesses of fabric. A square or rectangular frame is useful for larger pieces and can also double as a quilting frame for some projects. Both rings and frames can be purchased with a floor or table stand, which frees both hands to work—one underneath the fabric and one on top.

Stitching

When doing hand embroidery, study the diagram of the individual stitch carefully. It is important to notice in which direction the *stitching is progressing*, whether from right to left or from left to right. Additionally, pay close attention to the direction in which the *needle is pointing* as the stitch is made. Practice each stitch until you pick up its particular rhythm before you begin work on your project. In a row of stitches, all should be the same size, and they should be evenly spaced.

Work with a strand of thread or yarn about 12" (30cm) in length. A longer strand will become frayed and weakened as it passes repeatedly through the fabric. Place fabric in the embroidery frame so that it is taut and the threads of the fabric are at right angles to one another. Do not knot the end of the thread or yarn; instead, begin by leaving ½" (1.3cm) tail of thread on the right side of the fabric about 1" (2.5cm) from where you will begin. Work over the 1" (2.5cm) of thread to secure it. Clip off thread end on the right side of the fabric when you work up to it. At end of stitching, work the end of the thread or yarn back underneath the completed work on the wrong side.

Securing thread end

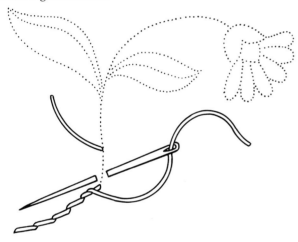

Machine embroidery

THREADS: For crewel-type machine embroidery, you will need invisible nylon thread and your choice of yarns—chenille, mohair, nubby and novelty yarns, or whatever suits you. Soutache braid, string, ribbon, and other unusual materials can be substituted for yarn. For regular machine embroidery, both free-motion and decorative stitching, a special high-sheen machine embroidery thread is available. Size 30 machine embroidery thread is coarser than size 50, which is fairly fine. Select the size which gives the desired effect.

NEEDLES: Either a sharp or a ballpoint needle can be used, preferably a size 9 or 11.

TWEEZERS: In crewel-type machine embroidery, tweezers are a good idea for holding the yarn under the needle to eliminate the risk of a wounded finger.

FRAMES: A frame is an asset for regular machine embroidery, but not necessary for crewel-type embroidery. Choose a small ring frame, and put the fabric, wrong side up, over the smaller of the two rings; then fit the larger ring in place. Turn the frame over to work on the right side of the fabric; this enables the work to lie flat on the bed of the machine as you stitch. (This is opposite from the way the fabric is placed in the frame for hand embroidery.)

Stitching

When embroidering by machine, practice each individual stitch and technique until you are confident of the results. Practice turning corners and making smooth curves with the individual stitches. Always begin work on your project with a full bobbin and full top spool. If you have to interrupt a row of stitching, write down exactly what the settings are for tension, stitch length, and stitch width; do not trust your memory. Always practice before beginning work on your project with a swatch of the fabric and thread you will use to get the correct tension and pressure. On free-motion embroidery, practice machine circles to get the smooth, steady motion necessary for even stitching.

Machine crewel techniques

Use clear nylon as the top thread on the machine and a thread which matches the color of your fabric on the bobbin.

➤ Choose a light pressure setting on your machine, or eliminate pressure completely by setting the pressure dial at 0.

➤ Loosen top tension to prevent thread breakage.

➤ Remove the presser foot *and* the presser foot shank. (You might forget the shank if you have a snap-on type foot.)

➤ Do not forget to lower the presser foot bar to engage the tension setting. It is easy to forget to do this since you have removed the presser foot and shank.

Place one end of a length of yarn at a starting point on your design, and stitch back and forth across the yarn to anchor one end. Move the yarn to one side out of the needle's path, and stitch with a straight stitch to the next angle or point of the design. Using tweezers to hold the yarn in place, anchor the yarn at this point of the design. Continue in this manner until the design is completely executed.

(If the design is one of mostly straight lines, you can sew directly over the yarn, braid, or embroidery floss with a zigzag or blind hem stitch.)

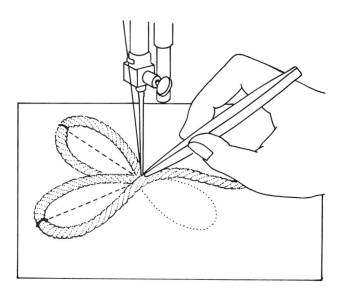

Free-motion machine embroidery

Use machine embroidery thread in the top threading of the machine. If machine embroidery thread is not available, use mercerized cotton. Do not use polyester thread. It breaks.

In the bobbin, use a regular sewing thread either in white or a color which matches the fabric.

- ➤ Select a loose tension setting to avoid thread breakage. The top and bottom threads should pull almost evenly when you tug on them, but the top thread should be a little looser. The bobbin thread should not show at all on the right side of the fabric.
- ➤ Choose a short, narrow zigzag stitch.
- ➤ Place fabric in an embroidery ring, especially if the fabric is lightweight.
- ➤ Remove the presser foot and presser foot shank, but do not forget to lower the presser foot bar before beginning to stitch. Otherwise, the tension on the machine will not be engaged.

- ➤ On older machines, drop the feed dog to "darn" position.
- ➤ Bring the bobbin thread up through the fabric to the right side. Hold both threads taut at the beginning of the stitching to avoid a knot of thread at start of stitching.

Begin stitching at the center of your design, and work toward the outside edges. Stitch at an even pace at as fast a machine speed as you can maintain. The machine makes more uniform stitches at faster speeds. Hold the embroidery ring firmly, and guide it smoothly under the needle. Do not jerk the ring, or you will have skips in the stitching. Turn the ring gradually when you are making a curve; do not pivot sharply unless you want to make a corner. As your experience grows, you will find it easy to accomplish even intricate shading and the most sophisticated designs.

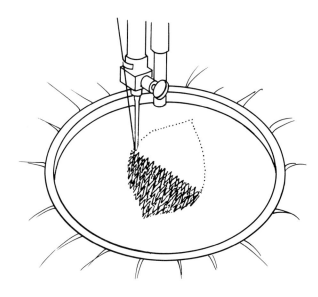

Decorative stitching

Machine embroidery thread is the best choice for decorative machine stitching as it shows up better than regular sewing thread. For the bobbin, use a thread color-matched to the background fabric. Check your sewing machine instruction book for the correct settings for specific stitches. Experiment on a scrap of fabric until you are quite confident of what to expect from the stitch.

Embroidery Stitches

Stitch	Use	Machine Equivalent (Parentheses indicate how specific stitch capability may be provided)
Running stitch	Basic stitch used for outlining shapes; for rapidly filling in shapes; also used for quilting and in joining patchwork pieces together. Can be even or uneven, and can also be threaded with another color.	Feather stitch set at 0 width (disc or built-in).
Back stitch	Very much like the running stitch, except much stronger. Often used to start and end a row of running stitches.	Feather stitch set at 0 width (disc or built-in).
Straight stitch	Also known as the single satin stitch. Useful for defining simple shapes.	Zigzag stitch (built-in) at maximum width—free motion work.
Satin stitch	Used to cover a small area solidly. May also be used for attaching appliqué.	Zigzag stitch (built-in) with width changed if necessary during stitching to make shapes.

Stitch	Use	Machine Equivalent (Parentheses indicate how specific stitch capability may be provided)
Long and short stitch	Used for borders, shading areas of a design, and appliqué.	Elastic stretch stitch (disc or built-in).
Seeding	A simple way to fill in an area. Utilizes small straight stitches of equal length.	Narrow zigzag stitch (built-in) guided randomly over area.
Arrow stitch	Used for lightly filling in an area or making a border.	Arrowhead stitch (disc or built-in).
Cross stitch	Used for borders and for light or heavy fill-in. Often used on gingham.	Multi-stitch zigzag; two rows overlapped (disc or built-in).

Stitch	Use	Machine Equivalent (Parentheses indicate how specific stitch capability may be provided)
Split stitch	For outlining and fill-in. Often used to outline a shape which will be satin-stitched to give a raised effect. Looks like a narrow chain stitch.	Very narrow, short zigzag stitch (built-in). Use with free-motion work.
Stem stitch	Also called an outline stitch, because it is used for outlining. Can be used to attach appliqué, fill in design areas.	Very narrow, short zigzag stitch (built-in). Use with free-motion work.
Buttonhole stitch	Useful for attaching borders and appliqué pieces. Also good for finishing off raw edges.	Paris point stitch (disc or built-in).
Feather stitch	Makes pretty borders and can also be used for fill-in. Very popular in "crazy quilts" to decorate edges of patches.	Feather stitch (disc or built-in).

Stitch	Use	Machine Equivalent (Parentheses indicate how specific stitch capability may be provided)
Chain stitch	Used as a decorative border and as fill-in.	Chain stitch built into machine or multi-stretch stitch disc.
Lazy daisy or detached chain	Used in groups to add a mass of color.	Yarn couched with clear nylon thread.
Herringbone stitch	Makes lines and borders and attaches appliqué. Can be open and lacy or closed and dense, depending on desired effect. Also a very popular stitch for "crazy quilts."	Honeycomb stitch (disc).
Chevron stitch	Used for lines and borders.	Turkish hemstitch (disc).

Stitch	*Use*	*Machine Equivalent* (Parentheses indicate how specific stitch capability may be provided)
Coral stitch 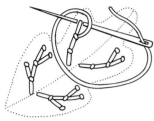	Also called a knot stitch, it can be used as an accent stitch, or as outlining or fill-in.	Star stitch (disc). 
Couching 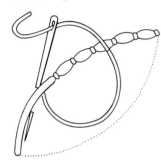	Used for fill-in or outlining shapes. Couching allows the use of materials too heavy to pull through the fabric.	Blind hem stitch (disc or built-in) used in combination with yarn or other desired material. 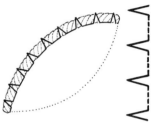
French knot 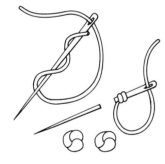	Used for flower centers, also as the tie-down stitch in couching.	Couch yarn with nylon thread. 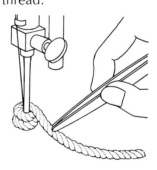
Bullion knot 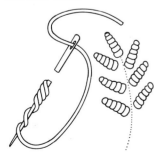	Used as an accent, or can be the single stitch used for flower petals. (Special hint: use a blunt needle when making this stitch by hand.)	Narrow zigzag (built-in). 

Fabrics

Much has been written about the types of fabric suitable for quilted projects, and it all adds up to the fact that almost any fabric can be used, but the following points should be kept in mind when selecting the particular ones for your project.

- The fabrics you use should complement one another and the design you have selected. The Design chapter told you how to choose fabric colors and patterns to enhance your design. Additionally, you should be sure that all your fabrics have the same care requirements. For example, are all the fabrics washable, and do they have approximately the same life expectancy? It is never easy to go back into a quilted project and replace portions of it which have worn away before others.

- Decide before beginning your project how much sentimental value you want to build into it. Do you really want to use all new fabrics which match each other perfectly, or do you want to use some from your scrap bag in the tradition of our grandmothers? The two ideas are not mutually exclusive because many times you can create a masterpiece from scraps you have on hand with the addition of some new fabric. There is nothing quite like the feeling you have when you find an old, familiar, and loved scrap of fabric in a quilt your mother made.

- Think about the use your quilting is going to receive. Match the fabric to the end use. For our upholstery projects, we chose very durable cotton and synthetic blends; for our evening jacket, we used fragile silks and brocades. A poignant example of matching fabric to purpose was demonstrated by a friend who made a quilt for a deaf and blind child. The fabrics used were a variety of interesting surface textures—velvets, vinyls, furs, taffetas, corduroys.

- Try to match your fabric to your sewing skills, especially if you are just beginning to quilt. The easiest fabrics to work with are firmly woven cottons and cotton/polyester blends, including broadcloth, percale, muslin, and gingham. Knits are very popular for garments now and will surely come under consideration for your quilted projects. But be certain that you examine any knit you are planning to use with a critical eye: single knits almost certainly will not do, as they are too stretchy. Doubleknits are generally sturdy but do not hold a crease well, which can be a disadvantage in trying to press under seam allowances. Doubleknits also tend to be very lofty, which means that some of your quilting stitches might well get lost in the bulk of the knit. If you must use doubleknits, they seem to do best in pieces with curved seams rather than those with sharp angles.

Working with fabric grain

It is very important to remember how fabric is constructed when you cut the individual pieces for your quilt. Otherwise, you cannot know how to avoid certain problems that could spoil your efforts at patchwork, appliqué, and quilting.

Woven fabric is made up of lengthwise and crosswise threads which cross over and under one another at specified intervals. These threads should form perfect right angles where they cross. When they do, the fabric is "on grain." When the angles are not perfect, the fabric is "off grain." You should make absolutely certain that your fabric is on grain before cutting out any of the pieces for your quilt. (The only exception is permanent press fabric, which has been finished with a solution that locks the grain as it is, whether perfect or not. You do not have to worry about permanent press fabrics, as they will not change grain position.)

To check whether your fabric is on grain, first make each cut end perfectly straight. Do this by one of two methods: either pull a thread across the width of the fabric and trim along that thread line, or lay a straight edge at a perfect right angle to the selvage of the fabric, draw a straight line across the width of the fabric, and trim on this line.

Next hold the fabric up and fold it in half crosswise. If the two cut edges hang exactly even with one another down their width, the fabric is on grain. If they do not meet exactly, the grain is off at the places where they do not meet. To put fabric on grain, you may carefully press it in the required direction, or you can pull it back on grain. (If you have a great length of fabric, you may need help.) Grasp the fabric at the center of a side diagonally opposite from the off-grain edge and tug firmly. Repeat this process along the cut edges of the fabric until they hang evenly along their full width.

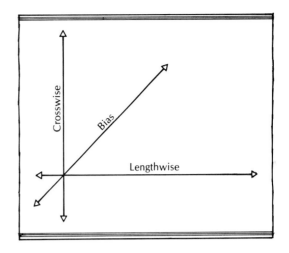

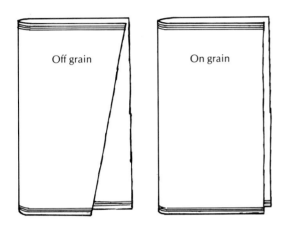

It is also important to remember that the lengthwise grain is the strongest; the crosswise grain is nearly as strong as the lengthwise grain; and any diagonal grain, or bias, is the weakest direction of woven fabric because it stretches the most. True bias is the diagonal direction of fabric which crosses the intersection of the lengthwise and crosswise threads at exactly 45°. Knits are an exception because they are constructed entirely differently. The crosswise direction of knits is the stretchiest, and the lengthwise direction is generally the most stable.

Most woven fabrics will tear on one thread across the entire width. Therefore, it is often easier to tear the fabric for a straight edge than to try to cut it straight. This will work with many lightweight cottons, and it is an easy way to tear strips to make sashing, borders, and bindings, but your fabric must be on grain, and you must check it to make absolutely sure the strip is a constant width its entire length. The exceptions to this are velvet and velveteen, and they pucker when torn; always cut them.

One more fact about woven fabrics you should keep in mind: the lengthwise edges are finished with a self-edge, or selvage. It is tempting to use this edge in your sewing, particularly if your are working with fabric that ravels badly. Be careful; the selvage can pucker when laundered, thus destroying any seam into which it is sewed. It is advisable not to use the selvage at all on small pieces and to clip it every four to six inches if you are using it as a seam finish.

Determining the lengthwise and crosswise grain of fabric is fairly easy when you have a brand-new piece, but what do you do with a scrap that has no selvage to guide you? Try unraveling an edge of the scrap—the crosswise threads usually come out more easily than do the lengthwise threads.

Fabric grain and individual quilt pieces

The reason you need to understand what grain in fabric is and how it functions is so that you can fit the pieces of your quilt block together with as little trouble as possible. A striking example of the difference grain makes is the problem encountered by an experienced quilt maker who had pieced together an enormous Lone Star top of many, many diamonds, only to find that it would not lie flat. She knew she could not quilt it until she had corrected the problem because the whole quilt would be puckered. The cause of her problem was several diamonds in one point of the star which had been cut off-grain. Although they fit perfectly with the other diamonds, they were pulling the whole area out of shape. The offending diamonds had to be taken out and replaced with others that were grain-perfect. In addition, differences in color sometimes occur when the same grain direction is not used for all pieces. This is particularly noticeable in napped fabrics such as corduroy and velvet.

A good general rule to follow when cutting out your individual pieces for your quilt blocks is to place the longest area of the piece on the lengthwise grain. If a need for fabric economy prevents your using the lengthwise grain, then use the crosswise. Diamond shapes, long rectangles, and triangles other than right triangles should all be cut with the longest portion on the straight (lengthwise or crosswise) grain of the fabric. For example, if there are five diamonds that go together to make a star, the long center of each diamond should be placed on the lengthwise grain of fabric. The same general rule applies to the irregular shapes often found in appliqué; the longest area of the shape should be placed on the straight grain.

There are exceptions, however, to the rule just given. Quite often, when you are working with a stripe, check, or plaid, you will prefer to place the sections on the diagonal to give your design more pizzazz. Go ahead; but remember that this may put some of your seamlines on the bias, meaning that they will stretch more than you had anticipated. Sometimes this can be helped by machine-stitching along the seamline with a very short stitch (16-18 stitch length) or by cutting a paper lining to fit underneath the piece; the paper is removed after the piecing is complete. Large curved pieces such as

half-circles or crescents fit together best when as much of the curve as possible is on the bias. In both of these exceptions, it is vital to make up a test block; moreover, if the blocks are to be set directly next to one another, with seams that must be matched exactly, two or more blocks should be made and stitched together. The third exception is with triangles; it is often wiser to position them so two sides are on the straight grain (one on lengthwise and one on crosswise), rather than placing the longest side on the straight grain, thereby throwing the other two sides on the bias.

Estimating fabric yardage

In order to predict accurately how much fabric you will need for a particular design, you will have to make a cutting diagram for each fabric. When you designed your quilt block, you decided on the number of colors and types of fabrics you wanted to interpret the design. Now, if you haven't already done it, is the time to make a drawing, no matter how rough, of how you are going to set the quilt blocks together. If you plan to make a garment, it is wise to draw your quilt blocks onto the paper pattern so that you can see how the design will fall and where you will need only portions of a block. (The alternative to this is, of course, to make up one big piece of fabric in your chosen design and then lay your pattern out on it.) Your drawing should indicate

Draw quilt design onto pattern piece

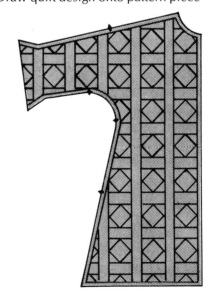

where you are going to need strips and borders, ruffles or collars, bound edges, etc. and what fabric you are going to use for these areas. Be sure to include allowances for the fabric to be used as the quilt backing or the garment lining if you want it to match one of the fabrics in the quilt block.

Study your drawing; then make a list of all the fabrics to be used in each block and the shape of each fabric piece. You might want to make a drawing of the template next to the name and color of the fabric. Be sure to note if a fabric is used for more than one shape. Next, count the number of blocks. Multiply each fabric piece by the number of blocks to see how many times each piece occurs in the final project. For example, if you had 3 solid yellow 5" (12.7cm) circles per quilt block, and you needed 20 blocks, you would need a total of 60 solid yellow 5" (12.7cm) circles for the finished project. To figure out how much solid yellow fabric you would need for the 60 circles, plan to use 45" (114.3cm) wide fabric unless you know for sure that you will be using a different width. Cut a strip of paper 45" (114.3cm) wide, or mark off 45" (114.3cm) on a cutting board if you have one.

Begin by determining how many circles will fit across the width of the fabric. Simple math tells you that 5" (12.7cm), the diameter of the circle, goes into 45" (114.3cm), the fabric width, nine times. But you cannot get nine circles out of one fabric width for several reasons: you must add a seam allowance of ¼" (6mm) around each circle which will increase the diameter of the circle by ½" (1.3cm); you cannot use the fabric selvage; and you should allow a bit of space between each circle for accurate cutting. (When you position pieces with straight edges, however, you can often lay two pieces next to one another so that one edge of each piece is cut at the same time.) Therefore, the actual diameter of the circles will be 5½" (14cm) with seam allowances, and by allowing ¼" (6mm) between circles, each circle will take up a total of 5¾" (14.6cm). With this new figure, you should plan no more than 7 circles across the width of the fabric.

How much *length* do you need from the fabric if you can get 7 circles in one row across the width? Divide the 7 per row into the 60 total circles needed for the quilt—8⁴⁄₇. You will therefore need 9 rows. (The partial row will need the same length as all the full rows; there will be just a little width left over.) Since each row requires a length of 5¾" (14.6cm) and you need 9 rows, the total length required is 51¾" (131.4cm), rounded to 52" (132.1cm). To find out how many yards (meters) of fabric you need, divide 52" (132.1cm) by 36" (100cm) (the number of inches [centimeters] in a yard [meter]), round up to the nearest fourth, half, or eighth, and you will get 1½ yards (1.3 meters). This is almost exactly what you will need for sixty 5" (12.7cm) circles, not allowing for mistakes. So you might add an extra ½ yard (meter) or so. If you do not use it, the excess will be a great addition to your scrap basket!

Estimating fabric yardage

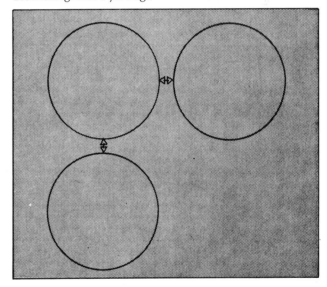

To estimate the amount of fabric needed for any shape, even irregular ones, you must go through the above process. Do this for each fabric you are using in your quilt, and you will be able to shop with confidence.

To estimate yardage requirements for sashing, bindings, or borders, first determine whether it is more economical to cut them on the lengthwise or the crosswise grain. Either direction is acceptable, and the fabric design may have a deciding effect on how these pieces are cut. Consider also that if the fabric width is not great enough to allow you to cut continuous strips, you may wish to cut on the lengthwise grain to eliminate piecing. From the drawing of your finished project, calculate the width each strip will be, and remember to add ¼" (6mm) seam allowances to each side *and* end. Multiply the number of strips needed in each width by the width of the strip, and add them together to see how many strips can be cut from a width of fabric.

Backing fabrics

The backing fabric should be chosen to complement the fabrics used in the quilt top, so the first things to consider are color and texture. The backing must also be easy to quilt through, so it should be soft and pliable.

Today, the best fabric for backing a quilt is cotton or a cotton/polyester blend. A traditional fabric for quilt backings is unbleached muslin; the kind you can buy today is usually wash-and-wear and much more durable than the kind your grandmother used. Batiste and bleached muslin are also good choices for a backing. Knit fabrics are not recommended because they stretch and tend to be difficult to quilt.

For large quilts, a percale or muslin sheet makes an excellent backing; there will not be any seams to detract from the pattern of your quilting stitches. It is traditional to use a solid color or white backing, but you could certainly use a patterned sheet set off with matching pieces (cut, perhaps, from pillowcases) somewhere in your quilt top design.

Polyester fleece makes an excellent combination filler and backing for small quilted pieces. Easy to stitch through by hand or by machine, it is also firm, so you will probably need no additional backing if the back will not be visible in your finished work.

Should you need to piece fabric for the backing, try not to place a seam down the center. Instead, place a width of fabric down the center and add half of what is needed down each side.

Preparing your fabrics for cutting

If you plan to make an item using fancy silks and brocades such as our quilted jacket (see page 48)—and intend to use it only on special occasions—you can plan to dry-clean it, and you will not have to worry about the washability of the fabrics. Fabrics that are not washable may need very little initial preparation.

Washable, shrinkable fabrics, however, must be washed in hot water and preferably machine-dried to preshrink them as much as possible before you begin working with them. Even bolts of the same type of fabric may not be exactly alike in washability, shrinkability, and colorfastness; since you may have several different fabrics in your work, it is important to do everything you can to take any unpredictability out of your fabrics *before* cutting and sewing.

Synthetic-fiber fabrics should be pre-washed, too, because even if the fibers do not shrink, the construction of the fabric could become more compact, causing shrinkage.

If you are using a fabric that has been used and washed before, such as old clothing scraps, pressing may be all that is required if the fabric is not stained. Check such second-time-around fabrics to make sure that they have not been weakened by wear.

If any of your fabrics are at all wrinkled, press them before you begin cutting. Steam ironing will produce the best results; use a press cloth on more delicate fabrics.

Any fabric which is excessively wrinkled after washing and drying should probably be avoided. It will only give you more problems later on in the finished work.

Cutting and sewing accurately is important in any quilted project, so you should always work with clean, smooth fabrics.

Filling materials

The kind of filler you choose for your quilted piece depends on three things: the *look* you want, whether puffy or a little flatter; the *degree of warmth* you want from a finished quilt; and the actual quilting *technique* you are using.

One of the best and most widely available filler materials for bedcoverings and other large quilted pieces is polyester sheets or batts. Some are small and thin enough for baby quilts; others are large and thick enough for double bed coverings. Polyester is a soft, fluffy, lightweight filler; it makes warm coverings and it is quite easy to stitch through. It comes packaged and pre-cut in three sizes: 81" x 96" (205.7cm x 240cm), 81" x 108" (205.7cm x 270cm), and 90" x 108" (225cm x 270cm). Polyester fleece is more compact than polyester batting, and it is available by the yard in 40" (101.6cm) widths. To join widths, slightly overlap the edges and stitch with a zigzag; then trim close to the stitching. This joining is very flat. Polyester fleece can be used as a combination filler/backing, as it does not shred. Because of its sturdiness and durability, it is perfect for use with handbags, garments, etc.

At one time, fillers for bedcoverings were all cotton or wool batting. These materials are thick, heavy, and very warm, and not the easiest thing in the world to stitch through. They also are not so widely available any more, yet some quilters prefer the flat, thick look of a quilt filled with this material. If you want this kind of look and have a hard time finding the batting, you may substitute ready-made mattress pads which won't have to be hand-quilted to the extent cotton batts would. For lighter weight and an even flatter effect, use a lightweight cotton blanket or flannelette sheet-blanket.

A good stuffing material for trapunto and other puffed or padded quilting is polyester fiber fill, which is usually packaged in plastic bags. Polyester or acrylic yarn is also good for use in trapunto designs. (See Trapunto.)

Patchwork

Patchwork, or piecework, is a means of making a large piece of material by joining together a number of smaller pieces. There are two types of patchwork, random and geometric. In random patchwork, the pieces are put together in an irregular, free-flowing manner to achieve the mosaic of colors and textures so characteristic of "crazy quilts." This type of patchwork does not require patterns and templates and is not the precision craft of geometric piecing. In geometric patchwork, the pieces of fabric are cut into squares, rectangles, diamonds, pentagons, hexagons, triangles, or one of many other shapes which fit together like the pieces of a tile floor. Two or more of these shapes may be used together; the combinations of shapes can be quite sophisticated, often in the manner of brain-teaser puzzles.

Geometric arrangements are generally based on the traditional four-patch and nine-patch arrangements. The design possibilities within these block frameworks are practically inexhaustible. A one-patch quilt is not even made up in blocks—the whole quilt top is made of pieces of various fabrics cut to one shape such as a rectangle or hexagon.

The cardinal rule for patchwork is accuracy since the pieces must fit together perfectly. Even if you are working with only a square—one of the simplest shapes—the squares must be sewed with precision, because it is very easy to see if one side is shorter than another.

Block chart and piecing plan

For any patchwork pattern, you should make a *block chart*—a detailed picture of how your finished block will look. Draw it to actual size on heavy paper. (If you are copying a block pattern, you may have to enlarge it to suit your needs; see page 54.) Use the block chart to work out a *piecing plan*. A piecing plan enables you to sew patches together in the fastest, easiest way because it utilizes a system of unit construction. As a general rule, you will work in units by joining small patches first, then adding larger ones. Make other units the same way; then join the units. The object is to put the pieces together in such a way as to take advantage of as many long, straight seams as possible. Try to join all straight edges first; then fit in the patches that have curved edges.

Naturally, your design will determine the piecing order. Study the example, following the numbers to determine the sequence of piecing. Notice that there are several similar units that are put together first, then joined to make larger units, which go together to make one complete block.

Another method, if your block has a center section, is to start with the center section and sew the surrounding patches to it. Continue adding to the nucleus until the block is finished. Such a piecing plan is particularly applicable to random patchwork and has been expanded into a "quilt-as-you-patch" technique.*

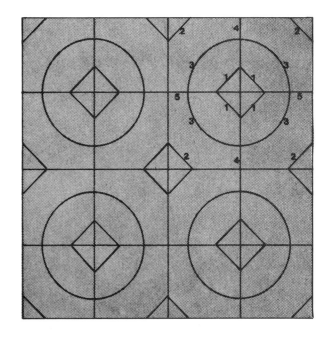

Glittering with golden brocade, sumptuous with silk, velvet, satin and lace, a quilted patchwork jacket proves that quilted keepsakes aren't always bedcoverings. A garment such as this is to be treasured equally by each generation who wears it. Pattern: Grandma's Favorite.

---

* This technique is covered in great detail in *Award Winning Quilts* by Effie Chalmers Pforr, Oxmoor House, Inc., 1974.

Cutting the patches

Each shape in the block chart must have a template. See the "Patterns and Templates" section for how to make the templates and how to mark and cut the fabric pieces. For patchwork, remember always to mark on the *wrong* side of the fabric.

Stitching

The order of stitching the patches together should follow your piecing plan, whether you stitch by hand or by machine. It can be to your advantage to use a combination of hand and machine stitches in one block. Small seams, curves, and corners can be more easily manipulated and eased into a perfect fit when hand sewing. Long, straight seams are stronger when sewed on the machine.

Accuracy and neatness are important in your stitching. Seams must be an even width: *stitch only on the seamline.* This is the only way the units will fit precisely together. At corners, stitch all the way to the end; then stop stitches, and start again on the adjoining side. Do not try to turn corners with continuous stitching.

Work in the following manner whether joining one patch to another, one unit to another, or one block to another. Place two patches (or units, or blocks) together, right sides facing. Pin, matching seamlines exactly. If sewing by hand, use quilting thread and a size 9 "between" needle. (If you are experienced with another needle size and prefer it, then by all means use the needle which is most comfortable for you.) Make your stitches as small as possible; try for about 10 per inch (2.5cm). Use a running stitch to make the seam, and secure the seams with a few backstitches. If you are using the sewing machine, select a straight stitch, about 12 per inch (2.5cm), and a thread to match the fiber content of the fabric. Do not backstitch at the beginning and end of the seams. Instead, tie the thread ends together. If the seam is to be crossed by another seam, the crossing will secure first line of stitching.

As you sew, press the seam allowances to one side, preferably toward the darker colored patches. Never press the seams open, as this will weaken the construction.

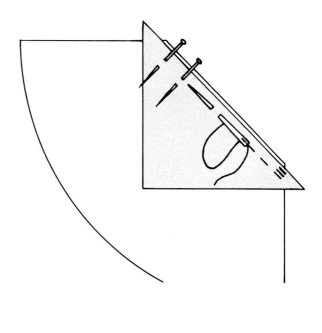

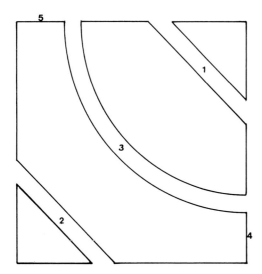

The English paper-liner system

A different hand-stitching method, the English paper-liner system is the only way to sew "true" patchwork according to some purists. Although a little more involved, this system assures that patches will fit together more exactly. It is especially useful for continuous one-patch designs, such as hexagons or diamonds, which have some straight and some bias edges.

Using your template, draw and cut as many finished-sized paper patches (meaning without the seam allowance) as you have fabric patches. Pin each paper patch to the center of its fabric patch on the wrong side. Press the fabric seam allowance back over the paper smoothly; then baste the seam allowance in place, stitching through the paper. To sew two such prepared patches together, hold them with the right sides facing and stitch with a tiny overhand stitch; do *not* stitch through the paper this time. Make tiny knots at the beginning and end of each seam. Continue adding patches in the same manner until you have completed the block; then remove the basting stitches and the paper liners.

Press the block

When the piecing is done, pull the edges of the block straight and pin the corners to your ironing board. Cover with a damp cloth, and steam press from the edges toward the center.

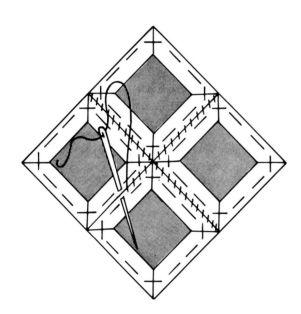

Patterns and Templates

The difference between a pattern and a template is that the pattern is not used on the fabric; instead, it is copied onto some type of sturdy material to make the template. The sturdy template is then placed on the fabric and traced the required number of times. This way, the pattern is not damaged and remains to be used for many more quilts. Additionally, tracing around templates assures greater accuracy in cutting the fabric pieces than would pinning the paper pattern in place and cutting around it.

Patterns

If you use an established pattern from a commercial source or a book, all you must do is check the pattern by making a test block; then make your templates. The purpose of making a test block is not only to see how well you like working with the pattern, but also to check the fit of the pieces as well. In the printing process, a pattern piece can sometimes lose some degree of its accuracy; it is a good idea to check each pattern piece before cutting all the pieces for the quilt.

However, if you have created your own quilt design, you must make your own pattern for the quilt block. The best way to do this is to start by drawing your design, actual size, onto a large sheet of ¼"

(6mm) graph paper. On another piece of graph paper, trace each shape individually, leaving plenty of space in between the shapes. Carefully add a ¼" (6mm) seam allowance around each shape. The first line you traced is the stitching line; the second line is the cutting line. Identify each pattern piece in some way, either with a name, a letter, or a number. It is also wise to put the name of the quilt pattern on each piece.

If your quilt block design is to be executed in a free-form appliqué, as is common with scenics or fabric paintings, you will have a fairly easy time drawing your pattern pieces. The main concern is that each shape be smoothly formed and pleasing to the eye and has a seam allowance for turning under and finishing the edge if necessary.

Geometric designs, particularly for patchwork, must be drawn precisely if the pieces are to fit together properly. Straight lines must be perfectly straight, angles must be accurate, curves must be smooth. Working on graph paper will help insure accuracy, as the grid of lines serves as a sort of governor to prevent mistakes. A small investment in a good ruler, preferably marked off in ⅛" (3mm) squares, a plastic or metal triangle, a French curve (also known as an S-curve), and a compass will pay off many times over.

Here are some of the more common geometric shapes. Use these as guides to help you draw your geometric patterns perfectly.

Square

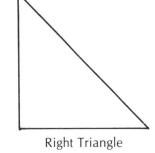

Right Triangle

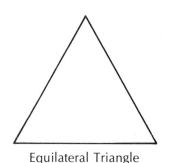

Equilateral Triangle

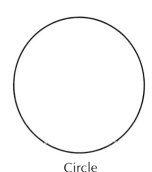

Circle

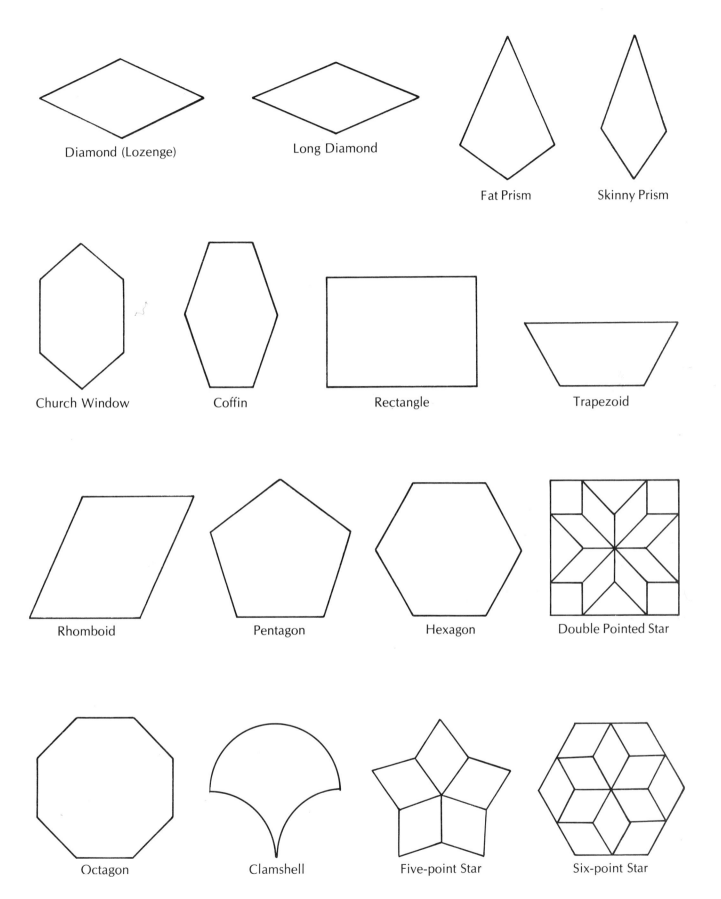

Diamond (Lozenge)

Long Diamond

Fat Prism

Skinny Prism

Church Window

Coffin

Rectangle

Trapezoid

Rhomboid

Pentagon

Hexagon

Double Pointed Star

Octagon

Clamshell

Five-point Star

Six-point Star

Enlarging patterns

It is seldom that you find a pattern that is exactly the size you need. Do not let this inhibit your creativity; enlarging or reducing a pattern is quite simple.

The very easiest way to size up a pattern is to have it photostatically enlarged. Simply instruct the photostat company as to what size you want the pattern pieces to be. The cost will vary and this service is usually found only in larger towns and cities.

You can easily enlarge or reduce a pattern yourself by using ¼" (6mm) graph paper. You should be able to tell in advance whether or not the piece you want to enlarge will fit on one sheet of paper, or whether you must tape several pieces together to get the area you need.

First trace the design you wish to enlarge onto graph paper. If the design is to be twice as large, use two blocks for every one block on the original. Copy carefully, transferring what is in each square to the larger scale. It is helpful sometimes to outline the design with a series of dots, then connect the dots using your straight edge and French curve to make the lines smooth. Study the following examples carefully.

In example A, we want to enlarge a church window. The original scale is that each block equals ¼" (6mm). To make it twice as large, each space which is presently contained in one block must be stretched to two. The length of the church window from end to end is eight squares; the width is four squares. When enlarged, the length should be sixteen squares and the width eight. Count off sixteen in length and eight in width on graph paper as shown. Draw the lengthwise and crosswise lines every two blocks to give yourself a larger scale. Draw the church window onto the new scale, transferring exactly to the larger squares what is in each of the smaller squares.

Irregular shapes are just as easily enlarged. Draw your new scale onto your graph paper, then copy exactly what is in each of the smaller squares. In example B, you see how easy it is.

A regular shape such as a diamond or a square can be enlarged by merely extending the sides with a straight edge to the desired length, as shown in example C.

A

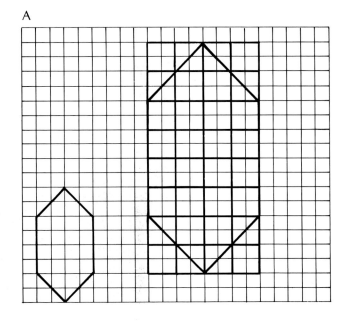

B

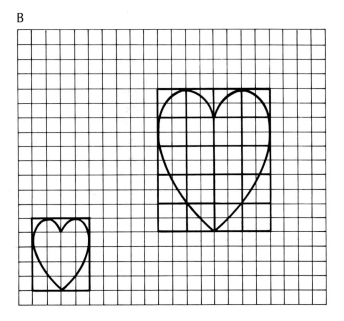

C

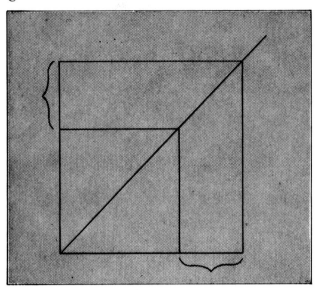

Templates

A template should be made of durable material, as you will be drawing around it repeatedly, and it is important that the sides remain true. The sturdiest materials readily available are acetate, which comes from art supply stores in sheets, and plastic, such as the lids from coffee and shortening cans or margarine tubs. Sometimes the flat sides of plastic bottles can be used. Transparent plastic is easiest to work with.

Sandpaper and cardboard have been traditional choices for templates, but the edges fray and become soft with repeated use, making it necessary to remake the templates. However, an identical piece of sandpaper (size 00) glued to the bottom of a plastic or acetate template prevents the template from slipping. If the sandpaper wears away, it is easily replaced, and the plastic is sure to remain the true shape. Many fabric or craft shops have metal templates in popular shapes and sizes, which can be ordered by mail; look for ads in the shopper section of craft and women's magazines. The commercial metal templates are ideal, but plastic templates are just as durable and are simple and inexpensive to construct.

Window templates

The patterns in this book all include a ¼" (6mm) seam allowance. The inside line in each pattern is the seamline; the outside line is the cutting line. A window template is one that is solid only in the ¼" (6mm) between these two lines; the center shape is cut out.

Window templates are recommended for marking fabric because these will allow you to mark both the seamline and the cutting line at one time on your fabric, as well as to see the exact design of each individual fabric piece.

To make a window template, you must first transfer the pattern to the template material so that you can cut out the template. If you are using transparent plastic, simply place the plastic over the pattern, and very carefully trace the cutting and seamlines onto the plastic with a ballpoint pen or sharpened crayon. It may help to use a ruler to keep these lines straight. If your plastic is not transparent, place a sheet of carbon paper behind the paper pattern and your piece of plastic beneath the carbon, and trace the pattern lines onto the plastic.

Carefully cut out the template with a sharp scalpel, modeling knife, matte knife, or similar razor-edge cutting tool. Cut along the outside cutting line first, then along the inside seamline. You now have a plastic window. The inside edge, in the cut-out area, outlines the finished size of the shape and is used to mark the seamline; the outside edge includes the seam allowance and is used to mark the cutting line. Save the piece you cut from the center to use as an aid for turning under seam allowances.

Window template

Marking your fabric

When estimating fabric yardage, you figured out how many shapes could be cut across the width of the fabric. Marking the template shapes on the fabric should now proceed accordingly. Make sure the fabric is on-grain and wrinkle-free; then place the template near the edge, avoiding the selvage.

Squares and other straight-edged shapes should be placed on the grain of the fabric. Odd shapes should be placed with the longest direction on the lengthwise grain. (See "Working with fabric grain.")

When cutting patchwork shapes, mark on the wrong side of the fabric. When cutting pieces for appliqué, mark on the right side of the fabric.

With a pointed, soft-lead pencil or dressmaker's pencil, trace around the outside edge and the inside edge of the window template. Sharpen your pencil frequently to keep lines true; it is difficult to decide where to cut along a thick line. When you have marked all the shapes you need from that fabric, cut out the shapes with sharp scissors.

Tracing the template

If your pattern calls for many small rectangles or squares from the same fabric, these may be cut in strips without the use of a template. Lay the fabric out smoothly. Prepare a straight edge across the width, either by pulling out a crosswise thread and trimming along that line, or by folding the edge of the fabric back about 2" (5cm), evening the selvages on both sides, pressing the fabric smooth, then trimming along the pressed line. Figure the width of the strips, including a ¼" (6mm) seam allowance for each side; if your finished strips will be 1" wide (2.5cm), cut 1½" (3.8cm) wide strips from the fabric. With a long straightedge, mark the wrong side of the fabric all the way across. Beginning at the straightened edge, mark a ¼" (6mm) seam line across the width of the fabric; then another line across the fabric the width of the strip (1" [2.5cm] in the example given above), then another ¼" (6mm) seam allowance. This third line will be your cutting line for the entire fabric strip. Continue with as many additional strips as you need. Now mark and cut lengths from these long strips in the same manner, avoiding the selvages. Each of the pieces you cut in this way will then have the seam allowances marked for sewing.

To keep all like shapes together until you need them for stitching, string them together on one thread or stack them in a small plastic bag.

It seems natural to combine quilting, wicker, and a porch swing for a sunny, bright outdoor room. A quilted cozy, trimmed with an adaptation of the pattern on the swing upholstery, keeps coffee hot in the pot. The rocker cushions are tufted, and the throw pillow in the swing is big enough to serve as a floor pillow for a child. Patterns used: San José Rose, Grandma's Fan, Pride of the South.

Quilting

Quilting, joining the three layers of top, filler, and backing, serves two purposes. First, it holds the quilt together. Secondly, quilting adds dimension to the visual interest of the finished work; it is a highly individualistic part of the design process. In fact, there have been several periods in quilting history when elaborate, overall stitching designs have served as the single decorative element on plain (usually white) top and backing fabrics, creating a fascinating play of light and shadows.

Quilting may also serve to highlight and emphasize the design of the quilt top. For example, in a pieced quilt that contains both decorative and plain blocks, the quilting may follow and outline the patterns in the decorative blocks and form different contrasting designs in the plain blocks. Straight-lined designs in plain blocks contrast well with curved designs in decorative blocks and vice versa. If a decorative block is an appliquéd picture, the quilting may form additional details such as clouds, rays of sunlight, or smoke from a chimney. Distinctive running or repeat designs are often quilted on sashing strips and borders.

Traditional quilting patterns abound in books and many can be purchased, but whether you borrow from these or create your own quilting patterns, the variations are endless. Quilters for centuries have based quilting patterns on handy, familiar objects or shapes—stars, diamonds, bells, shells, chains, flowers, feathers, birds, baskets, ships, even utensils and tools.

When planning your quilting designs, there are a couple of points to bear in mind. Generally, diagonal stitching lines on a quilt will show up better and last longer than horizontal and vertical stitching lines. More specifically, stitching that follows the bias of a fabric rather than the grain will help prevent the fabric from tearing or pulling apart. The closer your lines of quilting, the stronger the construction of your quilt.

Marking the quilting pattern on the quilt top

It is best to mark the entire quilting pattern on the quilt top before you assemble the quilt.

If you do not feel comfortable about stitching freehand by sight around motifs in outline quilting, place strips of masking tape or special sewing tape marked in different widths around the edges of the motif and quilt along the edge of the tape.

Use a ruler and tailor's chalk to mark straight lines. Or use the traditional method of snapping a chalked string that you've pulled taut across the quilt top and anchored with pins. For circular patterns, use a glass, cup, or plate, or improvise a compass with a pin, string, and marker. For other simple shapes, you may make templates out of cardboard. Mark around the edges with tailor's chalk, dressmaker's pencil, or soap slivers; or scratch the fabric with a needle. Lead pencil marking is not recommended; it does not easily wash out.

You can make a perforated pattern for more complex designs. First, draw the quilting design on paper. Pierce the lines at regular intervals with a sharp pencil, needle, or tracing wheel. (This can also be done on the sewing machine with an unthreaded needle.) Position the perforated design on the quilt top and mark the fabric through the perforations with stamping paste or powder (available in fabric and craft stores, directions included), chalk, or ground cinnamon. You may find it even simpler to pierce both pattern and fabric at the same time with a needle and use the needle marks as a quilting guide.

Hand quilting

Traditional quilting is done by hand on a quilting frame. It is certainly not the only way, but it is one of the best ways to assure that a large, bulky quilt turns out smooth and properly rectangular. An important point to remember for frame quilting is that the backing fabric must be cut 3" to 4" (7.5cm to 10cm) larger than the quilt top all around to allow for frame-frayed edges.

Quilting may also be done on a large wooden hoop, usually 22" (55.9cm) in diameter. Quilting hoops may be round or oval and some of them also come with a floor stand so that you don't have to hold everything in your lap while you stitch.

Assembling on the floor

Before you begin quilting a large quilt, you must assemble the three layers—backing, filler, and marked quilt top—in such a way that they will hold together without slipping around or bunching up while you sew. One of the best and simplest methods is to spread the quilt out, layer by layer, on the floor (preferably uncarpeted) and baste the layers together. Pin-basting should be sufficient, or you may find thread-basting easier to manage than pins, particularly if you are using a hoop.

First spread out the backing fabric, wrong side up, making sure it is smooth. Gently and carefully roll out the filler onto the backing, easing out any wrinkles; then trim the edges of the filler even with the edges of the backing. Carefully spread out the quilt top, right side up, so that you do not shift the filling. Then adjust lightly until all three layers are smooth and square and there are absolutely no wrinkles.

Pin-baste very carefully with long dressmaker's pins: do not lift the quilt or shift or bunch the materials. Use plenty of pins positioned in close parallel rows. Be especially careful about wrinkling the quilt if you have to crawl onto it.

If you choose to baste with thread, stitch at least eight long rows: two full-length diagonals, from opposite corners; two perpendicular lines, one across the center width, and one down the center length, and four outside basting lines, one across each end and one down each side. Or substitute diagonals for the side and end seams so that all basting lines radiate from the center.

You are now ready to attach the quilt to your frame according to the specifications of your individual frame.

Method 2

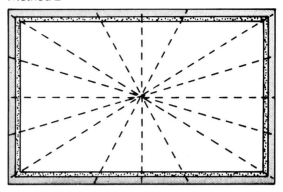

Assembling on the frame

It is also possible to assemble the layers of the quilt and baste them right on the frame. Start with the backing (which should be 3" to 4" [7.5cm to 10cm] larger all around than the quilt top) and stitch it with strong thread to the webbing or ticking on the side bars of the frame. Carefully unroll and spread the filling over the backing. Then very gently smooth the marked quilt top over the filling. Baste the top and backing together along the sides. The whole assembly will appear very puffy, but some of this puffiness will be removed when you roll the bars toward the middle of the quilt to begin stitching, and the quilting will take care of the rest.

However you go about assembling the layers, the important thing to remember is to keep every layer wrinkle-free, or the wrinkles will be quilted into the finished piece. Never stretch your filling, or you will leave weak areas in the quilt. Whether you baste with pins or thread, always baste closely enough to hold the work together securely throughout the quilting process.

Method 1

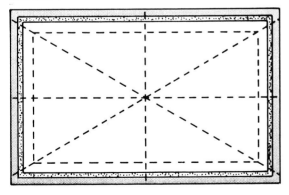

Quilting on the frame

If you are quilting alone, roll up the side bars so that the midline of the quilt is halfway between the bars and you have an arm's length of working area on either side. Start in the center and quilt toward you, following the quilting pattern markings. When you have quilted the entire area from both sides of the frame, unroll one side another foot or so at a time and continue quilting toward you. Quilt all of one side in this manner; then roll up that side and quilt the other.

Work with your right hand on top of the quilt (if you're right-handed) and your left hand underneath to guide the needle. You may find this position a little awkward at first, but it will not take long to get used to it, and you will find that it is a very efficient way to quilt.

Quilting on a hoop

Place the center of the basted quilt into the hoop so that the working area is smooth and taut. Any puffiness should be gently squeezed out at the edges. Begin stitching in the center of the hoop and work toward the edges, turning the work as needed so that you are always working toward you. Work outward from the center of the quilt, moving the hoop in circular positions toward the edges. When you reach the edge, you may work with smaller embroidery hoops.

Stitching

A beginning quilter should experiment with stitching a small layered sample piece (you could make it into a potholder) of a similar thickness before quilting a carefully planned heirloom-to-be. Not that quilting is difficult; you will simply want to establish a comfortable rhythm and even spacing for your running stitch through the thick material; experiment with needles; get used to a thimble, if you are not already, on either the index or middle finger; and practice starting and stopping a line of stitching so that the interruptions do not show.

Quilting is usually done with a relatively short straight needle, size 8 to 10 sharp or between, and with quilting thread in about 15" to 20" (37.5cm to 50cm) lengths at a time. (Too long a working thread will tangle easily.) The shorter, thicker needles will

not bend or break as easily as longer ones, although some quilters even prefer curved needles. Most quilting thread is coated with silicone to help it slip through the layers of fabric and filler, but you may also use #50 cotton thread or cotton-covered polyester thread. Never use doubled thread for quilting; threads rubbing together weaken each other and don't last as long as a single strong thread. Coating each needleful of thread with beeswax will help prevent knotting. A thimble is a must in quilting to protect your stitching finger, and you will also need to protect the guiding finger on the hand beneath the quilt with a rubber cap or a strip of adhesive bandage.

Take small running stitches along the pattern marking lines. Traditional quilters will tell you to make anywhere from six to twelve stitches per inch, but the shorter the stitches, the better they will hold when the quilt is washed. Many experienced quilters can take several even stitches at once on the needle; others quilt quite rapidly taking one stitch at a time, down through all the layers, then back up again, making stitches the same length on top and bottom.

There are two methods of starting and stopping a line of stitching: knotting the thread and locking it. Most quilters stick with one method and vow that the other is all wrong, but both work well.

If you *knot* the thread, begin with a small knot at the end of a single thread. Bring the needle up from the bottom through all the layers; then tug gently until the knot pulls through the backing and rests hidden in the filler. To end the stitching line, stop before your last stitch and knot the thread close to the quilt top. Make the last stitch, and tug the knot through the top into the filler. Run the remaining thread an inch or so through the filling so that the next stitches will secure it; then bring the needle out and cut the thread even with the quilt top.

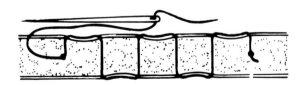

To *lock* your thread, start by inserting the needle through the top into the filler only, about 1" (2.5cm) down the stitching line from your actual starting point. Run the needle back through the filler, and bring it out again at the starting point for stitching. Leave a little tail until you pass it on the way back with your running stitches; then clip it off. When you are almost out of thread, lock the end of the stitching line the same way, by slipping the needle back about 1" (2.5cm) through the filler; bring out the needle and snip off the tail of thread.

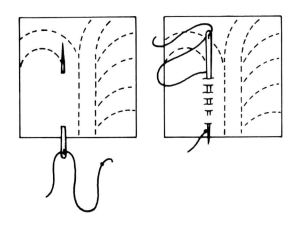

Machine quilting

Anything that can be quilted by hand could conceivably be quilted by sewing machine, up to and including a full-size bedcovering. But to be realistic, there are times when machine quilting can be advantageous, and other times when it is really not the better method. Machine quilting is not recommended for very large items; it is extremely cumbersome and offers too many chances for error. It requires such close thread-basting beforehand that you would undoubtedly save time and trouble to pin-baste and hand-quilt instead.

On the positive side, machine quilting can work extremely well on small, lightweight pieces, from potholders to pillow tops to baby quilts. It can be a very effective decorative detail on simple garments such as a long, slightly flared skirt. Use a commercial pattern, and for each pattern piece, cut two pieces of fabric, a top and a backing. Each must be slightly larger than the pattern to allow for shrinkage

caused by quilting. If you want a less bulky look, separate sheet batting into thinner layers. Thread-baste the three layers together; then machine-quilt in desired pattern before joining the pieces of the garment together.

Another consideration for machine quilting is the degree of elaborateness of the stitching design. Geometric designs with long, straight lines or simple large curves may be easily done by machine; intricate scrollwork and feather designs may not.

It is possible to machine-quilt even a large quilt if you use special methods. Apartment quilting can be done by machine, since you quilt small units first, then join units. (See "Apartment quilting.")

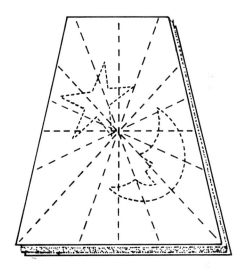

Stitching

You must test machine quilting methods on a trial piece which incorporates all the layers of the quilt. Although a straight stitch is the most usual choice for machine quilting, you might want to experiment with different stitches. Choose a lighter pressure setting and a looser tension setting; retain the presser foot. It is not necessary to place the work in a hoop. Practice stitching the quilting pattern until you are satisfied with the results, and write down the exact machine settings that give you these results. Do not trust your memory.

Apartment quilting

Apartment quilting, named because of the limited space in an apartment, is a practical solution to limited space problems and also makes your quilting project easy to take with you. It is a way of putting together a large quilt, yet taking up very little room in the process. Each quilt block, or perhaps as large a section as a fourth of the quilt, is quilted separately. When all the blocks or sections are quilted, they are then set together.

After all of your quilt top blocks are made and pressed, decide whether you prefer to work in blocks or in units. If you choose to work in units, go ahead and piece and press each unit before you begin quilting any of them. Then mark your quilting designs on individual blocks or units as needed.

Cut backing and filling for one block or unit to the same size as the block or unit. On a table, spread the backing layer wrong side up; smooth out the filler onto it; then carefully position the quilt top, smoothing the work until it is perfectly placed and wrinkle-free. Pin or thread-baste the layers together. Then quilt the piece, either by hand or by machine, to within ½" (1.3cm) of each edge. Use a hoop if you are quilting by hand.

When you have each block or unit quilted, join the sections together. Place two sections together, tops facing. Taking a ¼" (6mm) seam, sew only the edges of the tops together with a running stitch. (This also may be done by machine.) Next, open the work out again and arrange the filler pieces to overlap about ¼" (6mm). Then turn under each edge of the backings ¼" (6mm) and sew the backings together by hand with a slipstitch.

Continue joining all the sections in the same manner.

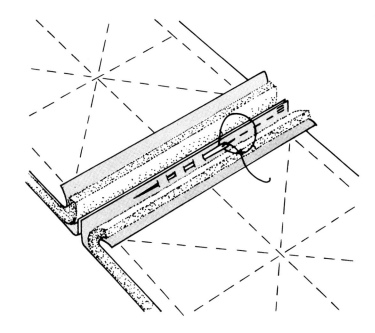

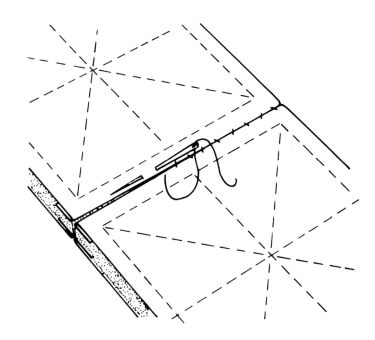

Setting a Quilt Together

Once you have decided on an overall pattern for your quilt, and have painstakingly made each of the quilt blocks and neatly pressed them, it is time to set them together to make the quilt top.

You are to be commended if you wish to hand-stitch the blocks together, but let's face it: machine stitching, especially at this stage, is not only fast and easy, it also adds to the sturdiness of the work.

If your design calls for some additional plain blocks, cut as many of those as you need from smooth, on-grain fabric.

Joining blocks in a rectangular pattern

Lay out all the blocks in order according to your design. Pin them all together to make sure that they fit properly. Make any adjustments or corrections to the blocks that you find to be necessary.

Work in vertical or horizontal rows. You may wish to pin-baste the ¼" (6mm) seams of all the blocks in the row as a safety measure before you stitch. Use a straight stitch, about 10 stitches to the inch (2.5cm), to join each block to the next one. When the row is all stitched, cover with a cloth and steam-press on the wrong side.

When each row has been stitched and pressed in this manner, join the rows to complete the quilt top.

Joining sashed patterns

You may have included harmonizing sashing in your original design. This is a very distinctive way of connecting individual blocks when each is a separate design with its own emphasis. Sashing (framing lattice strips of fabric between the blocks) is usually 2" to 3" (5cm to 7.5cm) wide. When you cut the strips (they may also be pieced, if you like), remember to include a ¼" (6mm) seam allowance on each side.

You will need long strips for either the length or the width of the finished quilt and short strips for the opposite direction. Assuming that you will work in vertical rows, you will first cut the long strips, one more strip than the number of rows of blocks. Cut shorter strips the width of each block. For *each* row, you will need the same number of short strips as you have blocks, plus one.

To make rows, join the first two short strips to the top and bottom of the first block; then join the remaining blocks and strips in the row. Join strips and blocks in each row in the same manner.

Sew the rows together with the long sashing strips between, taking care to match up exactly the crosswise strips as you join the rows.

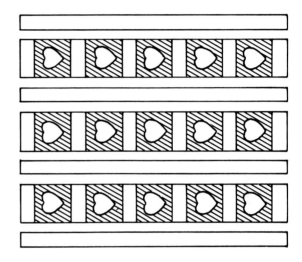

Other joining plans

If your overall pattern is other than rectangular (diagonal, for example), you will need to study your design sketch and decide on a joining plan, the same way you worked out a piecing plan for a patchwork block. Here again, for strength, take advantage of as many long, straight seams as possible.

Borders

You may wish to add a border to your quilt top before quilting, or make a border of the binding material after quilting. Refer to the "Borders and Bindings" section.

Pressing

After the quilt top is set together, give it a final pressing before you begin quilting to make sure the overall shape is properly rectangular.

Trapunto

The term *trapunto,* which technically refers to an Italian technique of corded designs, is sometimes used to describe stuffed or padded designs that are English in origin. The techniques are very similar and are often used in combination; the stuffing materials are the only real difference. The term as used in this book includes stuffed and corded designs. Trapunto is actually a method of quilting in itself, since it involves stitching a top fabric and a backing together with a filler in between. However, the filler material is inserted after the stitching is done and is used only in certain parts of a design for its relief effect; it is not a full-sized batting.

When the trapunto design is sewed through the two layers of fabric, the stitching is like the lines of a drawing. The filler material is inserted to raise and highlight parts of the drawing to create a sculptured surface effect.

The technique is not difficult to execute and its uses are unlimited. Trapunto makes interesting pillow tops, afghans, small appliance covers, potholders, clothing decoration, handbags, chair seat covers—the list could go on and on. Additional design possibilities exist when you consider combining trapunto with embroidery or appliqué.

Designs

Large, relatively simple outline designs usually work best with trapunto. But there are certainly no hard and fast rules. If you start out with a very simple floral motif, you might enjoy it so much that you could eventually try your hand at sculptured fabric portraits. It is not necessary to be an accomplished illustrator; the artistry lies in deciding whether to cord or to stuff, and which parts of a design to raise in this manner and which to leave flat.

Whether you create or borrow your design, play around with paper, pencil, and eraser until you achieve the desired effect, taking full advantage of trapunto's unique qualities.

Fabrics

Here again, the choice is almost unlimited. In general, however, plain, solid colors make an excellent mute background for fancy trapunto. On the other hand, if, in your travels through the fabric store, you spot a particularly exciting pattern, you might consider using that as a design, stitching around and highlighting parts of the pattern with stuffing or cording. A closely woven fabric works better with cording; terry cloth or even burlap works well with stuffing. In deciding on a top fabric, give some consideration to the kind of stitching you would like to use. There are all kinds of creative possibilities when you think about the combined effects of design; color, weight and texture of fabric; and the use of thread, yarn, or embroidery floss for stitching.

The best backing fabric is a crisp, woven interfacing. However, any coarsely woven fabric will do: muslin, scrim, or cheesecloth, to name a few. Sheer curtain fabrics such as marquisette and ninon make excellent choices for the backing fabric. The backing fabric should be strong enough to force the padding material to the front of the work, and the top fabric should be soft enough to give without puckering. The fabric back is generally covered with a lining of some sort when the trapunto piece is made into a finished item.

Stitching

The major decision in trapunto is whether or not you want the stitching to be a prominent part of the overall design. That decision will determine whether you use matching or contrasting colors;

A touch of quilting on each of these gift ideas turns the ordinary into the spectacular. The Sunflower *quilt pattern enhances the bib front of an apron; a stunning quilt block design,* Elkhorn, *appears on the back of a denim jacket; the quilt design* The Sunrise *sparks the hem of a bathrobe. A favorite toy for a little girl is a tiny doll crib with its own miniature quilt—made from just one quilt block of your design. The quilted banner is a beautiful personalized fabric painting, the design of which should come from your own observations.*

large or small stitches; yarn, embroidery thread, or regular sewing thread. You can machine stitch, if you like, and if you want it to show, use buttonhole twist. If you choose to hand-stitch, use either a running stitch or a back stitch, whichever works best with the chosen fabric.

Before you begin stitching, transfer your drawing in reverse onto the backing material. (Dressmaker's carbon paper is a handy aid here.) Pin or baste the two layers, *wrong sides together,* so that they do not slip as you work. Then stitch from the backing side following the design, and check the front of the work often to be sure the stitches look the way you want them to.

An alternative method is to mark the design on the top piece with small dotted lines that will be covered by your stitching. Then you are able to work from the front and will probably achieve neater stitching. If your stitching is not to be a prominent feature of the overall design, the stuffed or corded area will overshadow it to a small degree and hide tiny stitching errors.

Particularly with corded designs, it is best not to cross lines of stitching. If you sew by machine, do not backstitch to finish a line; instead, pull the threads to the wrong side and tie them. Or, move the stitch length setting on your sewing machine to zero and take about five stitches to lock the line of stitching. (The stitches will be on top of one another.)

Cording

For corded areas, you will make two *even*, parallel lines of stitching for a channel to pull the cording through. Depending on the size of the cording, make the parallel lines ⅛" (3mm) to ½" (1.3cm) apart. When stitching is completed, thread the cording material (usually yarn or candlewicking) into a blunt-end, size 18 tapestry needle. Spread the threads of the backing material, taking care not to break them, and insert the needle into the channel. Draw the cording the length of the channel and bring the needle out. Clip the ends of the cording; then tug the fabrics lightly until both ends of the cording are enclosed in the channel.

At curves and corners, bring the needle out through the backing, leave a small loop of cording for give, then reinsert the needle into the channel.

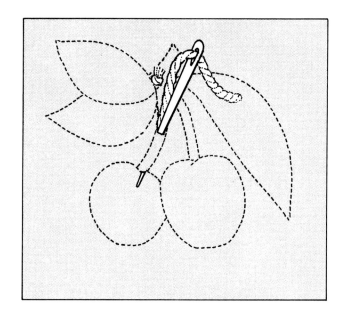

Stuffing

A good stuffing material is polyester fiber fill that comes in bags. You might also use small pieces of fabric, but these may have a tendency to bunch up if you wash the finished piece.

There are four ways to insert the stuffing:
1. Leave a 1" (2.5cm) opening in the stitching of the design; insert the stuffing through the opening with your finger; then finish the stitching.

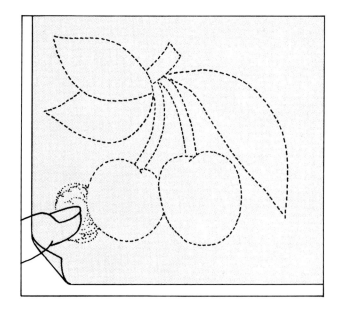

2. Somewhere near the center of the area to be stuffed, carefully separate the threads of the backing material without breaking them. Insert the stuffing through this opening, with the aid of a large crochet hook or knitting needle; then tug lightly on the backing fabric to close the threads again.

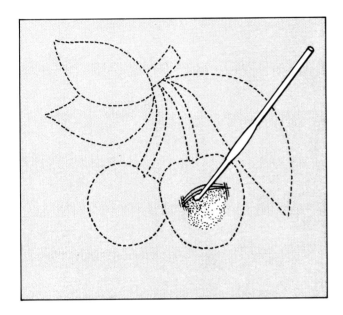

3. Make a small slit in the backing fabric, insert the stuffing material through the slit, and hand-stitch the opening back together.

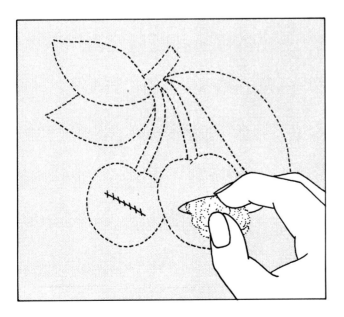

4. Use a large blunt needle (size 18 tapestry needle is good) and acrylic yarn. Start in the center of the area to be stuffed. Insert the needle at one side of the design between the two layers and pull it out the other side, leaving a long stitch of yarn in the area to be stuffed. Reinsert needle, leaving a small loop of yarn, and take another stitch. Continue working down to one end of the design; then fill in the other half. This method holds the stuffing (which is the yarn) in place for the life of the piece, eliminating the possibility of shifting and bunching.

Be careful not to overstuff and pucker your design. It does not take a lot of stuffing to achieve a striking effect.

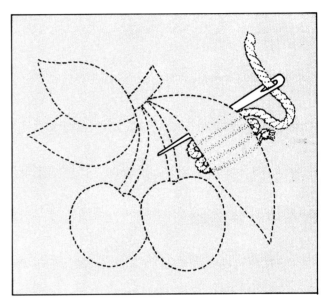

Finishing the work

The finishing technique depends entirely on how you plan to use the trapunto piece. Most uses will require that the inside of the piece be lined or finished off in some manner. The backing fabric does not always make a good-looking lining. Here are a couple of ideas for what to do with your first effort.

If you have worked your trapunto in a picture-frame size, why not frame the piece and hang it on the wall? Trim and hem the edges to the desired size, or add an interesting border. Mount the piece on cardboard or thin plywood and enclose it in some kind of frame. Or simply turn the edges over the board and glue them down.

If you have worked in a rather large size, make an afghan. Use another piece of fabric exactly like the top piece or in a contrasting color, in the same size. Place it on top of your trapunto design, right sides together; stitch around three sides and all four corners as if you were making a pillow cover; then turn the work inside out and hand-stitch the fourth side. Then topstitch all around the edge to hold the pieces of fabric in place.

Tufting

Tufting, or tying together the layers of an item to be quilted, has one big advantage over quilting: it is much easier and faster—which has a certain appeal for those who like shortcuts. Once upon a time, when laundering a quilt was no easy task, tufting was a way to simplify the process. (Some of our foremothers were eager to take shortcuts, too!) On washday, the ties could be cut, the quilt taken apart, the back and top washed and ironed, while the bulky cotton or wool batting got a good airing in the sun. The quilt could be retufted with little trouble.

That may not be a consideration today when laundering is easier and batting is so much better. But tufting is still one of the simplest ways to quilt, and it is possible to do as sturdy a job of quilting this way as with a simple stitching design. The technique can also be used in combination with stitched quilting for further decorative possibilities.

You can, if you wish, mark your quilt top with tailor's chalk as to where the tufts will be positioned. However, the design of the quilt top may dictate where the tufts should go, and no further marking will be necessary. Remember that the tufts, especially if you incorporate buttons or bows, add a strong element of surface interest and should be planned to enhance the theme of the quilt design.

There are two ways to make the tufts.

1. Use a needle with a large eye—an embroidery or yarn darning needle—threaded double with three or four strands of lightweight yarn. Make one stitch with this needle, down and back up through all the layers, pulling through all the yarn except a 2" (5cm) end on the surface. Clip the needle side to leave another 2" (5cm) strand; then tie the two strands together in a secure double knot. When you have made all the knots, trim the end of the yarn as evenly as possible, choosing a length which enhances your design.

2. You will need quilting thread or size 50 sewing thread and a supply of yarn, small buttons, bows, or whatever you wish to use to accent your design. Thread your sewing needle with the thread. Leave a long thread and make one stitch down and back up through all the layers; then clip the thread so that you have another thread end about 2" (5cm) long on top of the work. Make a double knot with these ends. Place three or four strands of yarn over the knot; then make another double knot with

the thread to hold the yarn in place. If you use buttons, place them so they are caught in the stitch, rather than just tied on; in fact, you may take two or three stitches through the buttons for strength.

Your tufting will be most satisfactory if it is done with the quilt on a frame, but that is not absolutely necessary. As long as you are careful, you can use a quilting hoop or even a table top. (See "Quilting—Assembling on the floor" and "Quilting—Assembling on the frame" for preparation of the piece for tufting.)

Method 1

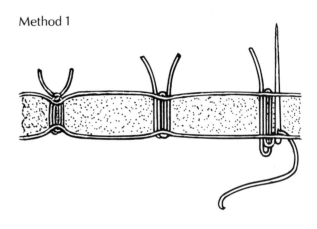

Method 2

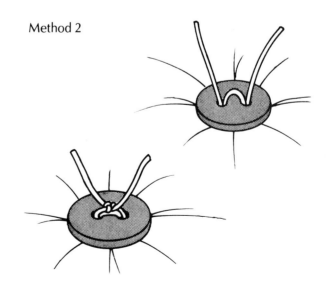

Prize Winning Quilt Patterns

Each pattern presented here received an honorable mention or was one of the three top prize winners in the *Progressive Farmer* quilt block contest. The patterns and color photographs are arranged alphabetically for easy reference, and each design is accompanied by the contestant's statement. (Please remember that the color blocks are photographs of the original entries in most cases, and you should feel free to adapt color schemes to your own preferences.) All patterns have been tested for accuracy, and quilt blocks have been made from each pattern in firmly woven fabric. Keep in mind that different fabrics and different people will cause quilt patterns to work up differently. Test any pattern you plan to make in the fabric you plan to use, and make sure the pattern works for you before you begin a major project with it.

The color photographs of the quilt blocks are arranged alphabetically by quilt block name. The patterns for the quilt blocks follow the color section and are also arranged alphabetically. Following the name of each quilt block in the color section is the beginning page for its pattern.

Second place winner in Progressive Farmer *magazine's quilt block contest,* The Courthouse Square *shows its winning ways in a full quilt. The bold design and striking solid-color fabrics combine to make a strong graphic statement. Note the three colored bands of fabric used for a border.*

Guide to Using the Patterns

- Wherever possible, the pattern pieces in this book are drawn to actual size. Exceptions are noted on individual pieces by either a fold line or a jagged line and instructions in the text for enlarging to proper size.
- All pattern pieces include a seam allowance of ¼" (6mm) except in special cases. Exceptions are noted on individual pieces.
- The number of pattern pieces needed for one quilt block are listed in the text accompanying each pattern.
- Quilting patterns are included for each block. The quilting patterns do not attempt to show size of stitches, only where the stitches should be placed. In outline quilting, the quilting stitches are placed ¼" (6mm) from the finished edge of the shape being outlined.
- If a quilt block was made of one small unit repeated many times, only the single unit is shown in the piecing and quilting diagrams in most cases. (The most common example of this is when the quilt block is made of four identical quarters.) When this integral unit is quite small, the entire quilt block, rather than just the single unit, is shown.

➤ If a pattern requires that a piece be cut for right and left sides, be certain to cut one side with the pattern piece right side up and the other side with the pattern piece wrong side up.

Key to Pattern Symbols

——————————————————————— Cutting line

——— — ——— — ——— — ——— Stitching line

⟵——————————————————⟶ Grain line (preferred direction for placement of pattern piece on fabric)

— — — — — — — — — — — — — — Gathering line (guide for placement of ease stitching)

·· Embroidery stitch placement

A section of the pattern has been omitted. Read the cutting instructions in the text.

Place on the fold. This indicates that only half of the pattern is given; the line on which this bracket appears must be placed on the fold *when making your pattern, not when cutting the fabric.* Make a full-size pattern to use to make the template for cutting the fabric. The place-on-the-fold-line edge becomes the center line of your pattern piece.

The last page of pattern pieces for this particular design. Be sure to turn the pages until you see this little quilt block to make sure you have seen all pieces for your chosen design.

Abundance–p.88

Bicentennial Quilt–p.96

Aunt Fanny's Flower Basket–p.93

Blue Bars, Gray Bars, No Stars–p.99

Christmas Poinsettia–p.101

Cotton Patch Treasures–p.105

Cotton Boll–p.103

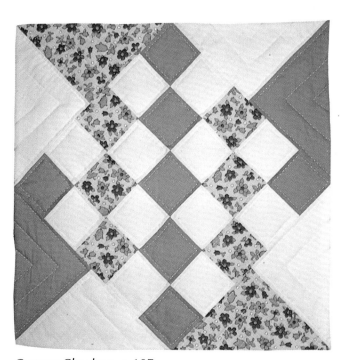

Country Checkers–p.107

East Tennessee Farm–p.109

Florida Forest–p.118

Elkhorn–p.115

Flower Bed–p.122

Garden Spot–p.124

Grandma's Fan–p.129

George Washington's Cherry Tree–p.127

Grandma's Favorite–p.132

Grandmother's Brooch of Love–p.134

Homestead–p.138

Holly Haven–p.136

Jack-in-the-Pulpit–p.140

Lily Garden–p.143

Lincoln's Hat–p.150

Lindbergh's Night Flight–p.145

Log Cabin–p.152

Morning Glory – p.156

Mountain Morning Glory – p.161

Mountain Homestead – p.158

Mrs. Feathersome – p.163

Oklahoma Trails and Fields–p.167

Old Rail Fence–p.173

Old Country Church–p.169

Pride of the South–p.175

Proud Pine–p.178

Rural Background–p.183

Red Barn–p.180

San José Rose–p.186

Southern Dogwood–p.188

Summer Leaves–p.193

Starflower–p.190

Sunflower–p.195

Sunshine and Stained Glass—p.198

The Courthouse Square—p.202

Texas Bicentennial Star—p.200

The Hay Wagon—p.206

The Sunrise—p.209

UNITED WE STAND

DIVIDED WE FALL

United We Stand—p.215

Tulip Bowl—p.212

Wheels—p.217

Wild Flower –p.219   *Windmill* –p.221

Quilted Fabric "Paintings"

In addition to the designs for which patterns are included, we share with you some of the favorite fabric "painting" quilt blocks submitted. Each is charming in that it captures some special memory or beloved scene of the artist. This type of design works well only when it is drawn from the actual experience of the person making the quilt block. That is why we do not give patterns for these designs, but present them in the hope that they will serve as a stimulus to your own creativity.

Precious Memories
Myrtle McRorey
Blackwell, Texas

Country Memories
Mrs. L. B. Southerland
Mt. Olive, North Carolina

Our Heritage, The Church
Nora Yount
Lenoir, North Carolina

Little Country Church
Erma Keyes
Crossville, Tennessee

The Good Life
Mrs. Wooster Atkinson
Bishopville, South Carolina

Mobile Bay
Eugenia Youens
Saraland, Alabama

The Outhouse
Mrs. E. L. Sturm
Holland, Texas

Little Red Schoolhouse
Georgia Humphrey
Cynthiana, Kentucky

Memory Box
Miss Carolyn Bogard
Clarksville, Tennessee

Precious Memories

Our Heritage, the Church

The Outhouse

The Good Life

Memory Box

Country Memories

Mobile Bay

Little Country Church

Little Red Schoolhouse

Abundance

Glenna Hayes
Roanoke, Virginia

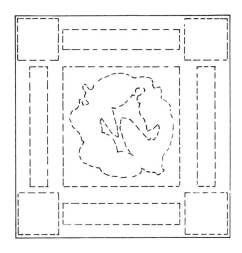

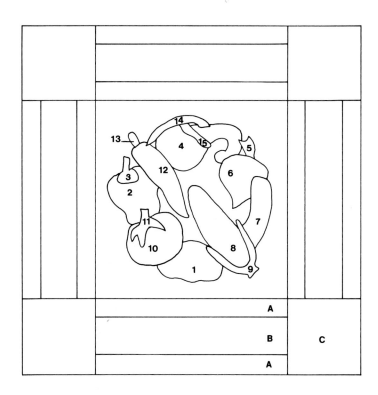

"My own vegetable garden is the inspiration for my design. Abundant homegrown vegetables, eaten fresh in summer, canned or frozen for winter, are an integral part of our rural heritage. Today there is renewed interest in home gardening due in part to a new awareness that better diet, including more vegetables, means improved health. Working with one's hands and enjoying the results of one's own creative labors, whether it be in making a garden or making a quilt, are also part of our heritage.

"Color is a main consideration in the overall plan of this quilt. Vegetable colors are bright and cheery and do not necessarily have to be nature's own to be effective. By varying these (for example, the tomato could be deep pink and the beet purple) and by changing the accent color and coordinating print, the design can be adapted to conform to any room color scheme, reflecting the personality and taste of each individual seamstress."

The center design of Miss Hayes's quilt block is appliquéd onto a background square of 10" x 10" (25.4cm x 25.4cm). The striped sashing and corner squares provide a perfect balance for the design. The square with the sashing measures 18" x 18" (45.7cm x 45.7cm).

One block takes the following:
One of each of the pieces numbered
    1 through 15
Background square—10" x 10"
    (25.4cm x 25.4cm)
A—8 narrow strips
B—4 wide strips
C—4 corners

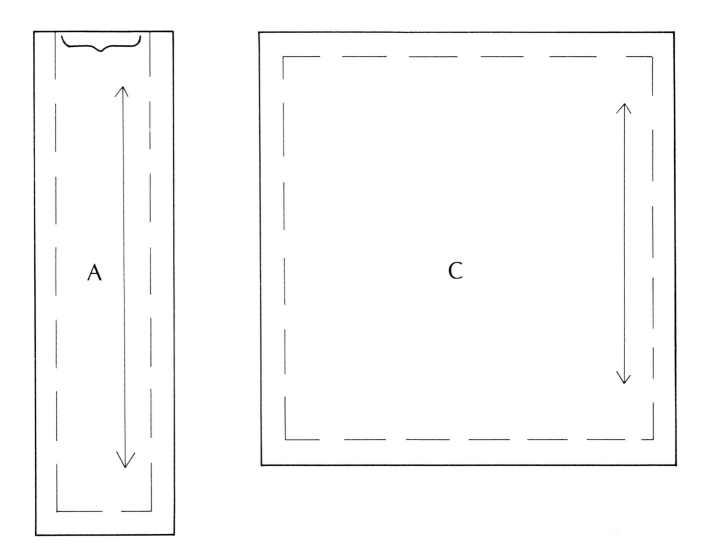

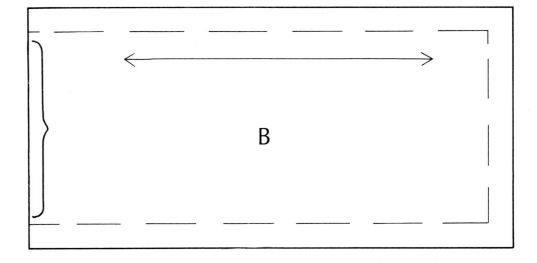

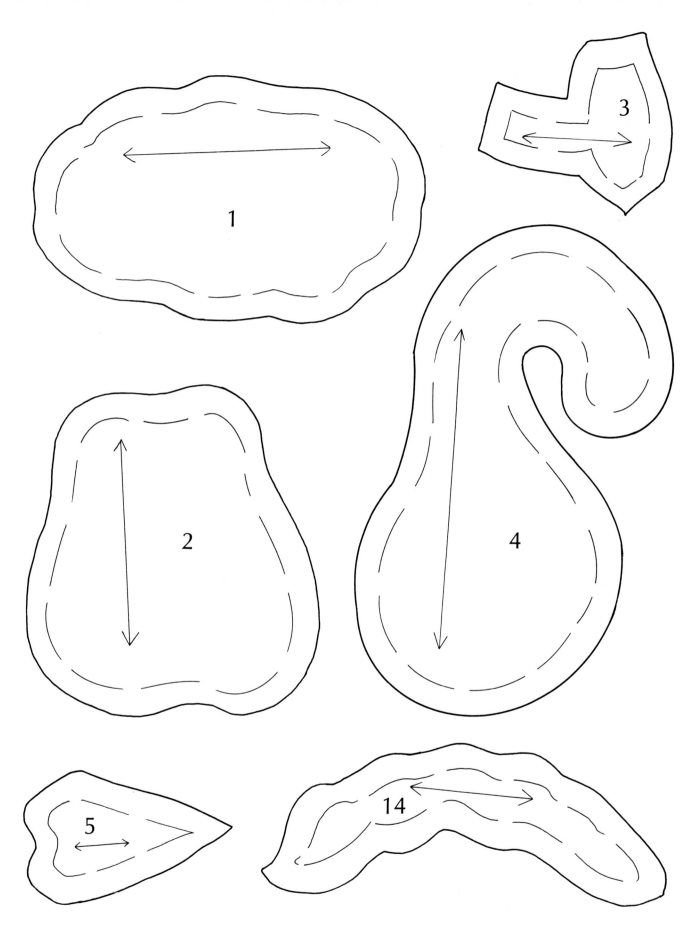

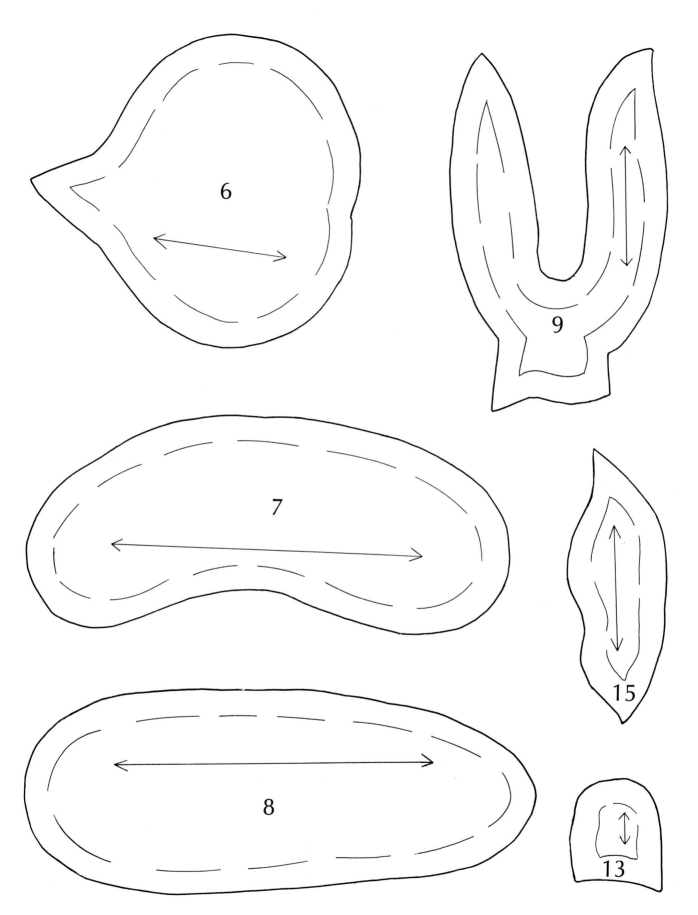

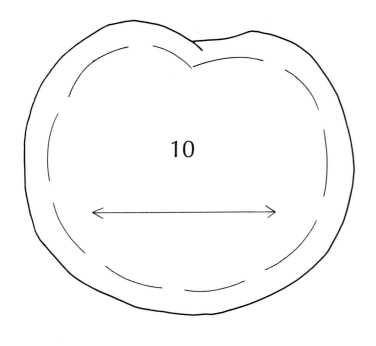

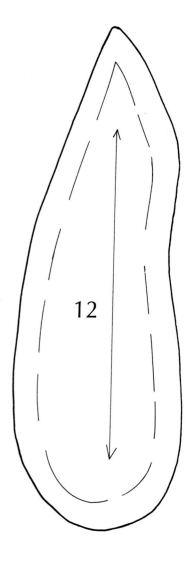

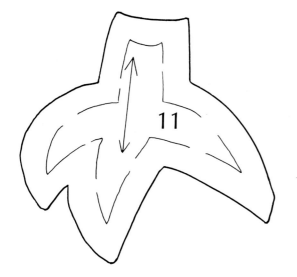

Aunt Fanny's Flower Basket

Margaret Eason
Williamston, North Carolina

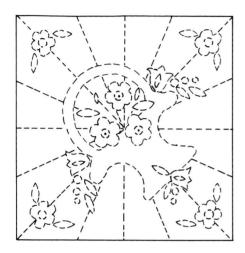

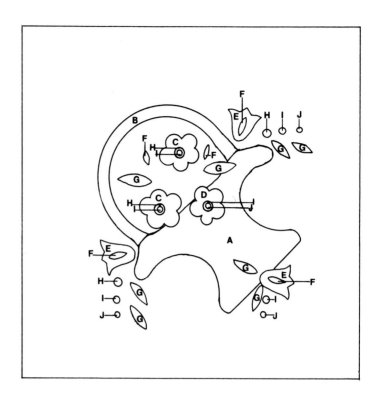

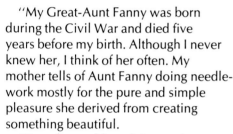

"My Great-Aunt Fanny was born during the Civil War and died five years before my birth. Although I never knew her, I think of her often. My mother tells of Aunt Fanny doing needlework mostly for the pure and simple pleasure she derived from creating something beautiful.

"Somehow, although I never knew Aunt Fanny, I feel a strong tie with her. I, too, enjoy needlework, especially quilting. I have always found working with my hands fascinating and relaxing. One might say I learned needlework the hard way as there was no one, other than Aunt Fanny, in my family who knew the art of needlework well enough to teach me, and I had to learn on my own. I cherish the thought that my children may enjoy needlework and other handcrafts as much as I do.

"I have named my youngest daughter in memory of Aunt Fanny. I sometimes envision Aunt Fanny, as she probably appeared during her childhood, when I see my daughter laughing and playing with other children. She and I love flowers as Aunt Fanny loved them. My mother has related on many occasions how Aunt Fanny would pick only short-stemmed flowers so that smaller buds could blossom for others to enjoy.

"When I saw *Progressive Farmer's* announcement of the quilt contest, I again remembered Aunt Fanny and wished to make something beautiful in memory of her. I chose a basket of short-stemmed flowers representative of her love for flowers and quilting. I wish to share her love for both with others."

This lovely quilt block utilizes the relief appliqué technique to make the design of the quilt top. Flower centers and berries are edge-finished with a buttonhole stitch. The floral motif is carried through with the quilting pattern. Place this quilt block design on the diagonal for maximum impact in whatever project you choose.

One block takes the following:
A—1 basket
B—1 handle
C—2 large flowers
D—1 small flower
E—3 tulips
F—5 total:
    3 tulip centers
    2 small leaves
G—8 leaves
H—4 total:
    2 outer flower centers for large
    flowers
    2 large berries
I—6 total:
    2 inner flower centers for
    large flower
    1 outer flower center for
    small flower
    3 medium-size berries
J—4 total:
    1 inner center for small flower
    3 small berries
Background square18″ x 18″
    (45.7cm x 45.7cm)

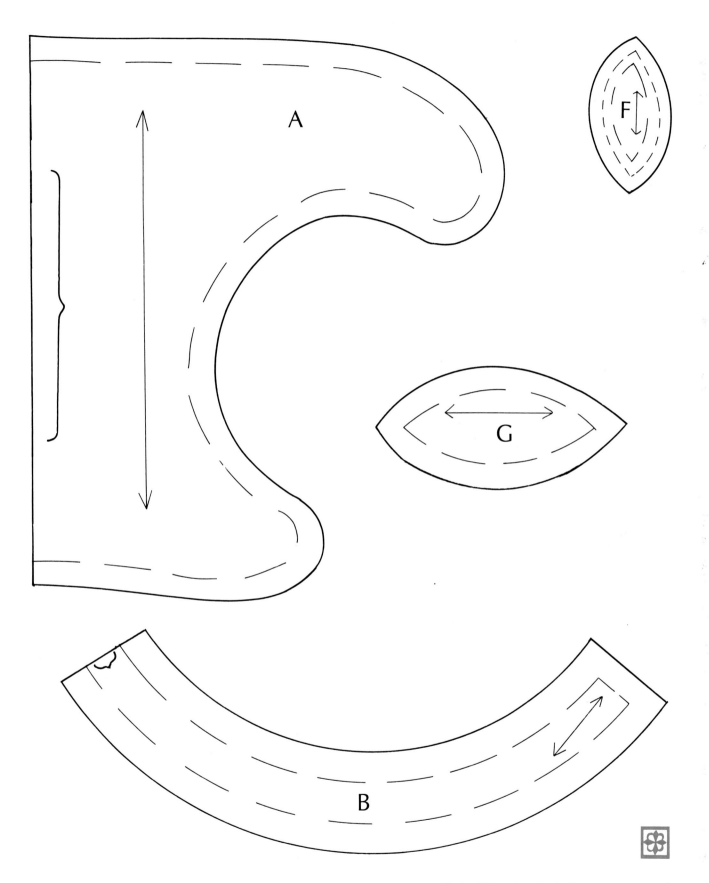

A

F

G

B

Bicentennial Quilt

Edna Underwood
Piggott, Arkansas

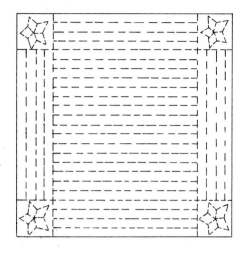

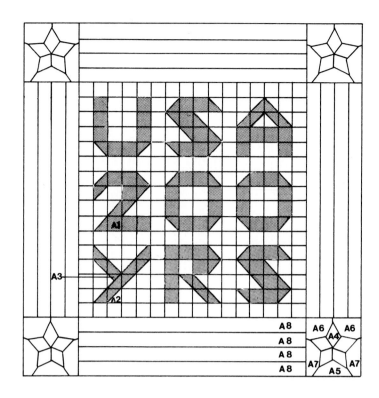

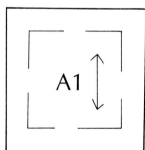

"This Bicentennial year is so special to each American that I wanted to make each of my five children a quilt keepsake. I knew what I wanted to say in the pattern, and I drew several pictures before I got the pattern to come out right for the letters. This block is a scaled-down model of a quilt I have made. Six of these blocks, each 27" x 27" (68.6cm x 68.6cm), will make a large quilt."

Mrs. Underwood's unique idea for patchwork letters can be used to make monogram, date, or name quilts by varying the letters you make. Although the piecing of the design is not difficult, it is time-consuming because of the number of pieces. Simple outline quilting is recommended for purity of design.

Mrs. Underwood included two patterns for this quilt. The pattern pieces labeled A will make a 27" x 27" (68.6cm x 68.6cm) square. The pattern pieces labeled B will make an 84" x 96" (210cm x 240.cm) quilt consisting of one big block. (See last page for this pattern for piecing diagram for B.)

One 27" x 27" (68.6cm x 68.6cm) block takes the following:
- A1—201 squares:
  - 55 light colored
  - 146 dark colored
- A2—108 triangles:
  - 55 light colored
  - 53 dark colored
- A3—2 small triangles:
  - 1 light colored
  - 1 dark colored
- A4—20 diamonds for stars:
  - 5 for each star, light colored
- A5—8 bottoms of stars:
  - 2 for each star, dark colored
- A6—8 top sides of star:
  - 2 for each star, dark colored (cut one for left side, turn pattern piece over to cut one for right side)
- A7—8 lower sides of star:
  - 2 for each star, dark colored (one for left, one for right)
- A8—16 stripes:
  - 8 of third color
  - 8 light colored

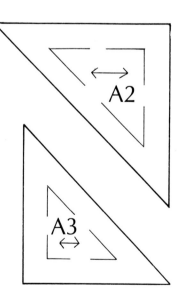

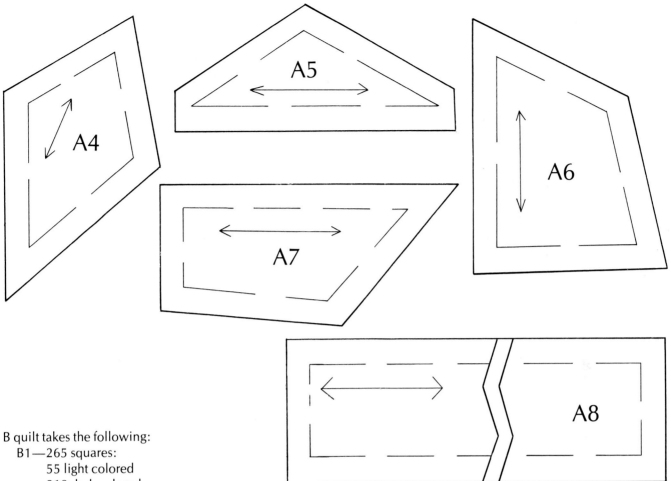

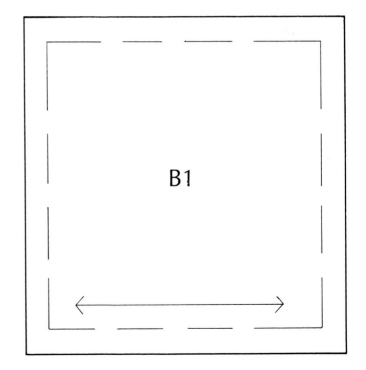

Extend length to 16½″ (41.25cm).

B quilt takes the following:
  B1—265 squares:
      55 light colored
      210 dark colored
  B2—108 triangles:
      55 light colored
      53 dark colored
  B3—2 small triangles:
      1 light colored
      1 dark colored
  B4—20 diamonds for star:
      5 for each star, light colored
  B5—4 star bottoms:
      1 for each star, dark colored
  B6—8 top sides of star:
      2 for each star, dark colored
      (1 left, 1 right)
  B7—8 lower sides of stars:
      2 for each star, dark colored
      (1 left, 1 right)
  End stripes 3½″ x 48″ (8.9cm x
      121.9cm):
      6 of third color
      6 light colored
  Side stripes 3½″ x 60″ (8.9cm x
      152.4cm):
      6 of third color
      6 light colored

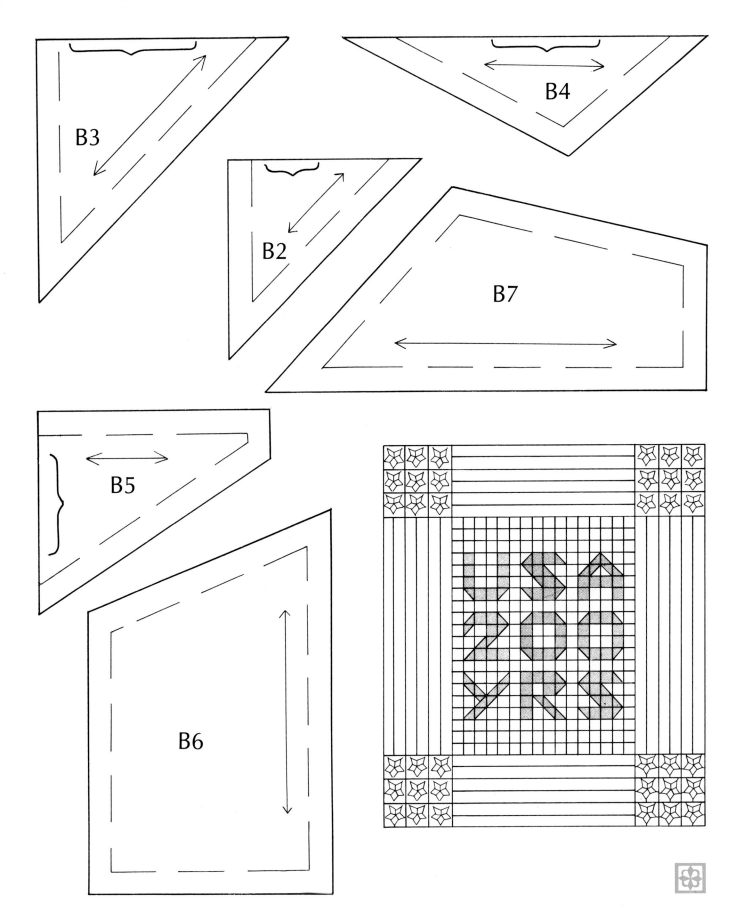

Blue Bars, Gray Bars, No Stars

Lloyd R. Smith, Jr.
Lebanon, Virginia

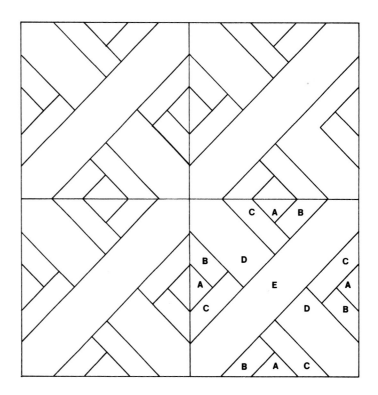

"The inspiration for this quilt block design is 'Stars and Bars,' the flag of the Confederacy during the Civil War. A part of every Southerner's heritage, the Civil War was a time when the North (the Blue) and the South (the Gray) met in conflict. Fortunately, that conflict was ended and the South has been recognized as the vital part of the Red, White, and Blue that it is.

"During this, our nation's Bicentennial year, it is important for all Southerners to recognize the significance of their agriculture, hospitality, and way of life. There are very few places left where people can have the joys of living in rural surroundings as we can in the South.

"In my quilt design the Blue and the Gray meet again, but this time they meet in unity. The gray bars, representative of the South, and the blue bars, representative of the rest of the country, seem to entwine to create this effect and say 'Friendship.' I've complemented the blue and gray bars with bordered squares of red and white, thereby making this an all-American

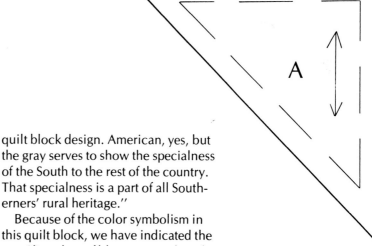

quilt block design. American, yes, but the gray serves to show the specialness of the South to the rest of the country. That specialness is a part of all Southerners' rural heritage."

Because of the color symbolism in this quilt block, we have indicated the specific colors of blue, gray, red, and white in the cutting directions. However, this is an extremely interesting patchwork pattern, especially when the quilt blocks are set side by side with no sashing between blocks. It would be equally beautiful done in a carefully thought out combination of colors and prints.

One block takes the following:

A—16 total:
    8 red
    8 white
B—16 total:
    8 red
    8 white
C—16 total:
    8 red
    8 white
D—8 total:
    4 gray
    4 blue
E—4 total:
    2 gray
    2 blue

    Notice that each 18″ x 18″ (45.7cm x 45.7cm) block is made up of 4 smaller squares, 2 with a predominant gray bar and 2 with a predominant blue bar. The duplicate squares are placed diagonally opposite one another to form the interlocking pattern.

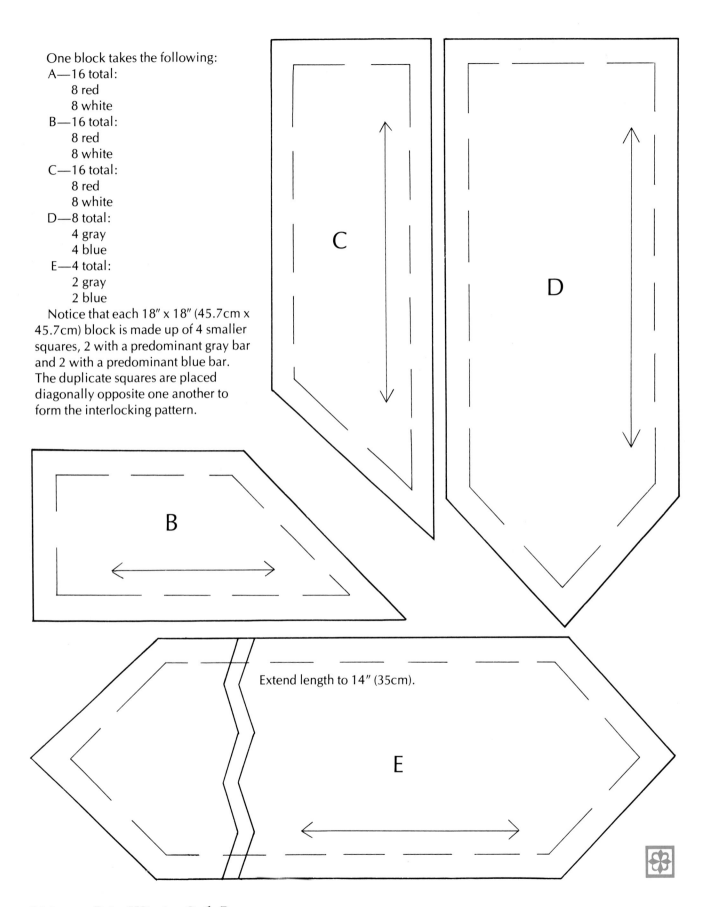

Extend length to 14″ (35cm).

Christmas Poinsettia

Jullia Mae Trammell
Cedar Bluff, Alabama

"I am entering this quilt design because I believe it is original and old fashioned. The design has only five pieces and two colors. This design was pieced by my great-grandmother and handed down to my grandmother, then my mother, and finally to me.

"I was raised on a farm in Cherokee County by my grandparents. The farm I lived on was large with lots of animals and flower gardens. My grandmother and I enjoyed quilting and sewing together in the winter. My grandmother taught me to quilt at an early age and I have been making quilts ever since as a hobby."

This unusual appliqué quilt design is relatively easy to construct and would make a beautiful Christmas banner or place mats for the holiday season.

One block takes the following:
A—1 red center
B—4 green stems
C—4 green leaves
D—8 red petals
E—20 small circles:
    16 green
    4 red
Background square—18" x 18"
    (45.7cm x 45.7cm)

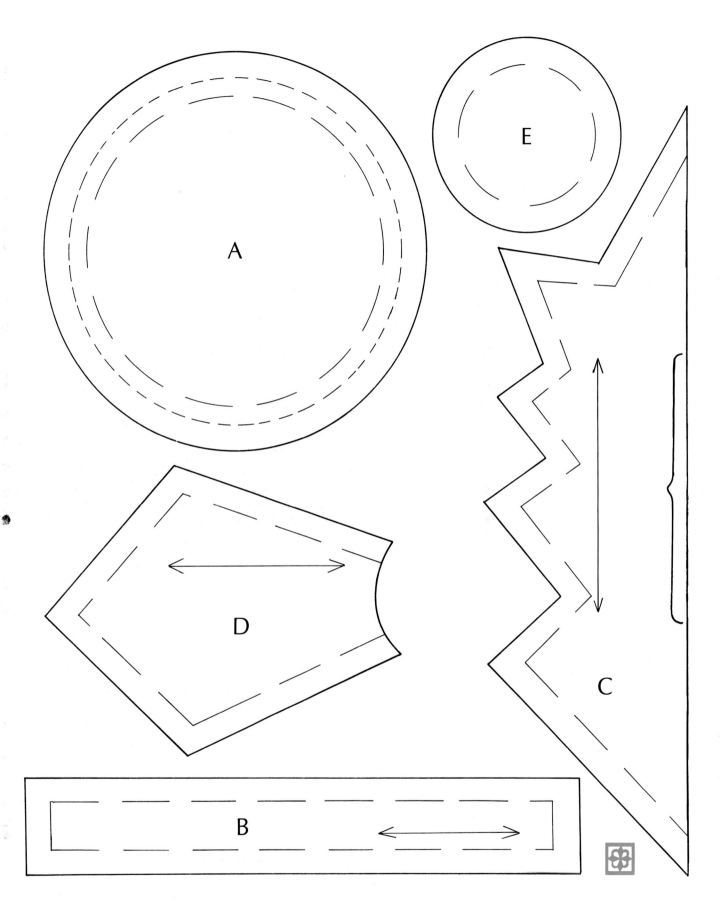

A

E

D

C

B

Cotton Boll

Mrs. T. W. Redding, Sr.
Asheboro, North Carolina

"In trying to think of something really original and pretty for a quilt design, I realized cotton, the 'King of Materials', was a natural for me. I grew up on a farm as one of ten children and my father raised cotton. We planted, hoed, and picked our cotton, and loaded it on the two-horse wagon to go to the gin. My father paid for fertilizer and bought our school shoes and clothes for the winter with the cotton money. Then Mama would take the children and pick the last of the 'yellow-scrap-cotton, shirt-tails' to go into the quilts. I learned to piece and quilt from my mother and loved it and still do. I make quilts for other people every winter. We have five children and have always used quilts to keep warm. (Our baby daughter went away to college this year and she took her quilt.) So this is my quilt design; I can well remember the beautiful blue sky above the pretty white and green cotton fields."

Mrs. Redding artfully employed the techniques of appliqué and embroidery for the major portion of her design; the sashing for her block is patchwork triangles. The stitch used around the outer edges of the cotton bolls is the blanket stitch; a chain stitch delineates the section within each boll.

One block takes the following:
A—4 bolls
B—4 burrs
C—36 triangles for sashing:
    20 of one color
    16 of second color
D—4 corner triangles to match
    second color in sashing
Background square for appliqué—
    12" x 12" (30.5cm x 30.5cm)
Approximate size of square with sashing—13½" x 13½" (34.3cm x 34.3cm)

Cotton Patch Treasures*

Mrs. Donnell Gowey
Seattle, Washington

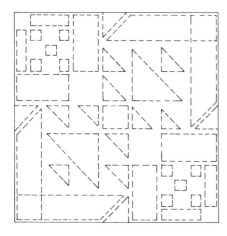

"I grew up on a North Carolina farm during the time when cotton was king. Schools observed 'cotton picking schedule' in the fall, dismissing students at noon to allow time for picking. I share with many others the memory of those days of blazing sun and aching back, of pride and disappointments at weighing-in time, of the ride home from the fields on the piles of soft cotton. I remember the laughter and song that eased the work. The clear, sweet melody of Negro spirituals rose across the fields, lifting the heart in the voice of faith and trust.

"And I remember my own secret pleasures discovered in the cotton fields. The mother killdeer nested on the bare earth, her colors blending with those of Mother Nature, her speckled eggs looking like pebbles. If approached, she would limp along, just out of reach, dragging one wing as if it were broken. When she had lured her pursuer a safe distance from her nest, she would spread her wings and soar upward. The nest would be in the vicinity where the bird was first sighted, and to discover it was joy for the day.

"Another treasure to be found was the flint arrowheads lost by the Indians 300 or 400 years earlier and uncovered by recent plowing. Unlike the killdeer's nest, the Indian arrowhead was a trophy to be carried home in a pocket and treasured in a collection.

"Cotton is no longer king in the South, but my quilt is reminiscent of those days. The white rows of cotton weave in and out across it. Tucked in and around the rows are the brown and red arrowheads left by the Indians and the nests of speckled eggs hidden by the killdeer. When the quilt blocks are joined, the white cotton rows meet in the design of the cross— that symbol of the greatest of all treasures."

This splendid patchwork pattern was selected as a Judges' Choice because of its outstanding beauty and

---

* Judges' Choice

workmanship. The large block, 27" x 27" (68.6cm x 68.6cm), shown in color on page 74 is made up of four of the squares, each 13½" x 13½" (34.3cm x 34.3cm), given on this page. A finished quilt of 81" x 108" (205.7cm x 274.3cm) would require three blocks across and four down.

One block takes the following:

A—8 large rectangles:
    4 white
    4 green

B—7 large squares:
    2 white
    2 red
    3 green

C—4 green small rectangles

D—20 small squares:
    2 green
    8 brown figured
    10 solid brown

E—36 right triangles:
    4 white
    6 red
    12 green
    14 brown

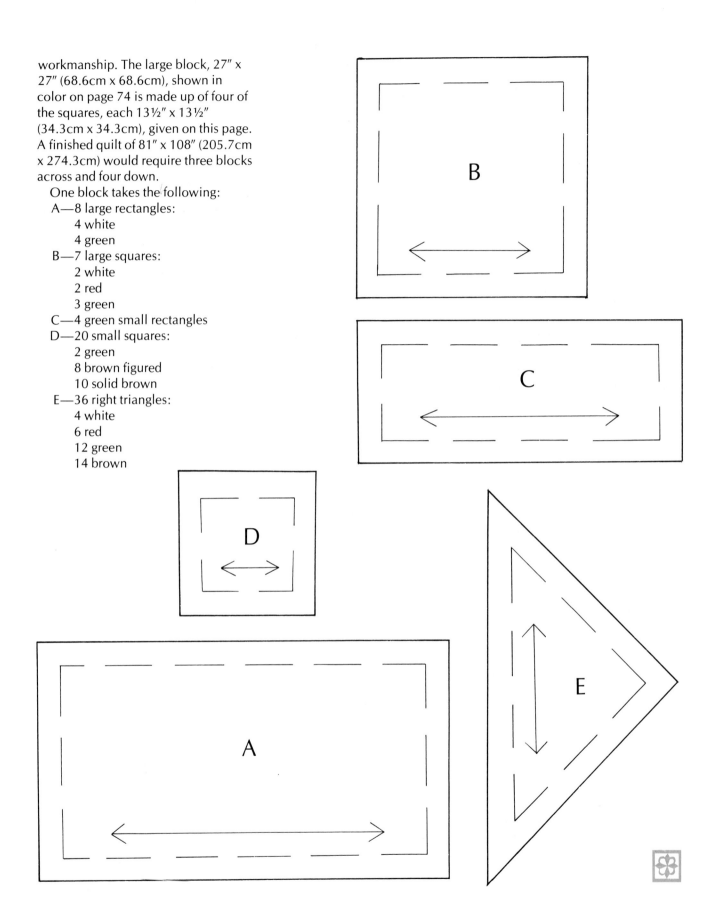

Country Checkers

Hope A. Shoaf
Edgemont, Arkansas

"*Country Checkers* reminds me of my grandfather. In winter when there weren't many outdoor chores, Grandpa used to love to play checkers. His eyes weren't too good in those days, so he couldn't pass the long winter evenings reading. He could see how to move his men on the old checkerboard and would delight in beating all of us kids at his favorite game. There was no television or radio in those days and no electricity, so we sat on the floor in front of the roaring fireplace. Shadows danced merrily across the old checkerboard, and the smell of pine logs filled the room. The only noise was the old clock on the mantel as it slowly ticked the minutes while he concentrated on each move.

"Grandpa has long since left us, but I can still see his eyes twinkle and hear him chuckle as he beat us in our game of country checkers."

Miss Shoaf's patchwork block surely brings back memories to all of us! Although this pattern is not hard to put together, care must be taken to keep perfect seamlines for perfect squares.

When the blocks are set together, two larger squares are formed at each side of the checkerboard.

One block takes the following:
A—25 squares:
    12 of first fabric
    6 of second fabric
    7 of third fabric
B—8 triangles:
    4 of first fabric
    2 of second fabric
    2 of third fabric
Each finished square measures 16" x 16" (40.6cm x 40.6cm).

Five squares across and six down make a quilt 80" x 96" (203.2cm x 243.84cm).

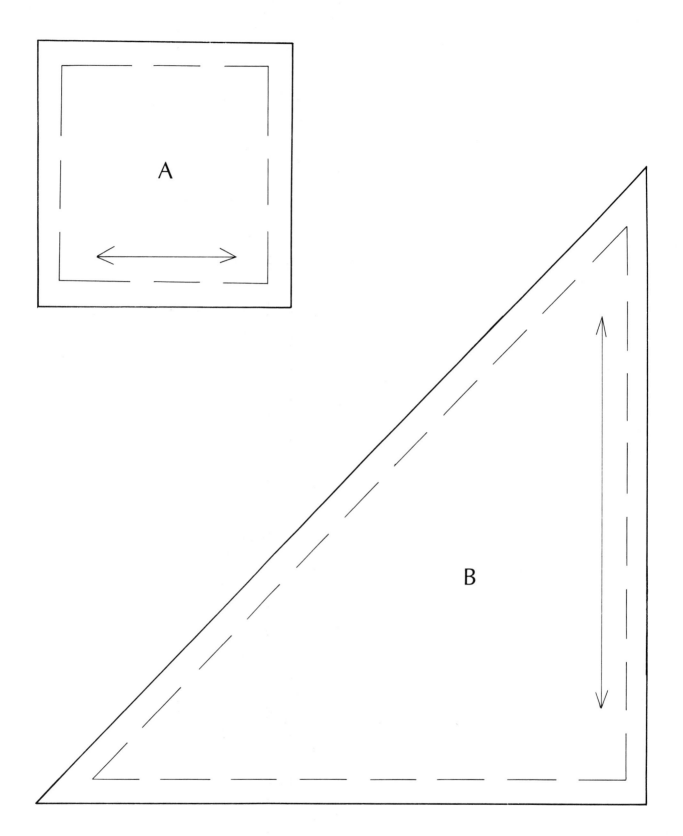

East Tennessee Farm*

Mrs. Leon L. Lenderman
Raleigh, North Carolina

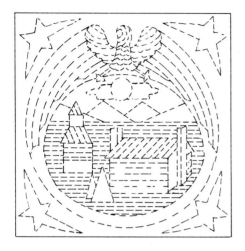

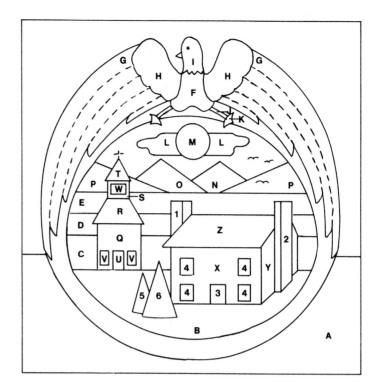

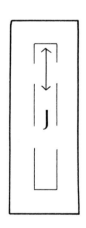

"The sun shines brightly on the fields of the Vinson Farm which was my home until marriage. The log cabin represents the original home of my great-great-grandfather who settled the land in 1788. It is part of the present house which is in the National Register of Historic Sites. For this reason, the American eagle is shown embracing the farm scene, and the national colors are used. At the beginning of the Missionary Baptist movement in East Tennessee, a church was organized in this cabin and the owner deeded part of his farm as a permanent site for the church. It became the largest in the county prior to the Civil War. Later my grandfather served as clerk for over 40 years. The church is still active. The peaks in the background are the Great Smoky Mountains which are less than 20 miles away.

"The birds are pigeons because the farm is on the Pigeon River. The calico floral foreground which surrounds the cabin represents the large

iris and daylily gardens that contain hundreds of varieties of these flowers. The four quilted stars represent the four major owners of the farm: the original owner, his nephew (who was my great-grandfather), my grandfather, and my father."

East Tennessee Farm took third prize in the contest. Here is what the judges said about Mrs. Lenderman's design: "We all agreed it is a medallion-type block, not repeatable, but what appealed to all of us was the good use of color and pattern, excellent craftsmanship, and charming naiveté of the American eagle. She also used appropriate early American type fabric in her selection of gingham."

This is a difficult pattern to sew primarily because it consists of 32 pieces almost all of which are different. Begin with a 20" x 20" (50.8cm x 50.8cm) background square, and cut pieces as directed on each pattern piece; then appliqué them in place.

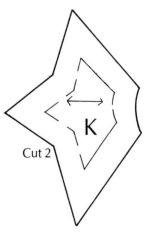

* Third Place Winner

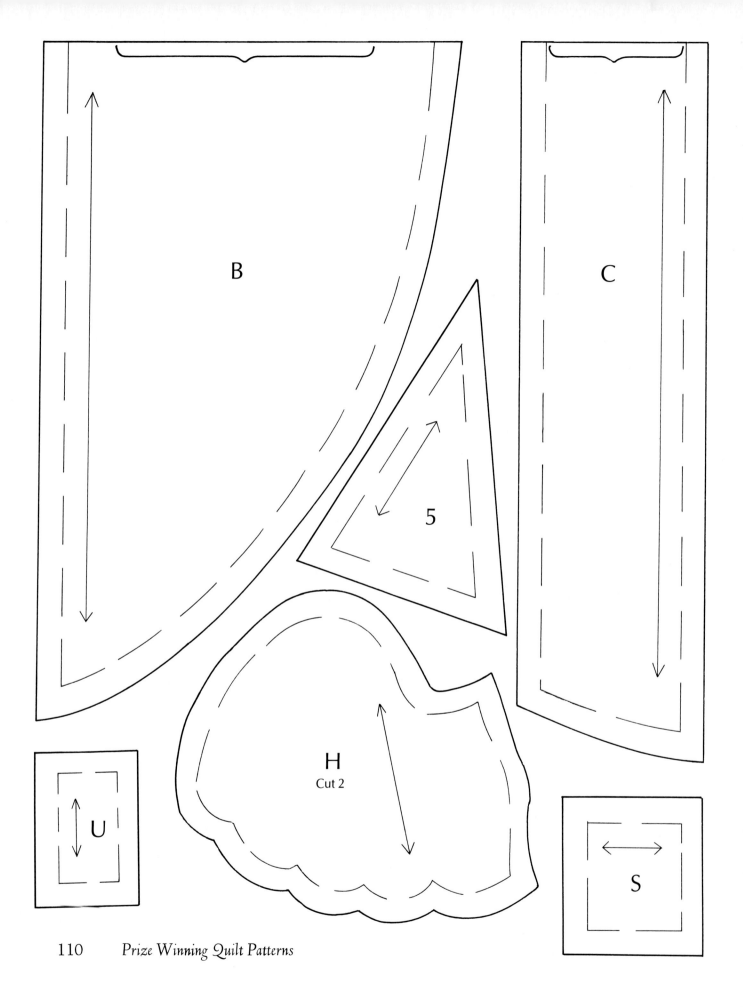

B

C

5

H
Cut 2

U

S

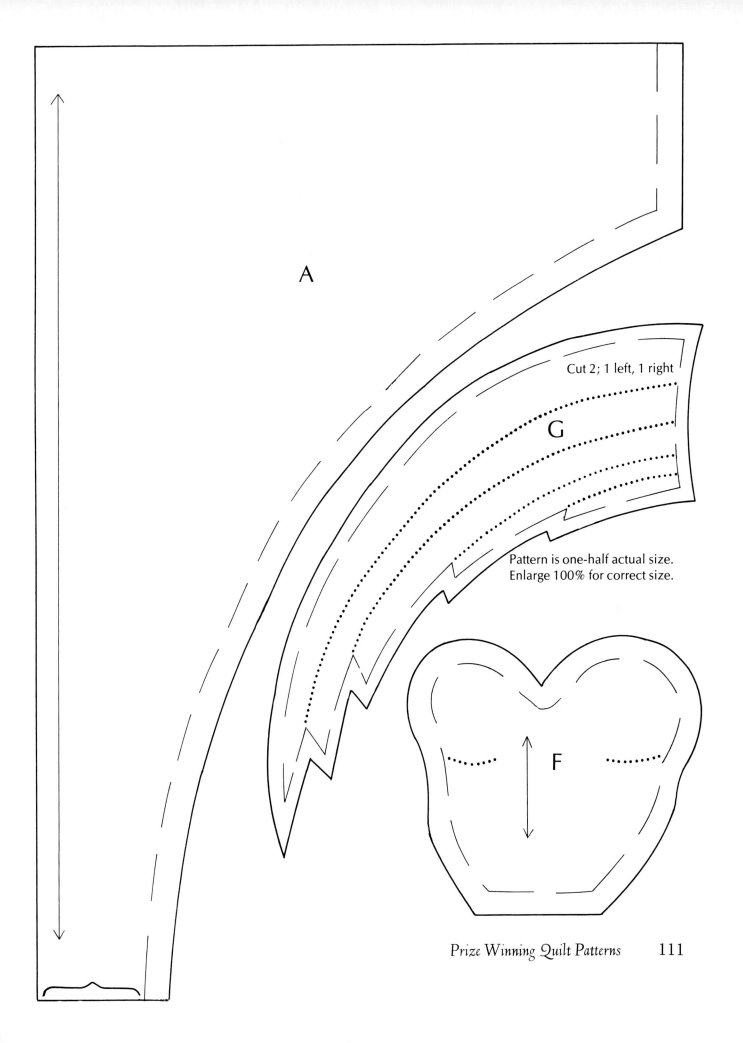

A

Cut 2; 1 left, 1 right

G

Pattern is one-half actual size.
Enlarge 100% for correct size.

F

Prize Winning Quilt Patterns   111

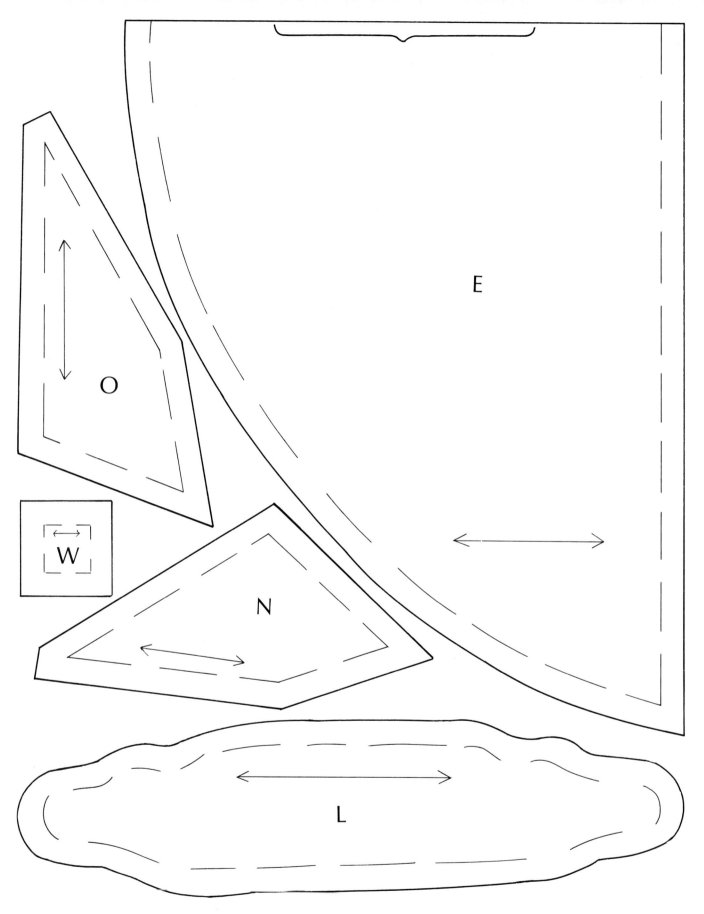

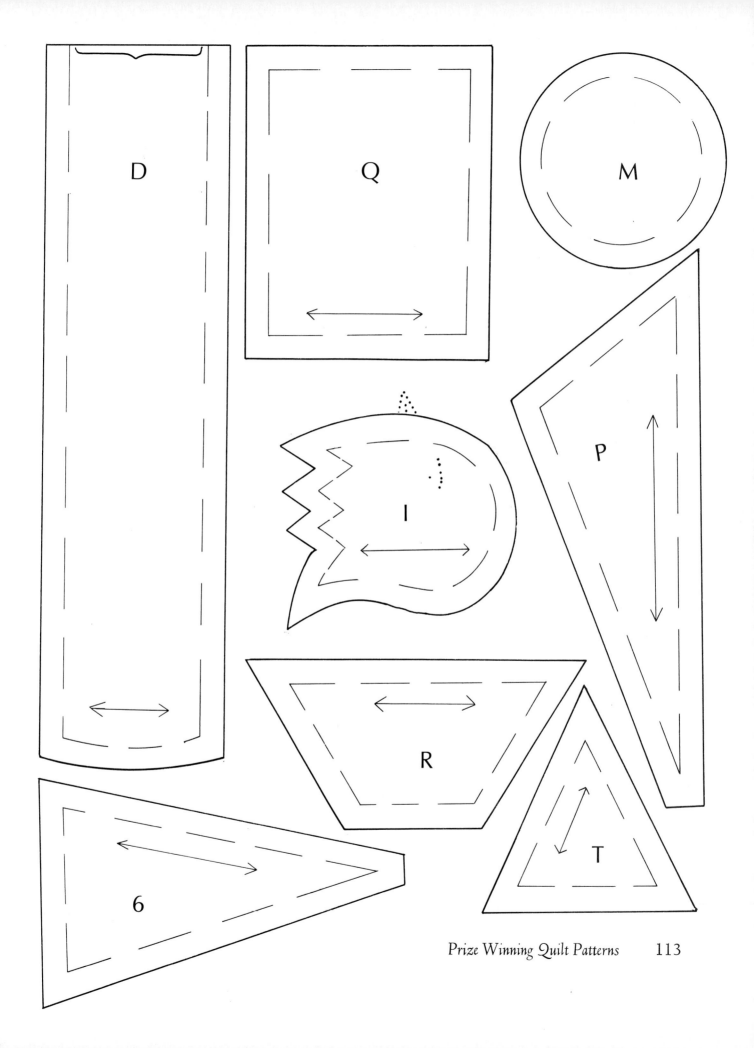

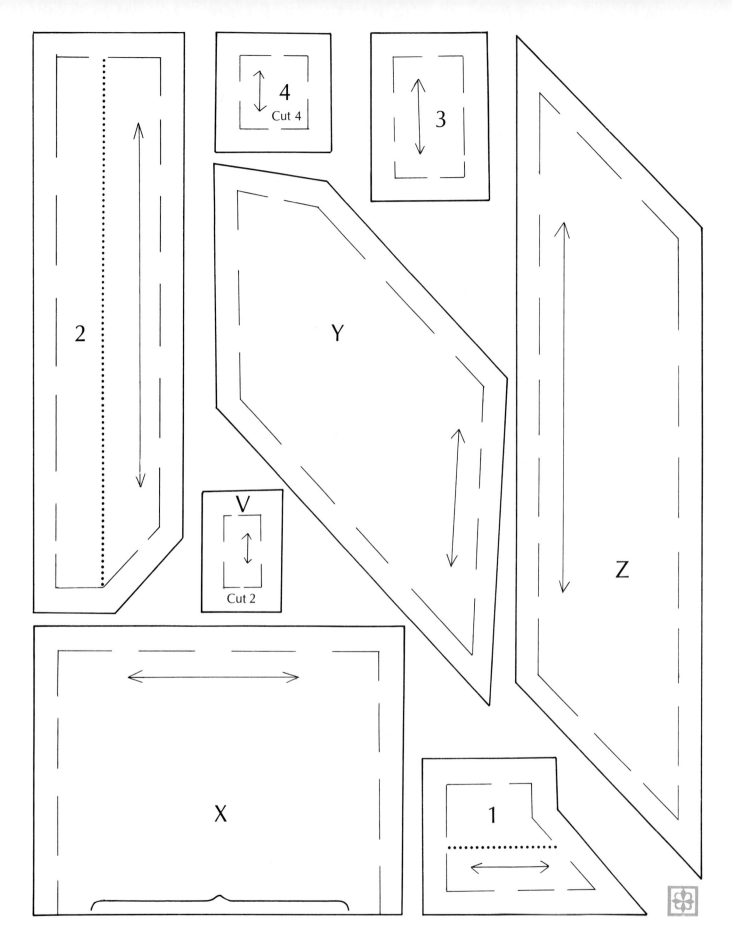

Elkhorn

Laura L. Allen
Jay, Oklahoma

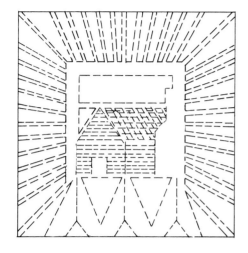

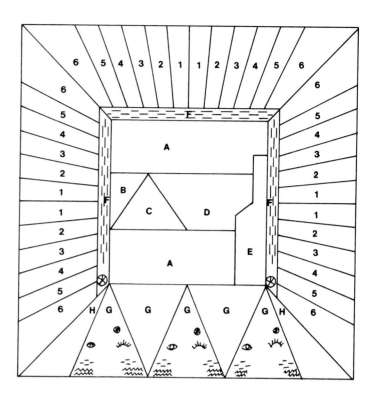

"The top and two sides are the Indian chief's headdress. In the center is the log cabin (with limestone fireplace) where Chief Elkhorn lived. Across the bottom are the tepees, or wigwams, that his tribe lived in. The embroidered work includes various Indian symbols: coyote tracks, sun rays, hogans, a mountain range, and the medicine man's eye.

"Our ranch is called Elkhorn because part of our land consists of the territory where Chief Elkhorn and his tribe lived. Our cattle drink water in the winter at the Elkhorn spring. Elkhorn's cabin was about one-quarter mile northwest of our ranch house. It was built of logs and had a fireplace of limestone. The cabin stood until 1931 when a farmer tore it down. About 20 years ago my husband moved the limestone rocks away. A cleared section of about 20 acres was surrounded with 50 or more mounds, which was where the tepees stood. Chief Elkhorn was the last Cherokee chief in this area to wear the old-time headdress."

Elkhorn was a perfect choice to dec-

orate the back of a denim jacket, as you can see on page 64. The strips around the top and sides of the quilt block give you an opportunity to make the block as colorful as you wish. Although it would be tedious to make enough blocks of this design to make a full quilt, one 10½" x 10½" (26.7cm x 26.7cm) block is fun to make in patchwork. Select appropriate embroidery stitches to carry out the designs on the teepees and around the central block.

One block takes the following:

A—2 total:	G—5 total:
1 cabin	3 teepees
1 sky	2 grasses
B—1 sky	H—2 grasses
C—1 eave	#1—6 in assorted colors
D—1 roof	#2—6 in assorted colors
E—1 chimney	#3—6 in assorted colors
F—3 bands	#4—6 in assorted colors
	#5—6 in assorted colors
	#6—6 in assorted colors

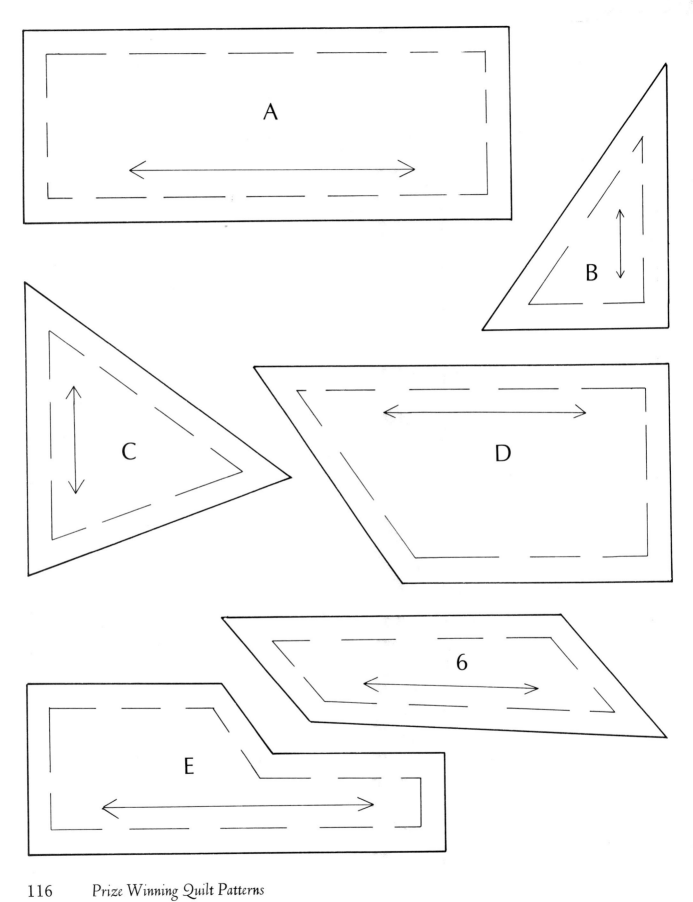

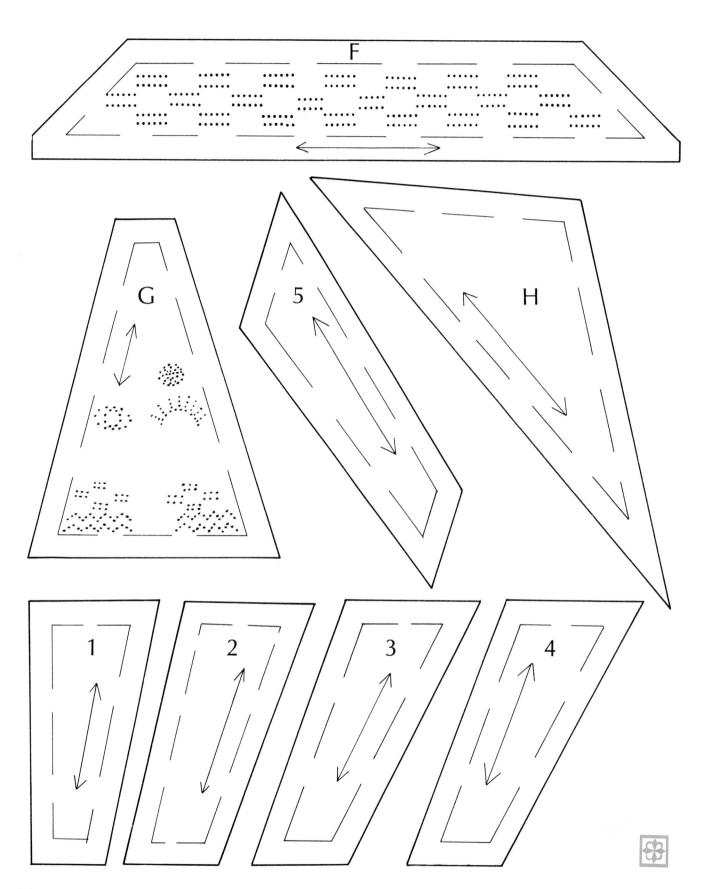

Florida Forest*

Mable Wolford
Lake City, Florida

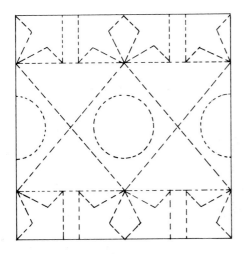

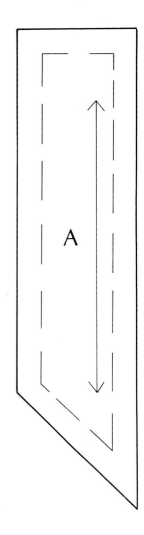

"My life and that of my ancestors is inextricably entwined with the beautiful trees, palmettos, and lakes of the Osceola National Forest. Its 157,000 acres provide sawtimber and other forest products. Ocean Pond, a recreational area containing a 2,000-acre lake, provides camping, picnicking, hunting, fishing, boating, skiing, and swimming.

"My great-grandfather came to Florida in 1853 and settled in this forest land where he married, built a home, and raised a family. He joined the Confederate Army in the 2nd year of the Civil War. He belonged to Company E of the 9th Florida regiment and was with Lee at Appomattox when he surrendered.

"In 1931 when Osceola National Forest was established, my grandparents could not bear to give up their land to the government. They were allowed to keep their land and live inside the forest. Some of the land still belongs to the family, and I have an

eighty-seven-year-old aunt living in the original house that was built by my great-grandfather.

"The walls of my home are paneled with red heart cypress which my husband and my uncle dragged from the forest floor. Because it takes a cypress tree 350 years to grow approximately twenty-four inches in diameter, these logs were probably growing before Columbus discovered America.

"I have many wonderful memories of this forest land, and this is what inspired me to make this quilt block."

This striking design, while more difficult than others, is certainly worth the effort. It was picked as a Judges' Choice. The background trees and stars are patchwork, and the large circles are appliquéd over the patchwork background. The large block, finished size 17" x 17" (43.2cm x 43.2cm), is made of four identical sections, each containing a tree and half a star. For each quarter of the quilt block you will need the following:

* Judges' Choice

Tree—Pattern pieces 1, 2, 3, 4, 5, 6;
    1 of each
Sides of tree—Pattern pieces A, B, C,
    D, E, F, G; 2 of each
Sides of star—Pattern piece H;
    4 total
Star—Pattern pieces I and J; 2 of I,
    4 of J
Circles—Pattern piece K; cut 1 full
    circle for each intersection
    of the 4 quarters of the de-
    sign; cut half-circles of L as
    needed to fill in design at
    the perimeter
Piecing order should be as follows:
1. Join the A through F sections to
    either side of the 1 through 6 sec-
    tions to make the tree.
2. Sew together each of the two HIJ
    sections to make the stars; then
    sew them to either side of the G
    strip.
3. Join the star tree trunk sections to
    the tree section.
4. Repeat above steps for each of
    the four quarters of the design.
5. Sew the 4 quarters together.
6. Appliqué the circle in place over
    the intersection of the 4 quarters.

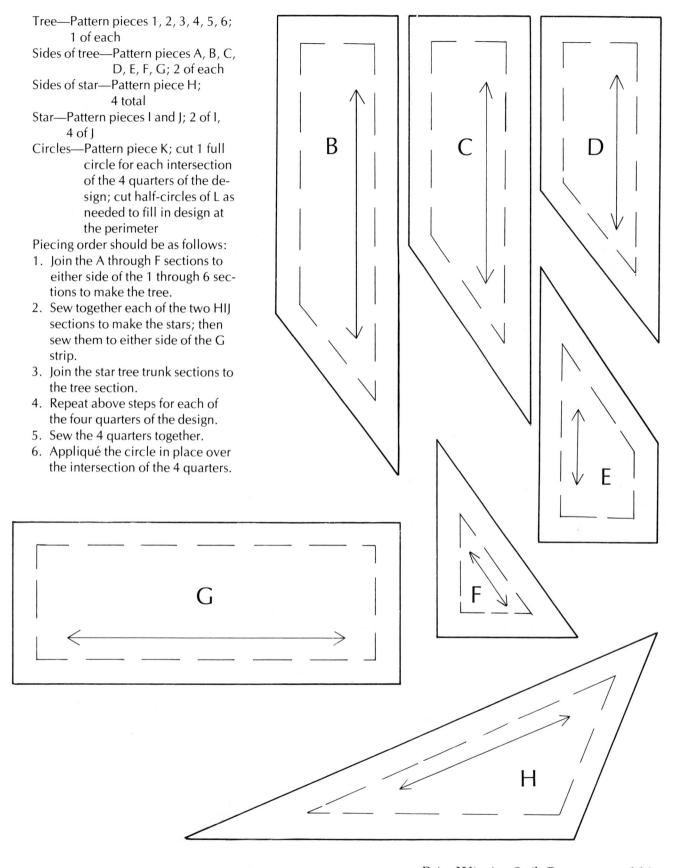

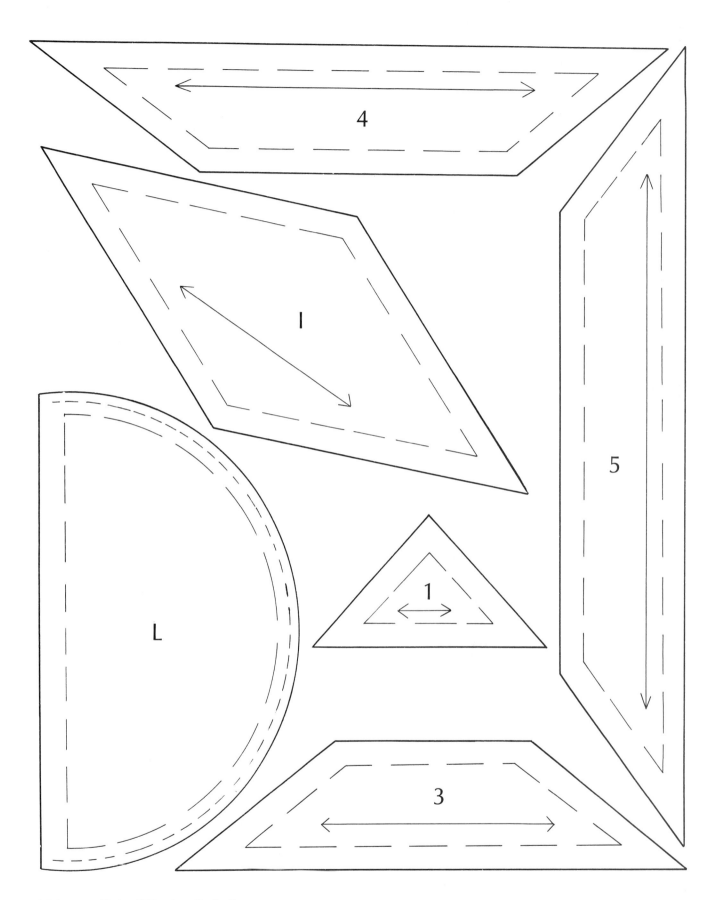

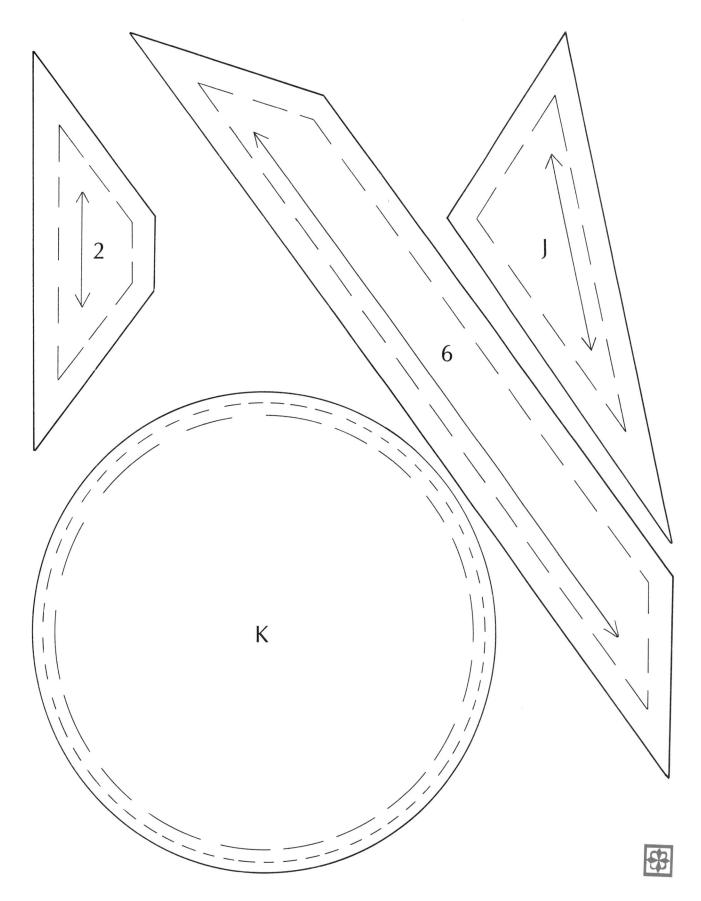

Flower Bed

Mrs. R. H. Fields
Ashville, Alabama

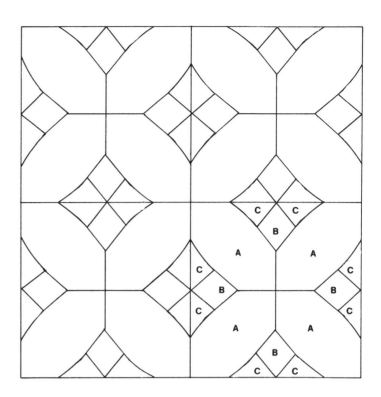

"My love for flowers and nature inspired me to design this pattern. You might call me a 'flower nut,' since I love anything called a flower. I really get close to nature and my Heavenly Father while working with my flowers. I can stand in my rose garden or flower garden and marvel at the wonders of nature. I see God all around me and really feel His presence. I just can't thank Him enough for creating all this beauty and giving me a chance to play a small part in helping create such beauty. I live in the country and love it. That is why I love the *Progressive Farmer* so much. I'm really a farmer at heart and love to see things grow.

"Anyone can change the color arrangement of this design to suit himself, but I think it will be prettier if it is made in two harmonizing colors and white."

Mrs. Fields made her 13″ x 13″ (33cm x 33cm) patchwork quilt block in polyester double knit, and it worked very well for this design. The edges of the major cross bars are slightly curved, and the doubleknit shapes eas-

ily to the curve. However, a woven fabric can be used, as demonstrated in the bolster pillows on page 12.

This quilt block is made up of four identical quarters.

For each quarter of the quilt block you will need the following:

A—4 center sections
B—4 diamonds
C—8 small triangles

Hint: This design is constructed more easily when the A pieces are sewed together in a clockwise fashion, rather than in pairs. Sew two Cs to each B; then fit the BC sections into the As. The design may be further enhanced by using a contrasting thread color to quilt the charming flower design.

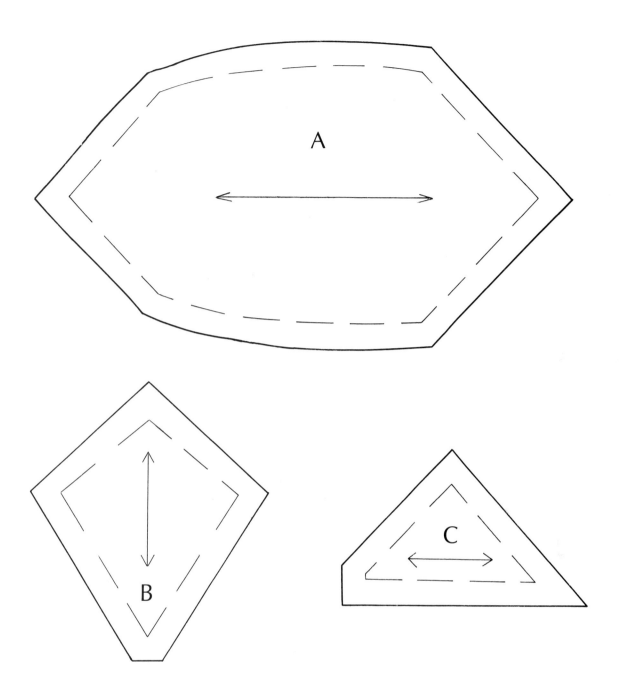

A

B

C

Garden Spot

Shirley Fulton
Mayslick, Kentucky

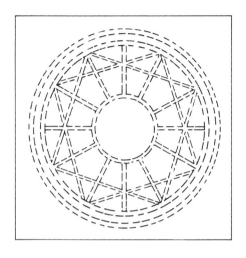

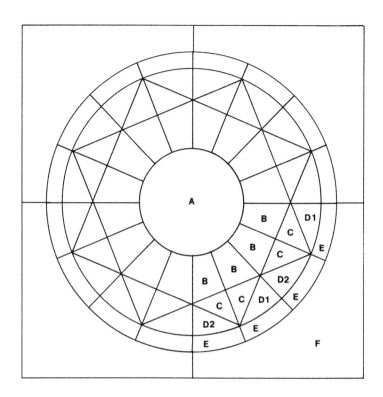

"Our little farm was once part of a larger estate. The estate owners and local people called what is now our farm their 'garden spot' because the soil was supposed to be the best and deepest in the area. This is the only name by which our farm has been labeled. The name of our farm inspired me to design this quilt block.

"Like an active, growing garden spot, the design from a distance looks very simple. A closer inspection shows it to be more complicated. The white areas with green quilting represent the non-growing times when the garden is a memory and an anticipation, existing in the thoughts of the gardener. The blues and aquas represent the cool dampness of the planting season. The colorful print represents the beauty and activity of the harvest season. Surrounding the garden is a band of yellow which represents the life-giving sunshine upon which we all depend."

Mrs. Fulton's design is a masterful piece of patchwork which should be put together to make four parts. Each of these is then attached to the center circle. This design would be especially complemented by patchwork sashing.

Each 17" x 17" (43.2cm x 43.2cm) block takes the following:
A—1 inner circle
B—16 total:
    8 of first print
    8 of solid
C—16 total:
    8 of second print
    8 of second solid
D—16 total of third print:
    8 for left side
    8 for right side
E—16 of third solid
F—4 of same fabric as center circle

Detail of corner quilting

Detail of center quilting

B

C

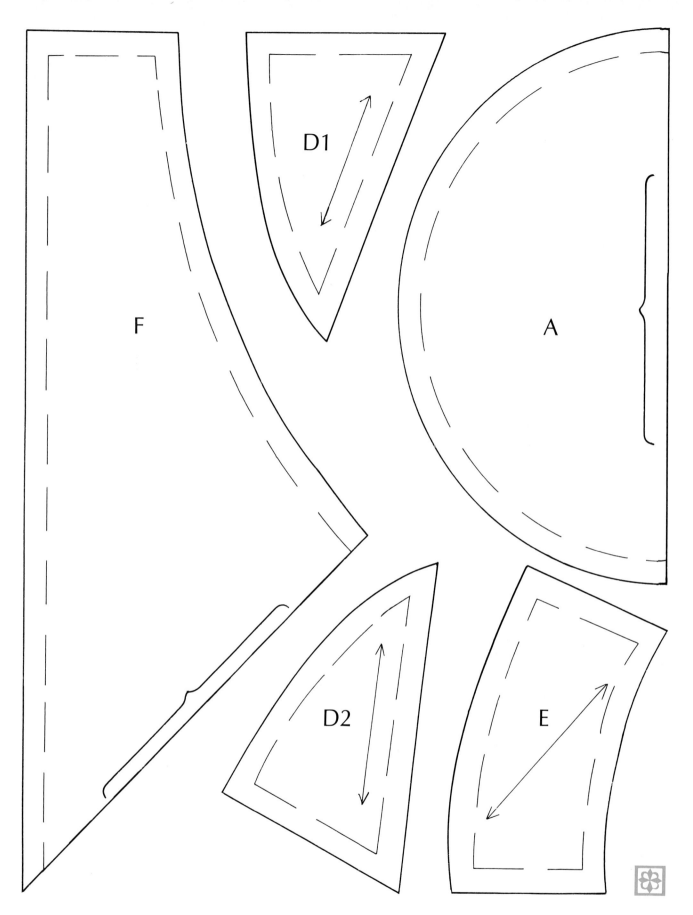

George Washington's Cherry Tree

Jewell Shores
Plant City, Florida

"This quilt is named in honor of the father of our country, but the original design was inspired by my grandson. I had told him, as a small boy, the story of George Washington and the famous words 'I cannot tell a lie.' I made this quilt up and presented it to him and his new wife as a remembrance of me and as a reminder of 'truth' to inspire their lives."

Mrs. Shores's beautiful quilt can be seen in all its glory on page 17. The tree trunk, leaves, and cherries are appliquéd in place, and the cherry stems and quilt title and signature are embroidered with an outline stitch.

Each block measures 17" x 17" (43.2cm x 43.2cm). For a finished quilt which measures 90" x 108" (228.6cm x 274.3 cm), you will need 13 whole blocks and 12 half blocks. The blocks are set on a diagonal so that the trees will be straight when the quilt is on the bed. They are joined with 2" (5cm) wide strips. Mrs. Shores used a dark green strip one way and a light green strip going the other way, and on both she appliquéd a white 1" (2.5cm) wide stripe down the center.

Mrs. Shores suggests a pale yellow or a white background. She used gold thread for quilting.

One block takes the following:

A—1 green tree trunk
B—6 green large leaves
C—7 green medium leaves
D—5 green small leaves
E—16 cherries:
    10 red
    6 gold
Background square—17½" x 17½"
    (43.7cm x 43.7cm)

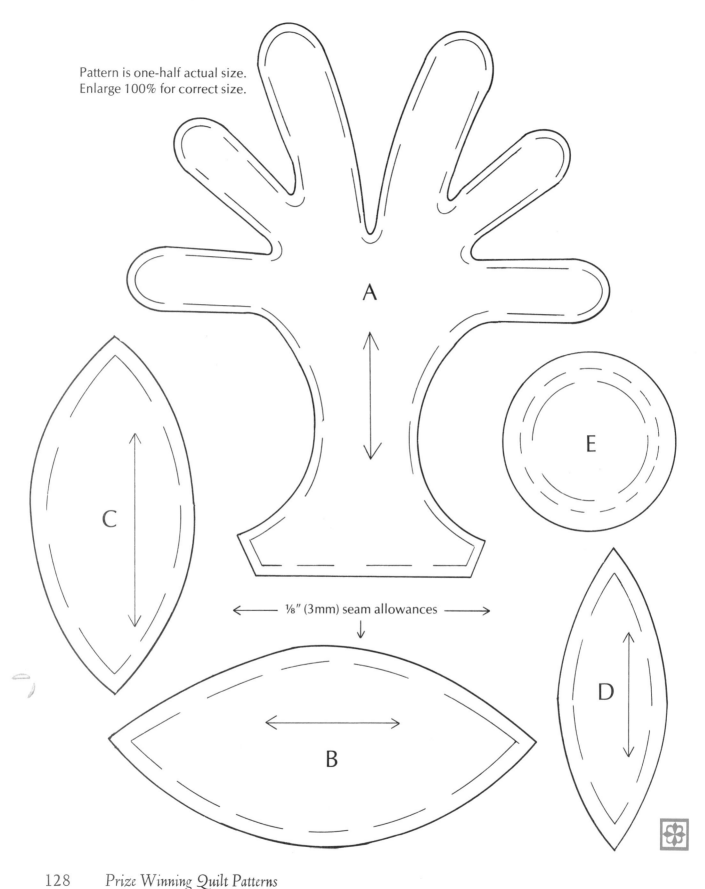

Pattern is one-half actual size.
Enlarge 100% for correct size.

A

C

E

⟵ ⅛" (3mm) seam allowances ⟶

B

D

Grandma's Fan

Mariena Bordelon
Bordelonville, Louisiana

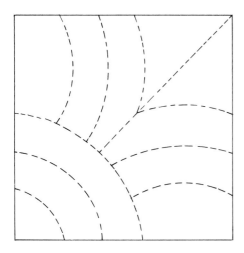

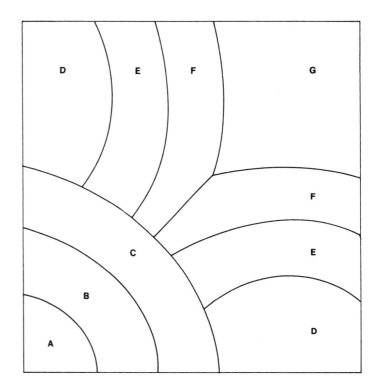

"This design is a link between the quilts of our grandmothers and those of today because the simple style of the fan is a favorite both then and now. I appreciate the knowledge which was handed down to us from our ancestors. It is to this knowledge that we owe, in good part, the progress of our nation.

"When several blocks of my quilt pattern are put together, they form a big fan like those used by our grandmothers."

Mrs. Bordelon's patchwork design can be seen in the chair cushions in our porch scene on page 57. Each finished square measures 11½" (29.2cm) on each side. Because of the curves and the necessity for the blocks to fit perfectly together, extra care should be taken in piecing this design. Be certain to make test blocks in the fabrics you choose, and you might even set two or three blocks together to make certain the seams match perfectly.

One block takes the following:
A—1 of first color
B—1 of second color

C—1 of third color
D—2 total of first color:
    1 for the right side
    1 for the left side
E—2 total of second color:
    1 for the right side
    1 for the left side
F—2 total of third color:
    1 for the right side
    1 for the left side
G—1 of first color

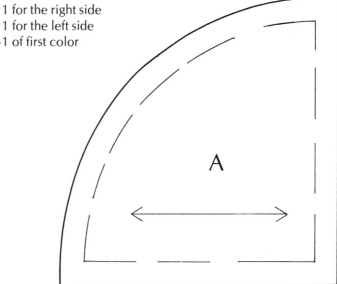

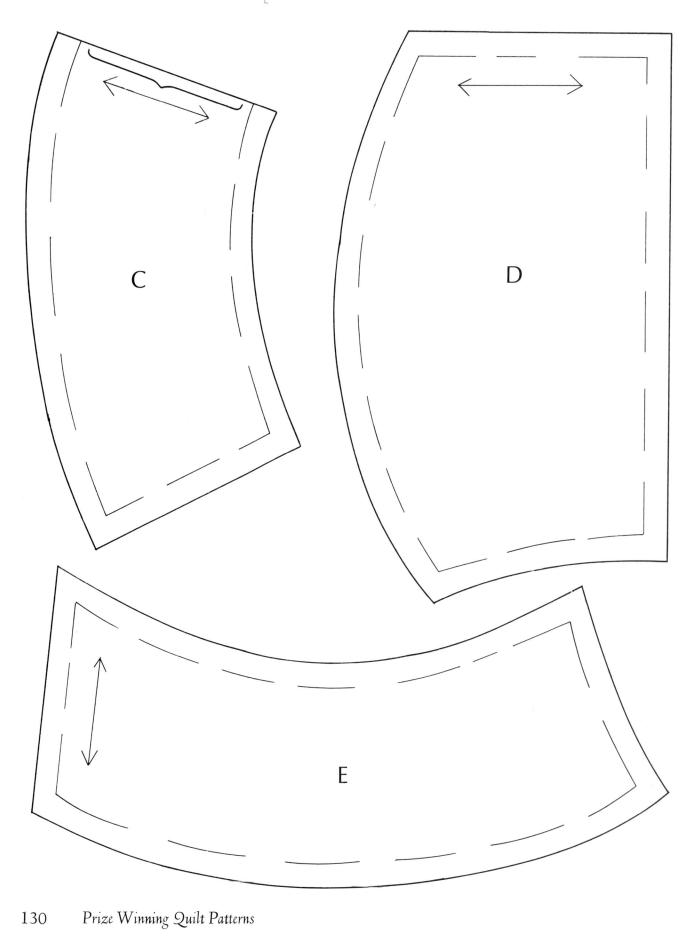

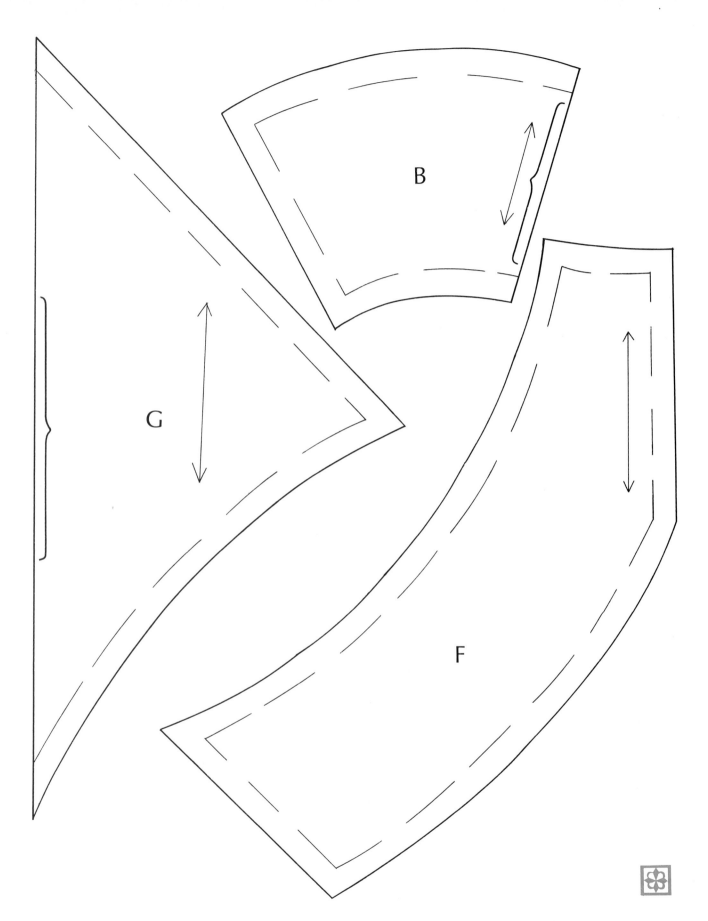

B

G

F

Grandma's Favorite

Annie McGukin
Starr, South Carolina

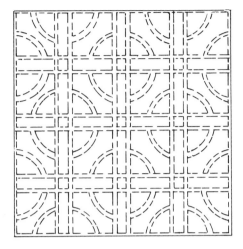

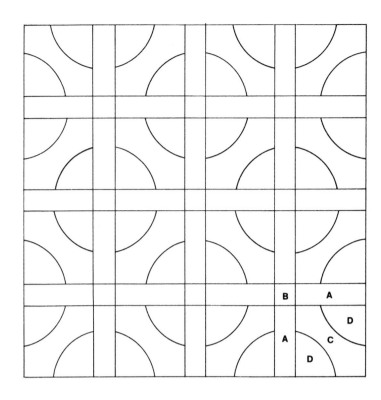

"This quilt design has evolved through the years and many generations of the McGukin family. I am calling it *Grandma's Favorite* because I believe it would be approved by not only Grandma but also the old quilters who traditionally sat around working out their own special patterns.

"It is red, white, and blue, very much like our national colors, but they also happen to be the family colors. The red represents strong military fortitude; the blue, loyalty; the white, sincerity.

"One of the virtues of this pattern is that it is made from small bits of cloth in the tradition of early quilt patterns. Cloth was scarce when quilting was at its peak, so every piece of woven cotton had to be used."

You will recognize this quilt pattern in the lovely silk, lace, and velvet jacket on page 48. Since the basic pattern is simple and relatively easy to piece, it is particularly appropriate for difficult fabrics such as these. The quilt block is made up of sixteen 3½" (8.9cm) squares set together with strips and corner squares.

One unit, consisting of the inner square and a portion of the stripping, takes the following:
A—2 rectangles
B—1 square
C—1 bar
D—2 wedges
Piece together these integral units first; then set them together. Because the stripping and corner square are sewed to the left and upper side of each square, the piecing of a large section of patchwork is almost automatic.

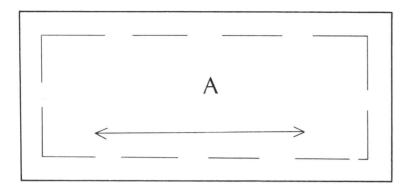

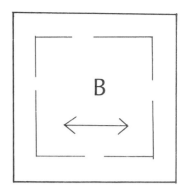

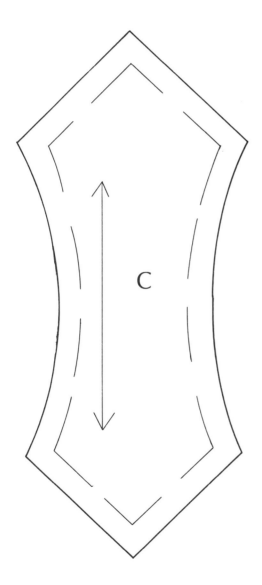

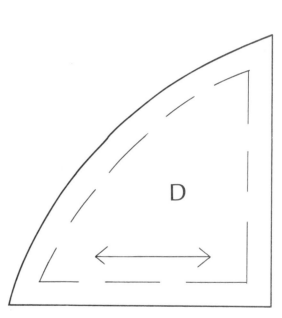

Grandmother's Brooch of Love

Edith Hunter
Marrowbone, Kentucky

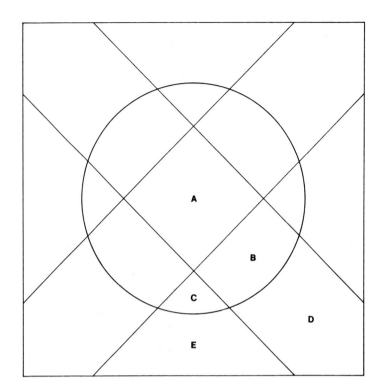

"When I was a child, I talked to my grandmother about the brooch she wore. I can still recall things she said about it. She told me the pin was the cross of love. When I asked why, she replied, 'It is love because it was given to me by your grandfather, and the cross represents Jesus. He died on the cross for us because he loves us so.' I have designed this quilt block in her honor. She was such a sweet grandmother.

"I am a grandmother now. I hope I can be as good and loving to my grandson as my grandmother was to me. I inherited so much love from her, and by doing this quilt design, I hope to pass some of that love on to my grandson."

This interesting design is interpreted in patchwork and is fairly easy to sew if the curves are handled carefully. The design shows up best with three different fabrics, and to get the full benefit of this strong graphic design, the 9½" x 9½" (24.1cm x 24.1cm) blocks should be set together with no sashing.

Each block takes the following:

A—1 of first color
B—4 of second color
C—4 of first color
D—4 of third color
E—4 of second color

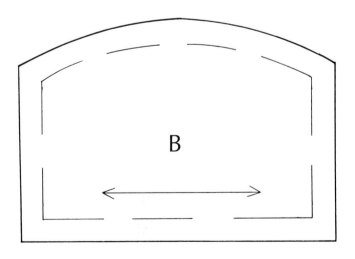

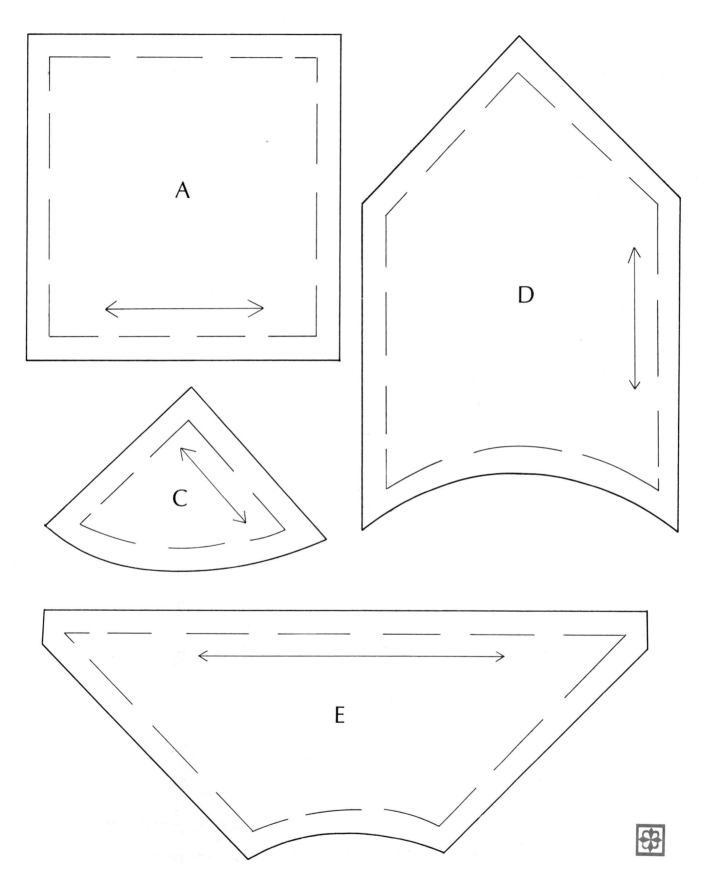

Holly Haven

Barbara Bogard
Clarksville, Tennessee

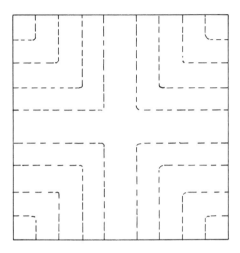

"I was inspired to make this quilt block because it took me back in memory to the youthful stories of my dad, growing and working on the farm where he and his brothers and sisters were raised. In their front yard their mother planted two holly trees, and my dad has told me of many hours he has spent watching the resident mockingbird eating the red berries on the holly tree. For years my family has gone back to the homeplace and gotten bouquets of holly for decorations. Now, after planting two holly trees in our front yard several years ago, we also have red berries in profusion. For the last two years we have had a mockingbird eating berries and singing in our trees. This has been a delight for all of us, and it brings back memories of home and his youth to my dad."

A charming feature of *Holly Haven* is the plump, stuffed holly berries in the center of the design. To make the berries, sew with small stitches and a double thread around the seamline of the flat circle of fabric. Place cotton or fiber fill in the center of the circle, and draw up on the thread to form the berry. Adjust stuffing to desired firmness. Stitch back and forth through base of berry to secure thread, tucking under the seam allowance. Tie off thread securely.

The embroidery stitch used for the detail on the leaves and the outline of the bird wings and tail is the outline stitch. The feather stitch is used in the center of the birds' tails; a satin stitch is used to shade the feathers of the wings; and French knots form the center of the berries and the birds' eyes.

This appliqué design is relatively easy to sew. The blocks would benefit from a well-designed sashing if many of them were to be set together for a project.

Each block takes the following:
A—4 leaves
B—4 birds
C—4 berries
Background square—10" (25.4cm) square

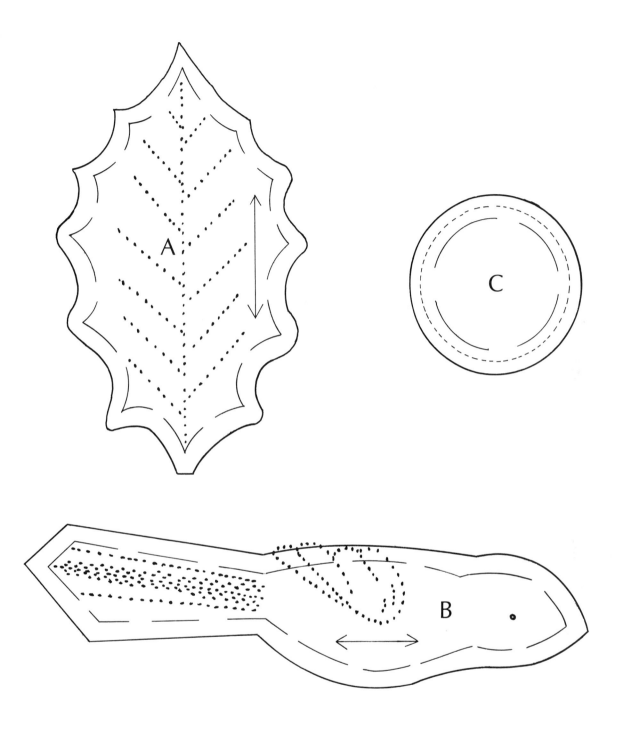

Homestead*

Alta Green
Brownwood, Texas

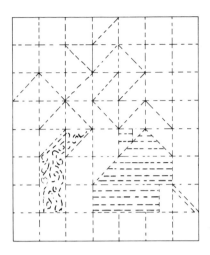

How dear to our hearts are the scenes of our childhood.

"We live on a farm in central Texas that was settled by our parents in 1887. The first house my father built on the new land was very similar to the one on my quilt block—one room, a half-story above, a lean-to, a fireplace for heating, and a tree for cooling.

"Actually the little house had been built onto more than once before my day (as the youngest of nine children). But when we think back over our heritage, the romance of those first families moving out to new, open land and making-do thrills every heart. So the little lean-to house will always be cherished.

"When my sister and I inherited the home place at our parents' deaths, we built a new house but preserved the old chimney. So on chilly evenings we can sit by an open, relaxing wood fire at the very hearth that our father built almost 90 years ago."

Homestead won a Judges' Choice award because of its rustic charm and

---

* Judges' Choice

ingenious adaptation of the basic one-patch form. Every shape in the quilt block is derived from a portion of a square. It is not difficult to piece but requires some amount of concentration to get each square in the right place. Note the vine quilted onto the tree trunk.

Each 16" x 14½" (40.6cm x 36.8cm) block takes the following:

A—whole block; 38 total:
    20 skies
    9 earths
    2 tree trunks
    4 houses
    3 print leaves
B—diagonal half block; 33 total:
    12 skies
    2 earths
    2 tree trunks
    3 houses
    9 print leaves
    5 solid leaves
C—vertical half block; 2 total:
    1 house
    1 door

D—1 chimney
E—1 sky above chimney
F—1 sky to side of chimney
   For supporting stake at side of house,
cut a 1″ x 3½″ (2.54cm x 8.9cm) bias
strip and appliqué it to the diagonal
edge of an earth diagonal half-block.

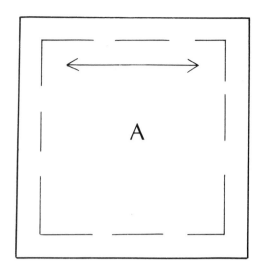

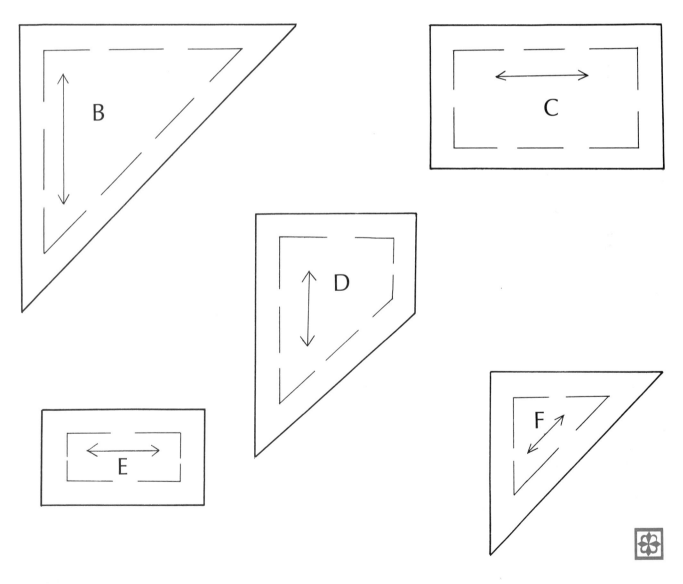

Jack-in-the-Pulpit

Ethel J. Bowman
Looneyville, West Virginia

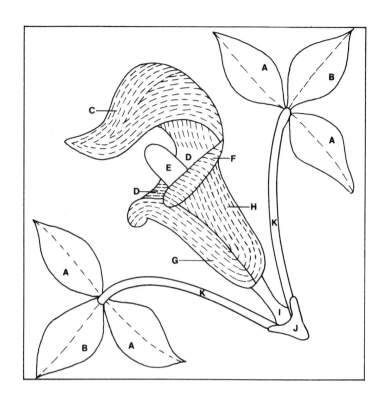

"The Jack-in-the-Pulpit is the only flower I can think of that I have never seen in a quilt book. Also known as the Indian Turnip, it grows in moist woodlands and is quite common in West Virginia. It is a beautiful wild flower, and I think it deserves recognition as such, along with the more highly praised roses, dogwoods, tulips, and poppies.

"Jack-in-the-Pulpit has been well named. The part that looks like the preacher is the smooth slender stalk called the spadix. The greenish pink flowers grow on a club-shaped spike on a pinkish green stalk. The pulpit is the leaflike growth which encloses the spadix like a trumpet. The spathe has a broad flap that extends up and over the spadix. It resembles the sounding board behind and over a pulpit. The spathe is green striped with pink or purple and/or brownish lines."

This exquisite appliqué and embroidery design works up rather quickly. The stitch used to highlight the blossom is a running stitch; the one used down the center of the leaves is an outline stitch. Mrs. Bowman bound her quilt block in bright pink to match the inside of the blossom, and that would be a good choice for sashing. The block should be set on the diagonal if a full quilt is being made; it would be lovely used in combination with plain blocks featuring a quilted design or with blocks displaying other wildflowers.

One block takes the following:

A—4 small leaves
B—2 large leaves
C—1 outer spathe
D—1 inner spathe
E—1 spadix
F—1 lip
G—1 left half of pulpit
H—1 right half of pulpit
I—1 stalk
J—1 spike
K—2 stems (Cut on the bias or use pre-packaged bias tape. Shape into a gentle curve.)
Background square—14" x 14" (35.6cm x 35.6cm)

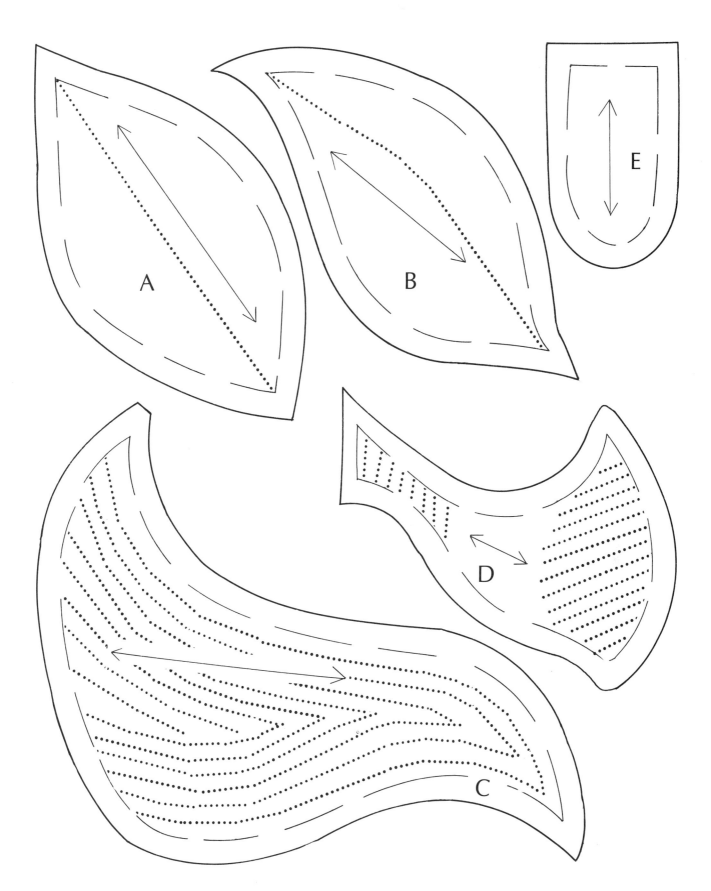

A

B

E

D

C

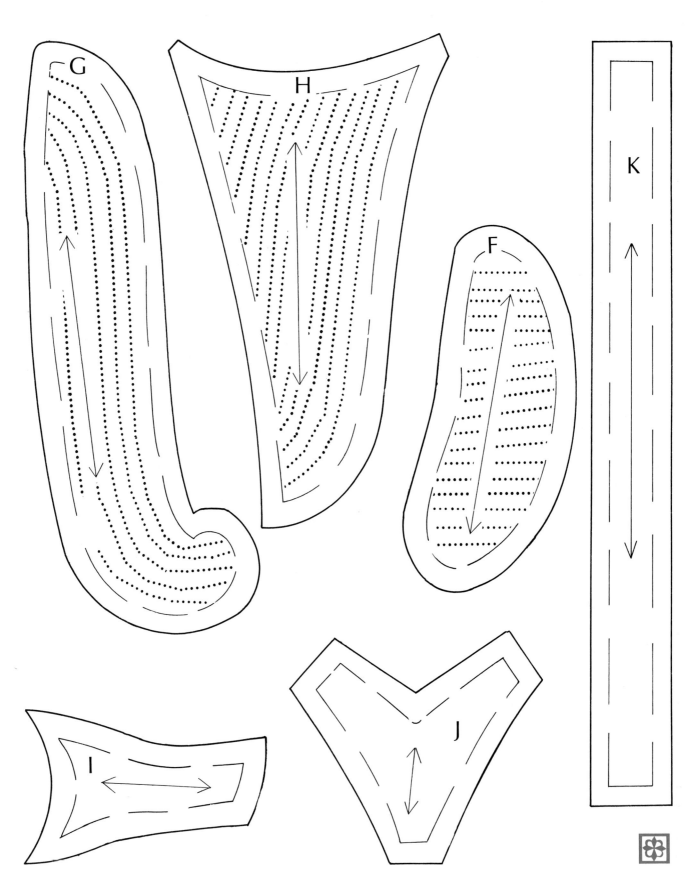

Lily Garden

Mrs. Gladys Smith
Moorefield, West Virginia

"Everyone must admire a garden full of lilies, especially on a bright sunny morning. To me this is one of the most beautiful scenes passed on to me from my Southern rural heritage. All through the years I can remember the majestic lily gardens of the surrounding rural community people.

"A garden full of lilies depicts a sense of purity given to us by God. Nothing is more stirring and full of beauty than lilies exhibited at Easter symbolizing the Resurrection. Thus, I am reminded not only of my Southern rural heritage but of my spiritual heritage as well."

Mrs. Smith's easy-to-sew appliqué pattern adapts well to a variety of color schemes. It also enlarges well, as you can see on our crawler quilt on page 31.

Each block takes the following:
A—1 center
B—4 flowers
C—8 leaves
Background square—12" x 12"
    (30.5cm x 30.5cm)

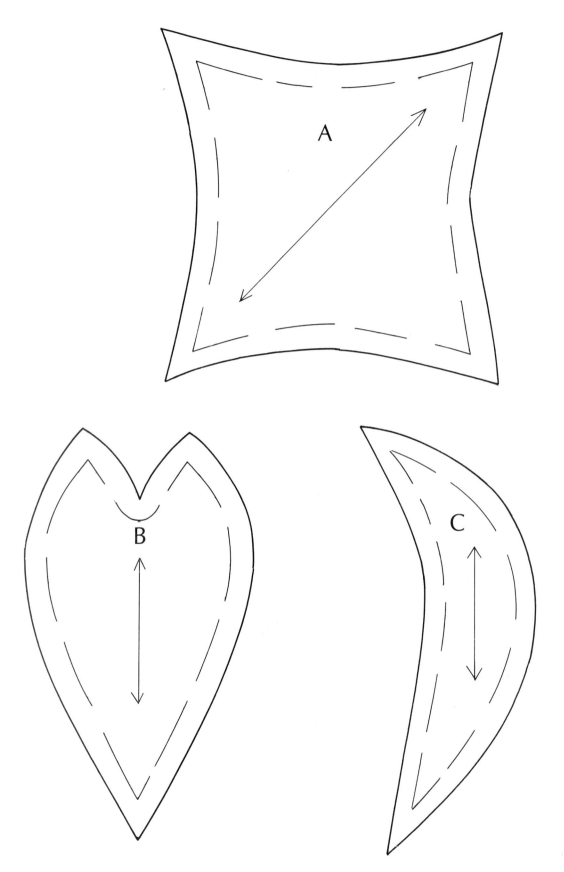

A

B

C

Lindbergh's Night Flight*

Ruby Magness
Jennie, Arkansas

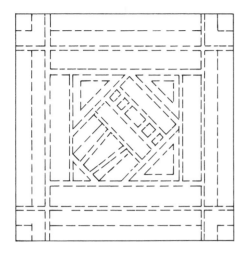

"Charles Lindbergh became a hero in 1927, but events that were to put him there started in 1923. Events that happened in Lake Village, Arkansas, gave him the courage and skill that later enabled him to successfully cross the Atlantic. In 1923, Lindy took all his savings and journeyed to Americus, Georgia, and purchased his first airplane at an auction. The WWI bi-plane trainer cost $500 and left him with no money. Friends suggested he try "barnstorming" (giving local townspeople thrill rides) in Texas to raise some cash. He flew westward from town to town giving thrill rides across Alabama and Mississippi. After traveling several days without a compass, he found himself over southeast Arkansas—125 miles north of his planned route.

"Lake Village offered only a golf course as a landing field, and after dinner that night at the country club, a full moon hung high above the Mississippi Delta. Always being a bit of a daredevil, Lindbergh jokingly invited

the groundskeeper to accompany him on a moonlight ride without mentioning that he had never flown at night. The keeper had refused earlier to get near the plane; but, to Lindy's surprise, at night he accepted. The two daring men soared high above the twisting Mississippi as the lights of Greenville and Lake Village twinkled below. After seeing the world as he had never seen it, Lindy set his plane down on the golf course with a perfect three-point landing.

"Lindy's night flight had been a success and prompted him to become proficient at flying in darkness—a skill he used in flying nonstop from New York to Paris in 1927. Today a monument stands in front of the old country club to commemorate that first daring night flight."

The strong lines and muted colors of this design seem especially masculine; indeed, *Night Flight* is a special favorite of the men who have seen it. It was also singled out for a Judges'

---

* Judges' Choice

Choice. It is not hard to piece, and would make a stunning wall hanging. Each block takes the following:

A—1 cockpit
B—2 skies with struts (note on pattern piece instructions for placement of appliquéd struts)
C—2 wings
D—2 skies
E—1 fuselage
F—1 tail
G—1 sky
H—2 skies
I—2 short bands
J—2 long bands
K—2 struts

Finished size of square is 16¼" x 16¼" (41.3cm x 41.3cm). You may wish to include sashing and corner squares as Mrs. Magness did, or you may decide on another plan. Mrs. Magness used 3½" x 17" (8.9cm x 43.2cm) strips with 3½" x 3½" (8.9cm x 8.9cm) corner blocks to make a 23½" (59.7cm) square.

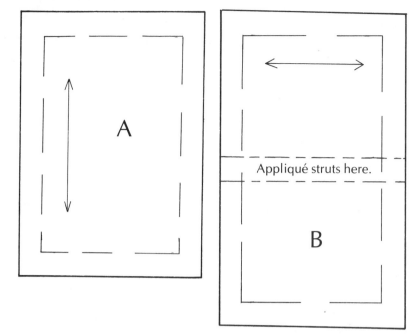

A

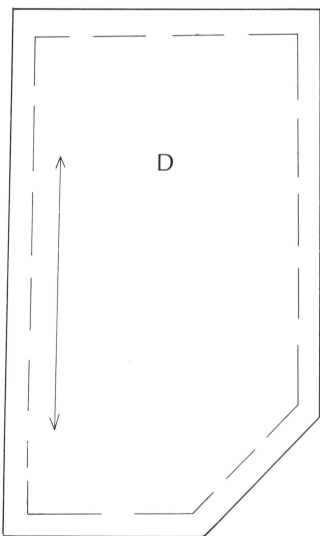

Appliqué struts here.

B

D

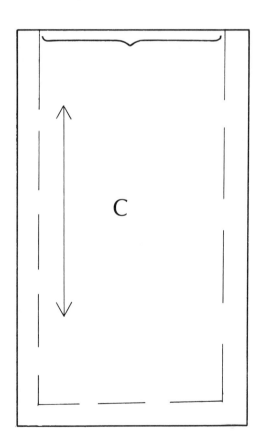

C

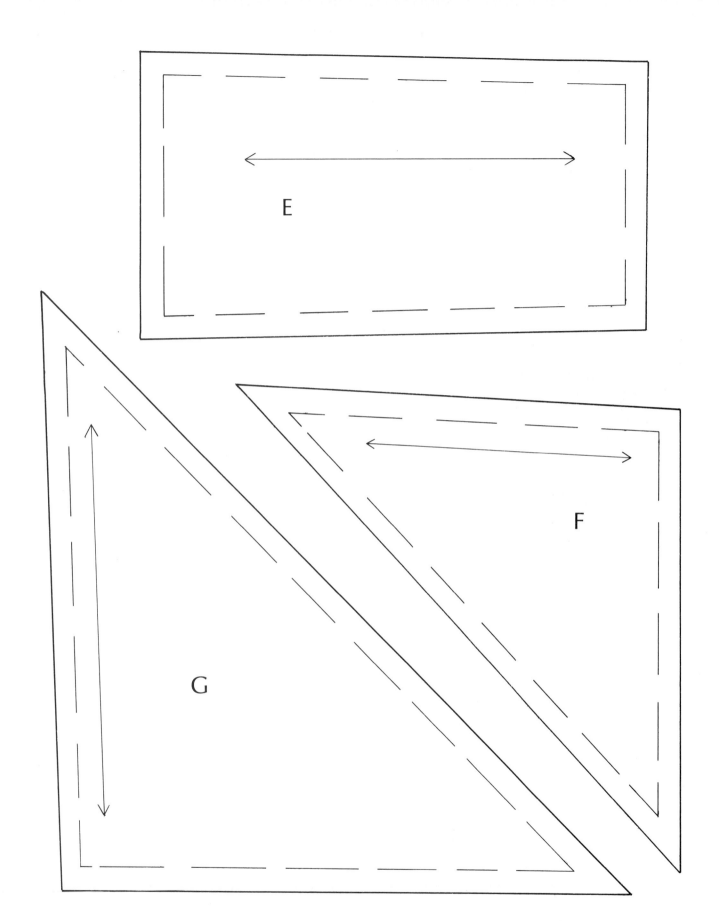

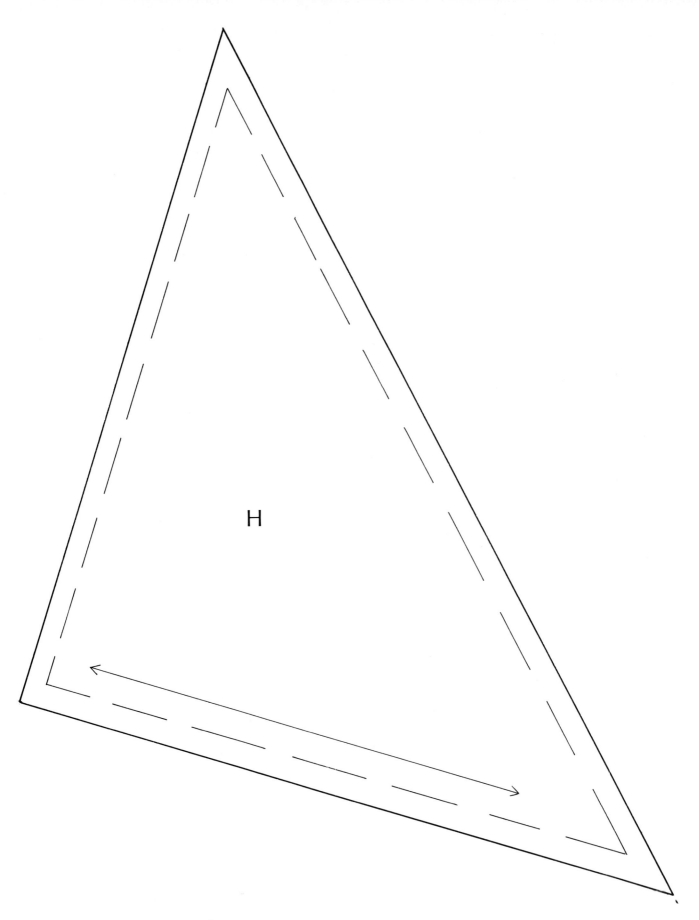

H

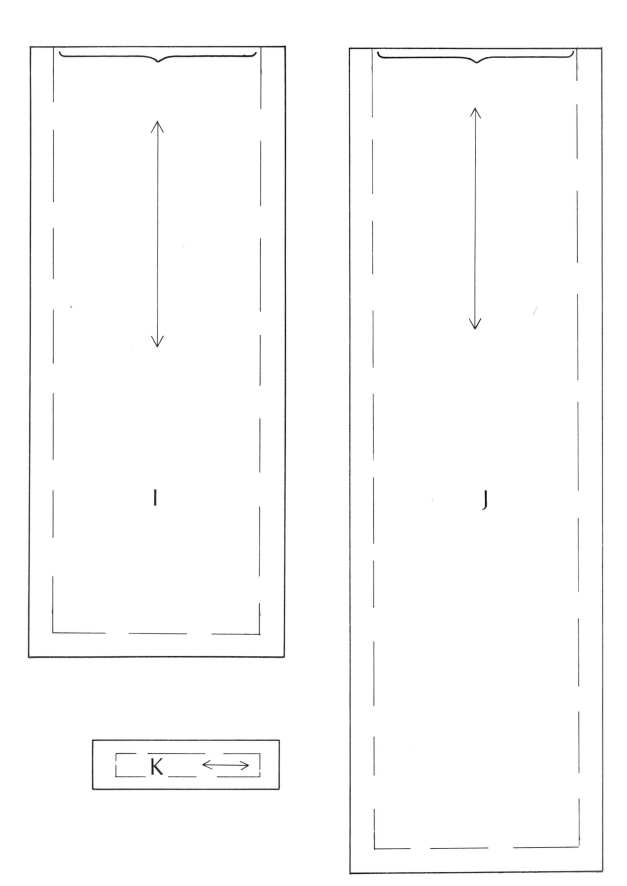

I

J

K ⟷

Lincoln's Hat

Gertrude Mitchell
Russell Springs, Kentucky

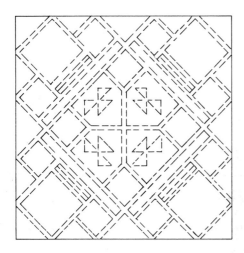

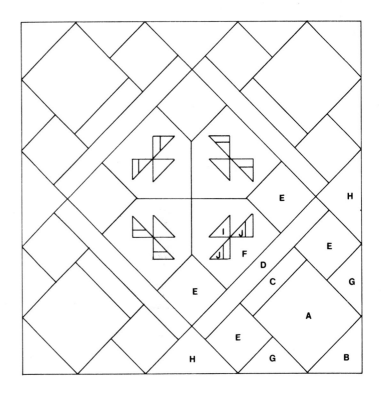

"This design, *Lincoln's Hat*, was selected by me because Lincoln was one of the most loved and admired heroes of the Bluegrass State as well as this great country of ours. The stovepipe hat was quite popular during the Lincoln years, and it became symbolic of this great leader. He and his wife, Mary Todd, were both native-born Kentuckians. They made great contributions to their home state as well as to the entire nation. His tender, friendly, understanding personality depicts the characteristic of Kentucky's people who are noted for their hospitality.

"This high hat made in our national colors brings to our minds the great principles upon which our country was founded as well as a great person who made the hat famous in his day."

This clever design is mostly patchwork—only the eyes and mouth are appliquéd in place with a blanket stitch. Mrs. Mitchell's fabric choices—a printed stripe for the face and a printed star pattern for the hatband—do much to enhance the design. A quilt in this design will probably be most effective when blocks are set together without sashing.

This 12½" x 12½" (31.8cm x 31.8cm) block takes the following:

A—4 hat tops
B—4 corner triangles
C—4 hat bands
D—4 hat brims
E—12 squares
F—4 faces
G—8 small triangles
H—4 large triangles
I—12 triangles with ⅛" (3mm) seam allowances:
    4 for mouths
    8 for eyes
J—8 triangles with ⅛" (3mm) seam allowances for pupils of eyes

Note: Use a closely spaced buttonhole stitch to sew eyes and mouths in place.

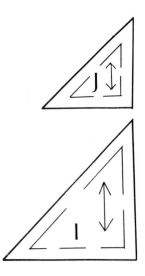

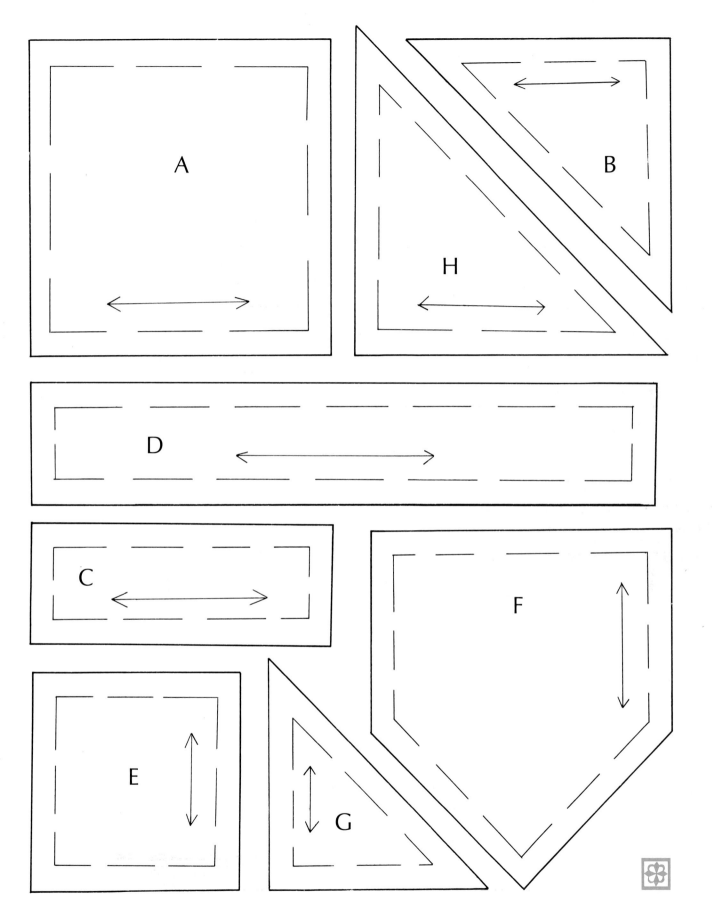

Log Cabin*

Edith McGlothlin
Siloam Springs, Arkansas

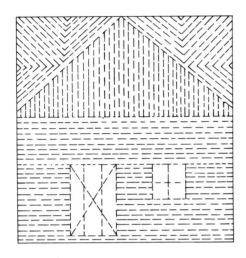

"I thought this log cabin pattern would be nice because it would bring back lots of old memories and history for the many people like myself who were born and raised in log cabins.

"I have watched several log cabins being built. When someone's home burned, or a new family wanted to move into the neighborhood, all the farmers planned a 'House Raising Day.' They stopped their work and got together with their saws, hammers, and nails, then sawed down trees and dragged them with a team of horses or mules to the spot for the house. Sometimes in only one day a log cabin was ready to move into. Women would get together and cook lots of food for the day. All who could built their cabins close to a spring, so that they would have their own water. Those who could not build close to a spring hauled their water in wooden barrels. In summer people would go to a river or creek to take a bath and do their laundry. All the cooking was done on

wood-burning stoves or outside on a campfire."

Mrs. McGlothlin effectively captures in her quilt block the mood she so vividly describes, taking a Judges' Choice special mention for her design. Mrs. McGlothlin is a master quilter; at first glance, her design looks as though the black and white house is pieced in strips rather than made from printed striped fabric! The piecing for this 12" x 12" (30.5cm x 30.5cm) square is not difficult; the close quilting is the challenge.

Each block takes the following:

A—1 roof
B—1 gable
C—2 ends of house
D—1 door
E—1 panel between door and window
F—2 total:
    1 window
    1 section below window
G—1 lower section
H—2 lower triangles
I—2 upper triangles

---

* Judges' Choice

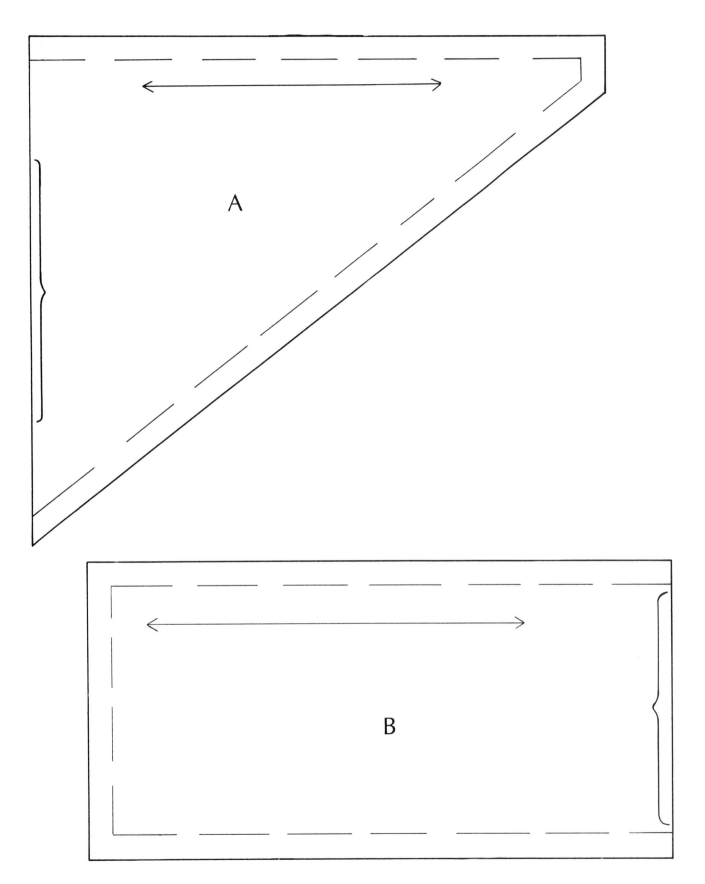

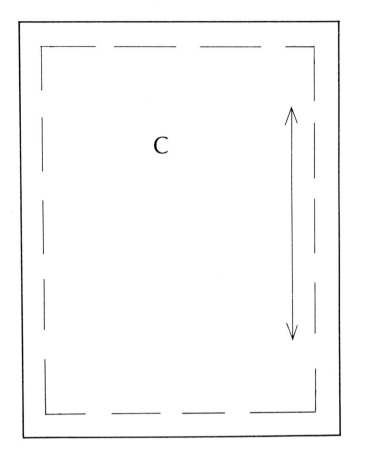

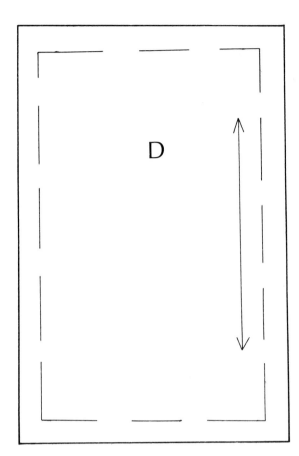

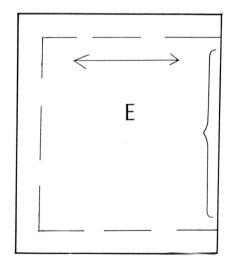

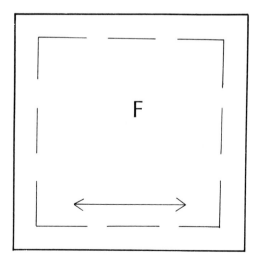

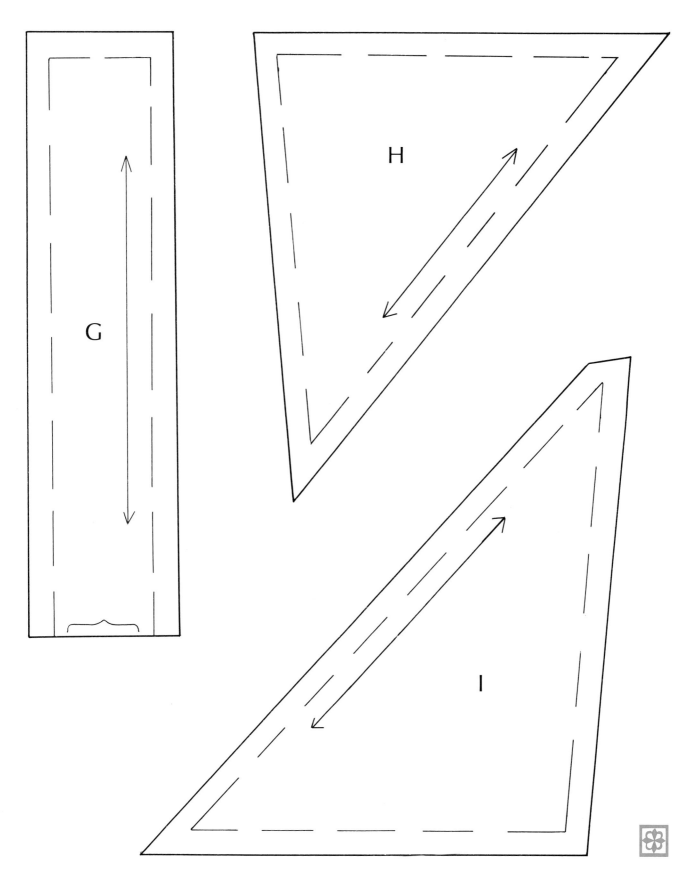

Morning Glory

Eunice McAlexander
Meadows of Dan, Virginia

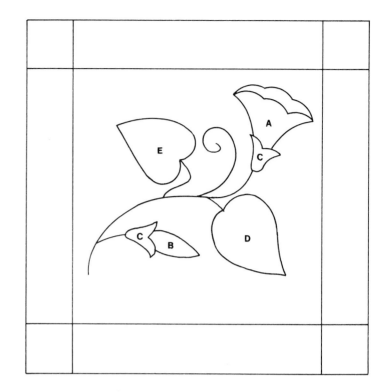

"I have chosen the morning glory as the motif for my quilt for several reasons. It grew around the window of my bedroom when I was a child, and I have loved it ever since. Even though it is considered to be a weed in some areas, it typifies the lush vegetation that covers the Southland.

"In the Blue Ridge Mountains where I grew up and where I still live, flowers and quilts were the two main means women had of satisfying their hunger for color, so a flower design for a quilt seemed most suitable."

This delicate pattern incorporates two of the favorite techniques associated with quilting—appliqué and embroidery. The blanket stitch is used to sew the pieces of the flower design in place. The turned-under seam allowance around all edges will eliminate the possibility of raveling, making the quilt block more durable.

Each block takes the following:
A—1 flower
B—1 bud
C—2 calices
D—1 large leaf
E—1 small leaf

The background square measures 12" x 12" (30.5cm x 30.5cm). The joining strips are 12" x 3" (30.5cm x 7.6cm). The corner blocks are 3" x 3" (7.6cm x 7.6cm). The stems are embroidered with two rows of outline stitch. The outer edges of the leaves, calices, and the bowl of the flower are finished with a blanket stitch. Veins on the leaves are made with a single row of outline stitch.

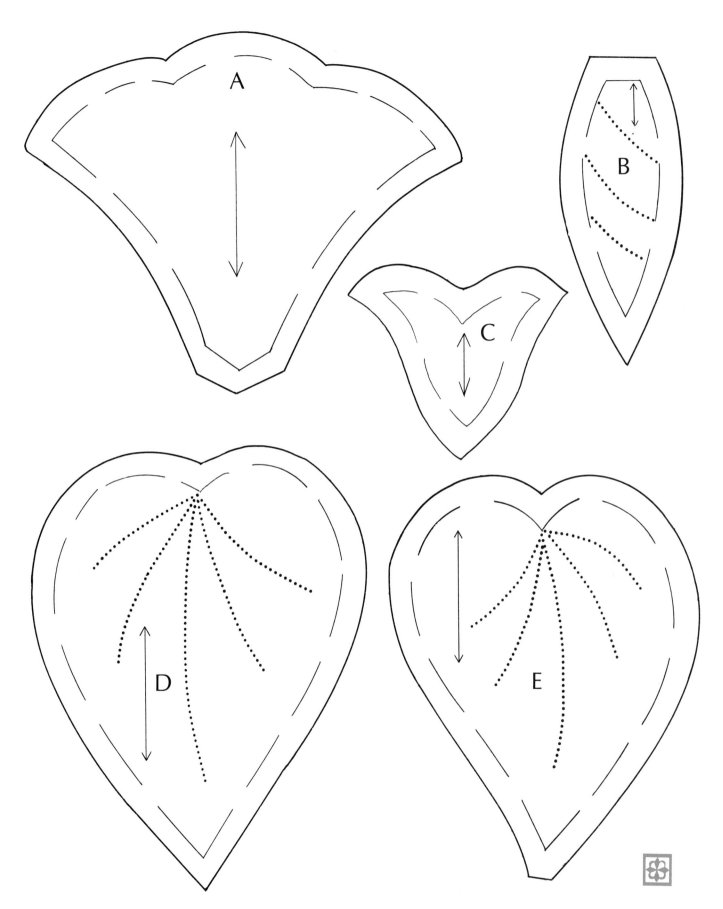

Mountain Homestead

Anna May Duke
Black Springs, Arkansas

"A lonely, scared girl, bereaved of her mother and not yet twenty years old, was sent to teach in a one-room school in the mountains. An elderly couple in a small, unpainted house on the farm they had cleared from the forest made her welcome, and for three years she was a part of their family, learning to sing folk songs, to carve spoons and wind vanes, and to piece and quilt bedcoverings. It was a leisurely pace, the seasons bringing work and ending it. The girl delighted in walks with the elderly lady, learning many things about people and nature that helped her find peace, if not always happiness. Memories of that small farm with its weathered gray house and outbuildings at the end of crooked paths remind her of the love given a lonely young girl.

"I remember the toolshed and forge next to the road, the wellhouse and smokehouse to the side, and the barn in the back. In spring and summer the yard and garden bloomed with flowers; the little fields were cleared and planted where the ground was most

level; the hillside orchard was pink and white with peach and pear blooms; and all around, the rail fences kept the dogwood-laced forests back with zig-zag lines. Little farms and the people who made a living from them are non-existent now, but their memory tells of a time when life could be savored to its fullest, and peace could be very real and God very close in the quietness of a little homestead surrounded by trees."

An intricate and demanding patchwork and appliqué design, this block is not for a beginner quilter. It is, however, quite beautiful and well worth the time it takes to construct. The major portion of the block is pieced; only the flowers in each of the four corners are appliquéd. They are made by first applying each inner section J to a corresponding outer section I, then piecing 4 of these IJ sections together to make a whole flower. Each of the whole flowers is then appliquéd to the background patchwork.

Each 14″ x 14″ (35.6cm x 35.6cm) block takes the following:

- A—1 center square
- B—4 curving sections
- C—4 large, 5-sided shapes
- D—4 pieces with one curved edge
- E—4 small squares
- F—4 double rectangles
- G—4 large triangles
- H—12 small triangles
- I—16 outer wedges
- J—16 inner wedges

Hint: Sew each BCDE section; then attach each one to center square A. Make two of the corner sections with two H triangles, and sew them to opposite sides of central block. Make other two corner sections with four H triangles, and sew them in place last.

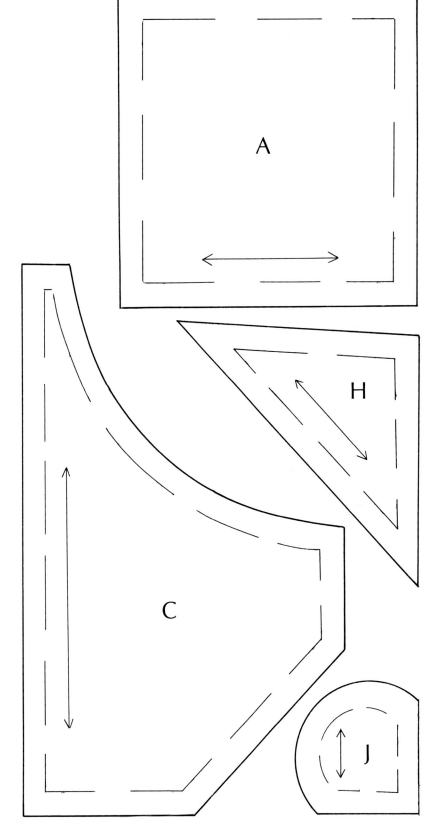

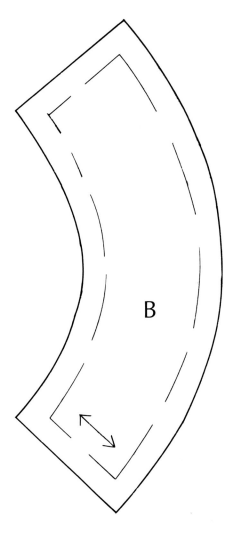

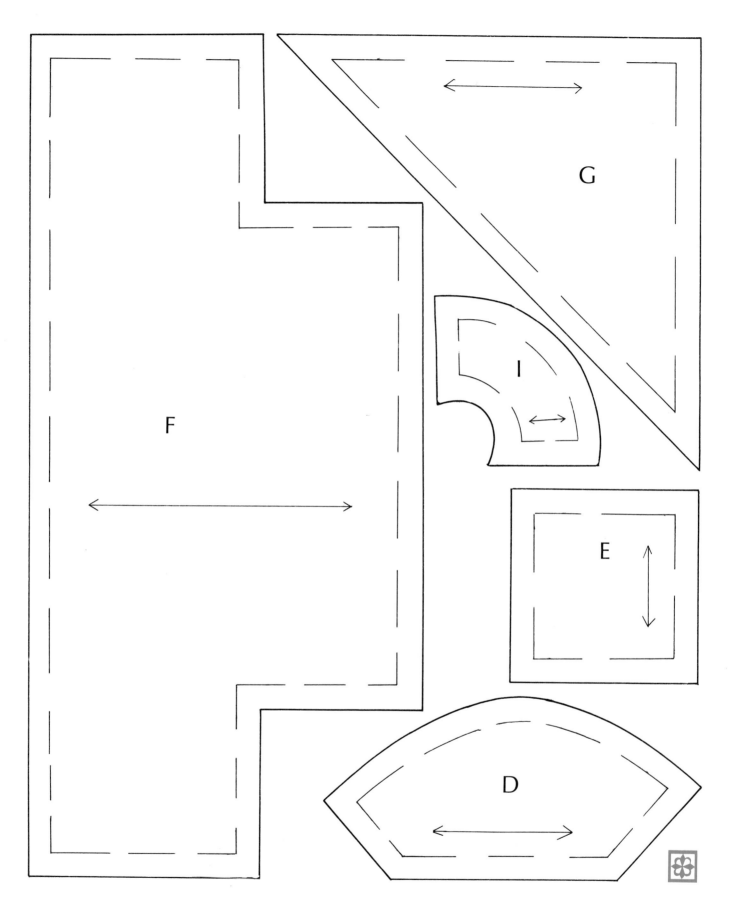

F

G

I

E

D

Mountain Morning Glory

Laura Estes
Franklin, North Carolina

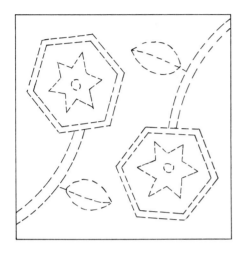

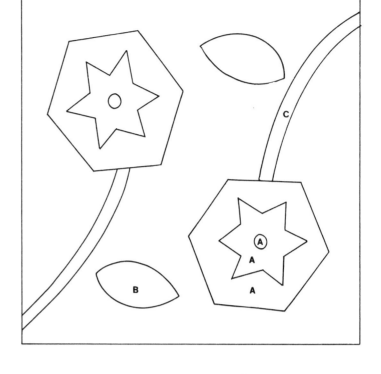

I will lift mine eyes unto the hills, from whence cometh my help.

"So often this verse from Psalm 121 adds comfort and inspiration. It seemed only logical to look to the mountains and to the natural beauty with which God has blessed us. The colorful flowers were my first thoughts. The question was—which one? There are so many with a wide variety of brilliant colors—the flaming azaleas, the wild roses, the ivy, the dogwood, and many more. So beautiful, so delicate, and colorful.

"The thought occurred to me to think about the one I come in contact with the most, the wild morning glory. This lovely little flower can be such a nuisance when it suddenly appears from what seems like nowhere in your vegetable garden. As it climbs through beans and up the cornstalks, you wonder whether or not it is so pretty. As is true with so many of the natural wonders that conflict with man's existence, the morning glory is another small example that everything God makes is truly beautiful in its own little way.

"I chose a combination of appliqué and reverse appliqué because this technique is fun to work with, and you can get very interesting results. Although orange is not a morning glory color, it does represent some of the brilliant colors scattered across the mountains, and it makes a quilt very eye catching."

As Miss Estes says, reverse appliqué is fun to work with, and this lively design will be a good introduction for you if you have never tried the technique.

These blocks set together without sashing would give good color and design saturation to a quilt top. The blocks would, however, work equally well with boldly-designed sashing.

Each block takes the following:
A—4 flowers:
    2 of one fabric; mark star design
    to be cut out
    2 of second fabric; mark center
    circle to be cut out
B—2 leaves
C—2 stems (or use packaged bias
    tape); shape into a gentle curve.
Background square—14″ x 14″
    (35.6cm x 35.6cm)

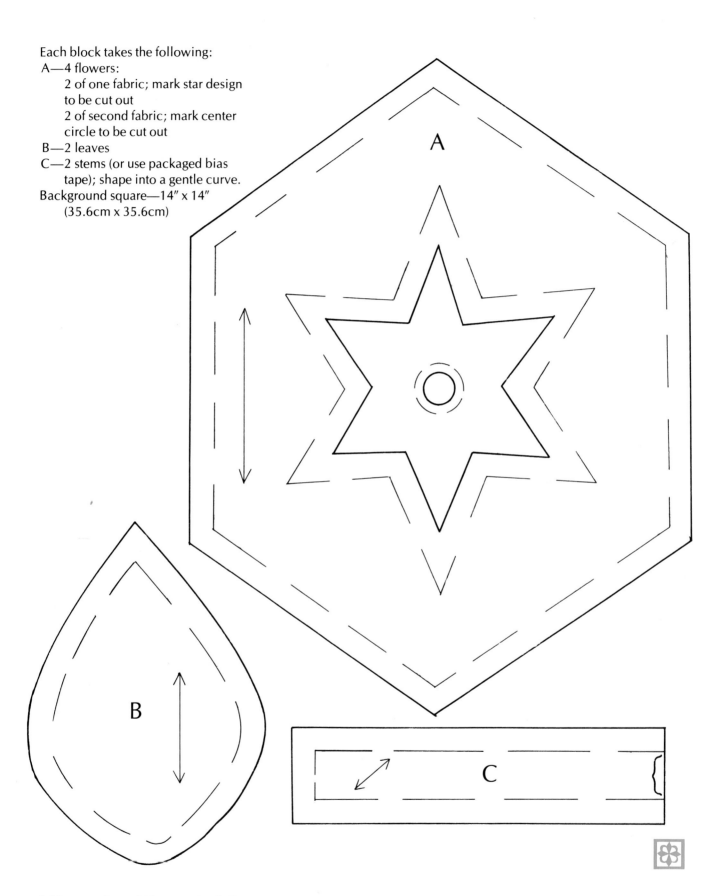

Mrs. Feathersome

**Mrs. Ray Kimbrell
Warren, Arkansas**

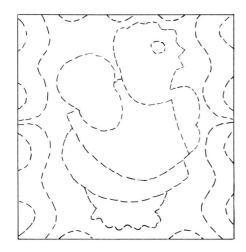

"This design of the prissy little hen called *Mrs. Feathersome* is an idea I chose from some stationery.

"Each finished block is 14½" (36.8cm) square. A quilt 88" x 105" (223.5cm x 266.7cm) requires 30 blocks set 5 across and 6 down. This original design is good for a child's room, or it could fit right in with the country look for adult bedrooms."

Mrs. Feathersome, when enlarged, also makes a charming baby quilt, as you can see on page 31. She is somewhat of a challenge to construct; the main part of her body is pieced and the details appliquéd and embroidered. When she is put together, she is then appliquéd to a 14½" x 14½" (36.8cm x 36.8cm) square and trimmed on all seamlines with rickrack. (See color photo, page 79.)

Each block takes the following:
A—Comb
B—Head
C—Wattle
D—Beak
E—Eye
F—Upper wing

G—Upper wing tip
H—Lower wing
I—Lower wing tip
J—Apron
K—Skirt
L—Pantaloons
M—Feet
Background square—14½" x 14½"
    (36.8cm x 36.8cm)

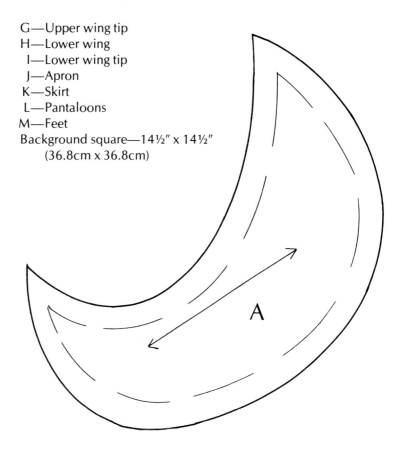

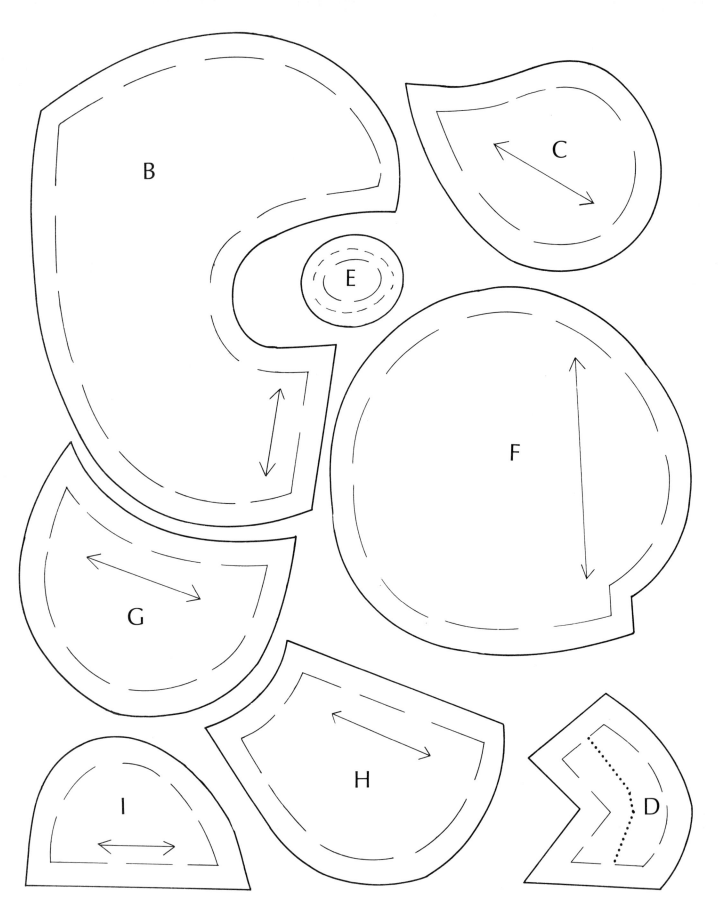

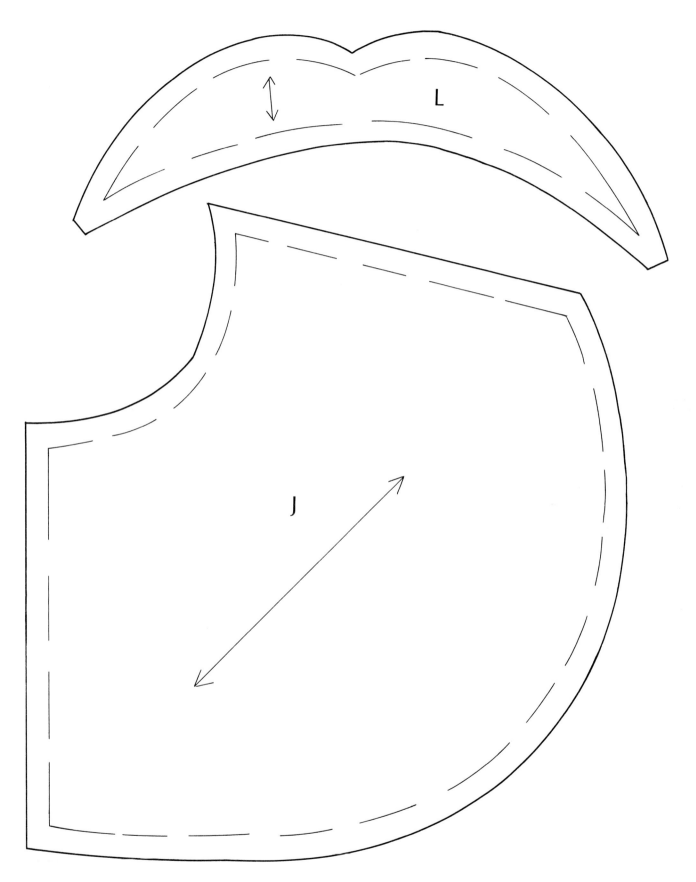

L

J

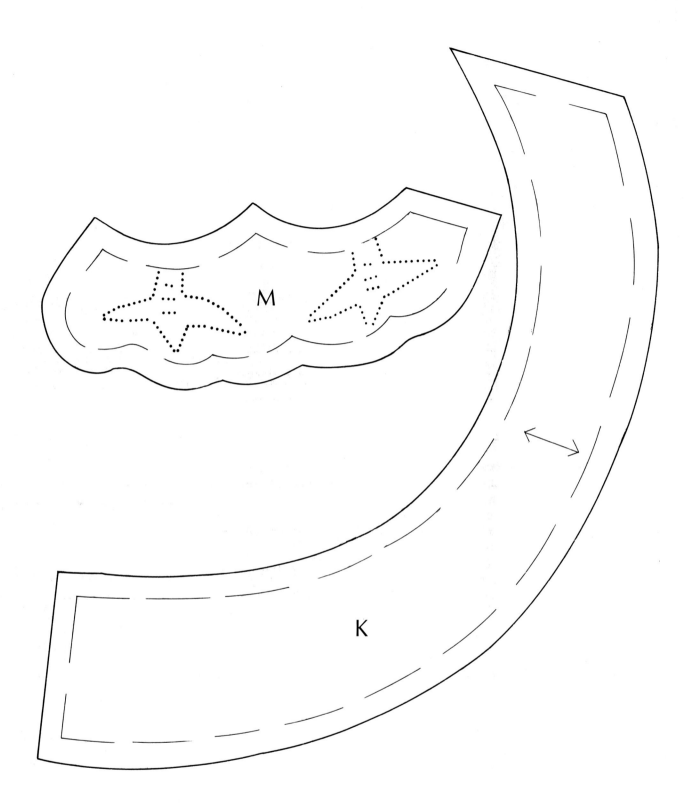

M

K

Oklahoma Trails and Fields

Mrs. Mildred Hardin
Walters, Oklahoma

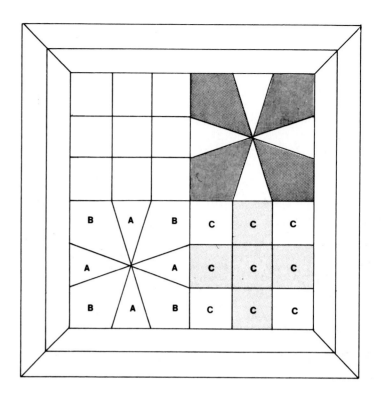

"In early 1900, my grandparents and their six children made the trip by wagon from northeastern Arkansas to Texas. When Oklahoma was opened to settlers in 1907, they obtained a farm in southwest Oklahoma in what is now called Cotton County, just north of Red River. These rolling plains were quite different from the hills they were used to. My parents bought their home place in 1920 and farmed it until their deaths. My husband and I are very proud of our farm and home. We plant mostly wheat, but do have some oats and feed for hay, and we raise cattle. The squares of red and white represent the fields, the blue is for trails (or it could represent windmills that were found in all pastures)."

A well-worked-out patchwork design, *Oklahoma Trails and Fields* requires only three pattern pieces. It is easy to put together and can be seen in the center of one of our floor cushions on page 12. Sashing should not be used around the sets of four blocks; the quilt is made up of these alternating blocks, and the outer edge of the quilt should be bordered and banded as shown.

One *Trails* block takes the following:
A—4 of first color
B—4 of second color
One *Fields* block takes the following:
C—4 of third color
5 of first color
Each block is approximately 5½"
(14cm) square when finished.

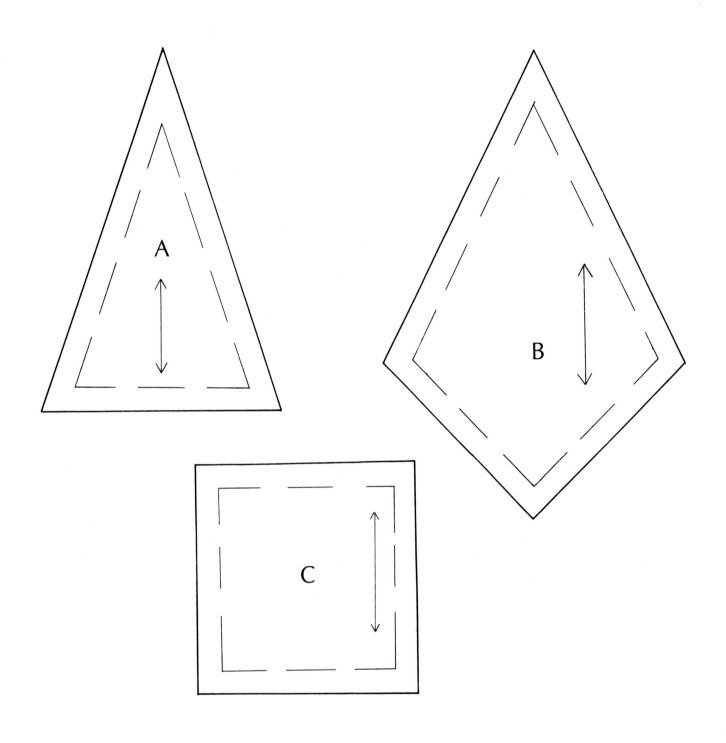

Old Country Church

Lois Bruner
Coeburn, Virginia

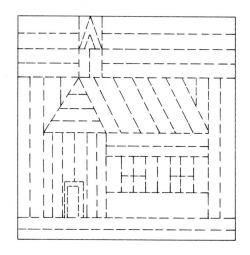

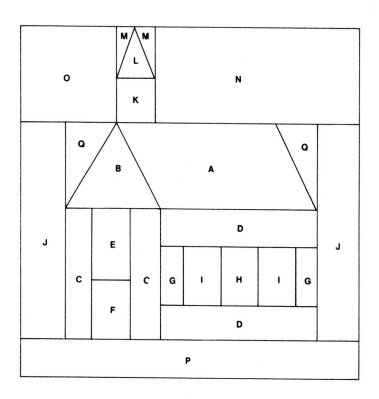

"The old country church played a major part in the laying of our nation's foundation. Through dependence on God and much faith in their beliefs, the early settlers formed a unified people strong enough to endure many hardships. The church was the backbone of their strength. They considered the church sacred and taught their children to respect it; no community was without its church building. Also, a church by the wayside meant comfort to travelers. Many tired, weary strugglers have found refuge in the country church, not only for their tired bodies but for their souls.

"Several of our patriots and statesmen were products of our early country churches. The traveling clergymen went forward searching out new places to build new churches, so that the strength of our founding fathers could survive and grow. As the population increased and cities were formed, churches became larger and lost their country feeling.

"But, there are still many old country churches where the word of God is preached and the church bell sends its tones across the countryside. There is nothing more comforting than to pass a church out in the country and hear the songs of the choir drifting through the windows. If you are homesick, come with me to our old country church where the welcome is so big that it pours out the windows and the door."

This design has a traditional feeling; it can be pieced in different fabrics for a totally different effect. Because of the many pieces in this block, it takes some time to put it together, although it is not difficult.

One block takes the following:
A—1 roof
B—1 gable
C—2 front pieces
D—2 long sides
E—1 piece for over front door
F—1 door
G—2 side ends
H—1 piece between windows
I—2 windows
J—2 sides of block

K—1 cupola
L—1 steeple
M—2 sides of steeple
N—1 sky
O—1 sky
P—1 ground
Q—2 skies
Finished size: 13" x 13"
(33cm x 33cm)

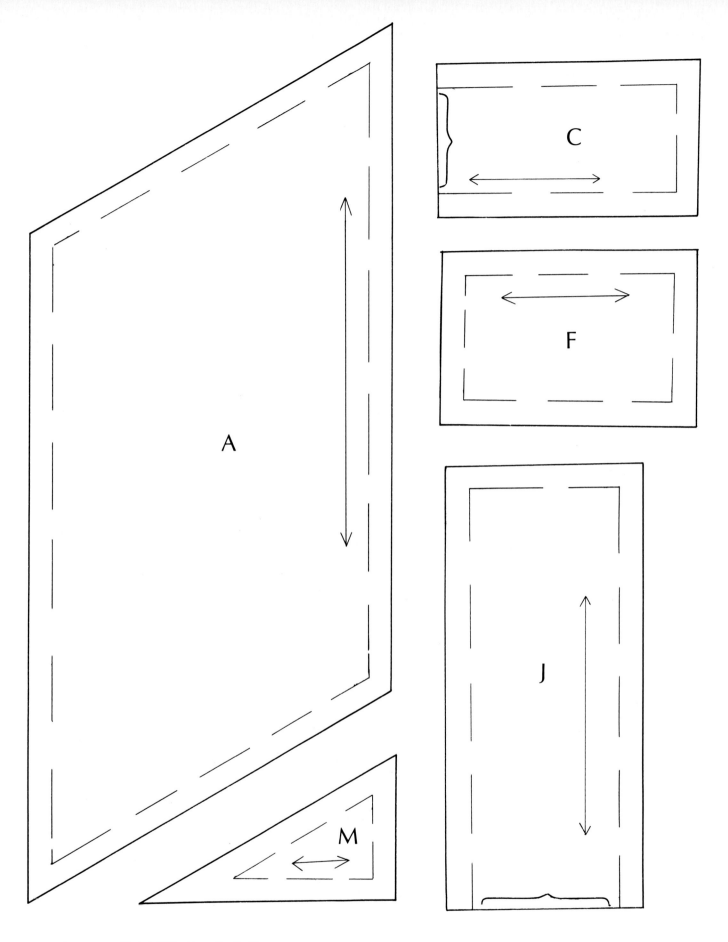

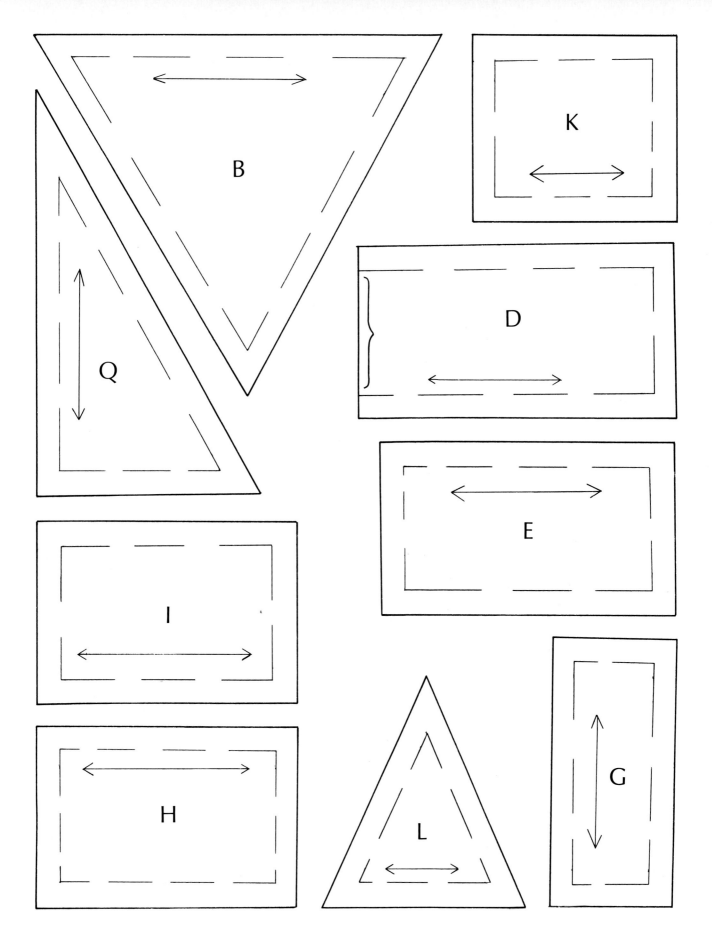

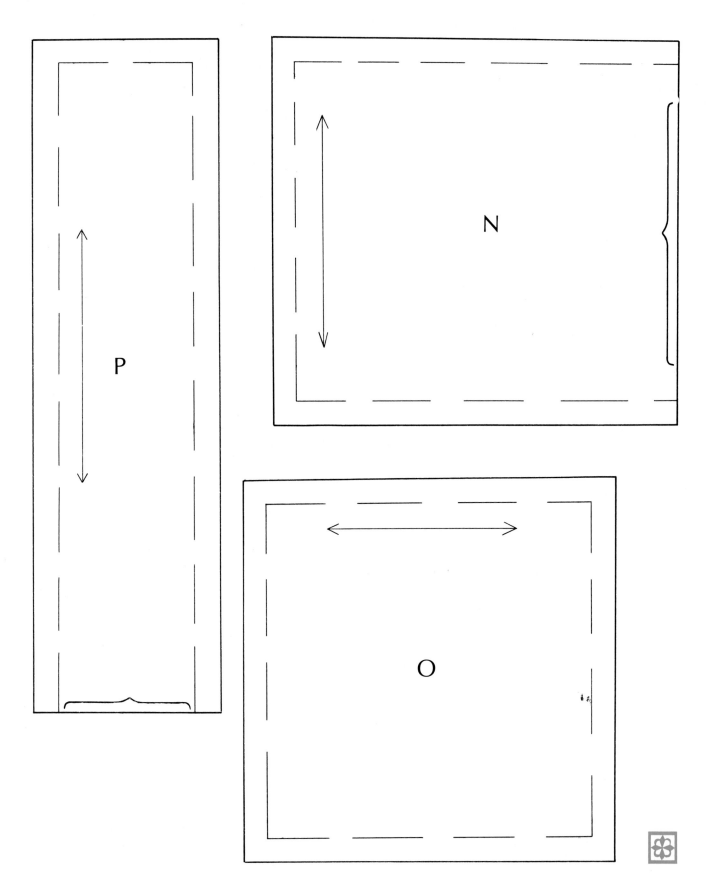

Old Rail Fence

Mary Williams
Timberville, Virginia

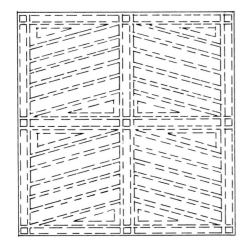

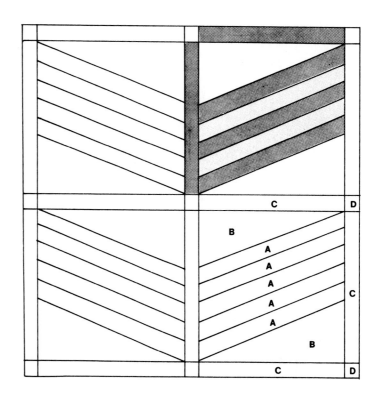

"For more than 50 years I have been piecing comfort and quilt tops. Of the more than 300 tops I have pieced, only one was partly done by machine. All others were sewn from start to finish by hand. This was the tradition of Americans at that time, and it is almost a vanishing art today.

"Farmlands have always been the backbone of America. Having always lived on a farm, I share a closeness to nature and God which one can only experience through living and working on the land.

"Typical of American farmlands is the rail fence. An invention of pioneers, a few remain as a symbol of our heritage. It is in tribute to this way of life that I have designed and pieced by hand this rail fence quilt."

This patchwork pattern has possibilities for taking on many different looks, depending on where the lights and darks are placed within the design. Notice that the big block is made up of four smaller squares, which are exactly alike except that two are mirror images of the other two. This means that you will cut fabric for half the blocks with the pattern right side up and cut the other half of the blocks with the pattern upside down. The sashing with small squares that Mrs. Williams shows seem perfect for this design. A finished block, composed of 4 squares and 3 rows of sashing in each direction, measures 20¾" x 20¾" (52.7cm x 52.7cm).

Each 9½" (24.1cm) block takes the following:

A—5 rails:
3 of first color
2 of second color

B—2 triangles of third color

To sash the upper and left side of each square:

C—2 side strips of first color

D—1 corner square of third color

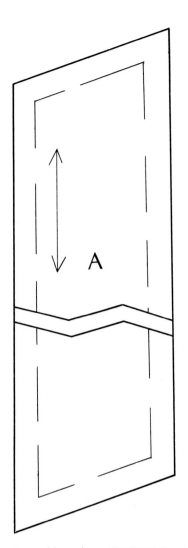

Extend length to 10¼″ (25.6cm).

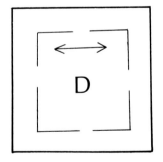

B

C

Pride of the South
Velma Perry
Winfield, Alabama

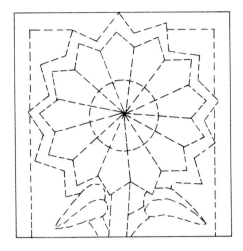

"Sunflowers have always held a fascination for me, even as a child. Their tall, strong stems with the weight of their lusty bounty of ripe seeds amaze me. Birds of the countryside are not the only creatures who seek their nutty goodness. We human beings run a good race in their harvesting. Their colors range from tones of yellow to gold and brown, reward enough for reserving a few feet of soil in which to plant and watch them grow."

Of the many, many sunflower quilt blocks submitted to the contest, Mrs. Perry's was certainly outstanding. You can see it in different fabrics in the throw pillow on the swing on page 57. Although there are many pieces to this pattern, it is a pleasure to sew. (Hint: We used fusible bonding web to hold our petals in place for stitching.)

Each block takes the following:
A—13 large petals
B—13 medium petals
C—13 small petals
D—1 center
E—1 stem
F—1 small leaf
G—1 large leaf
Background square—16½" x 16½"
    (41.9cm x 41.9cm)

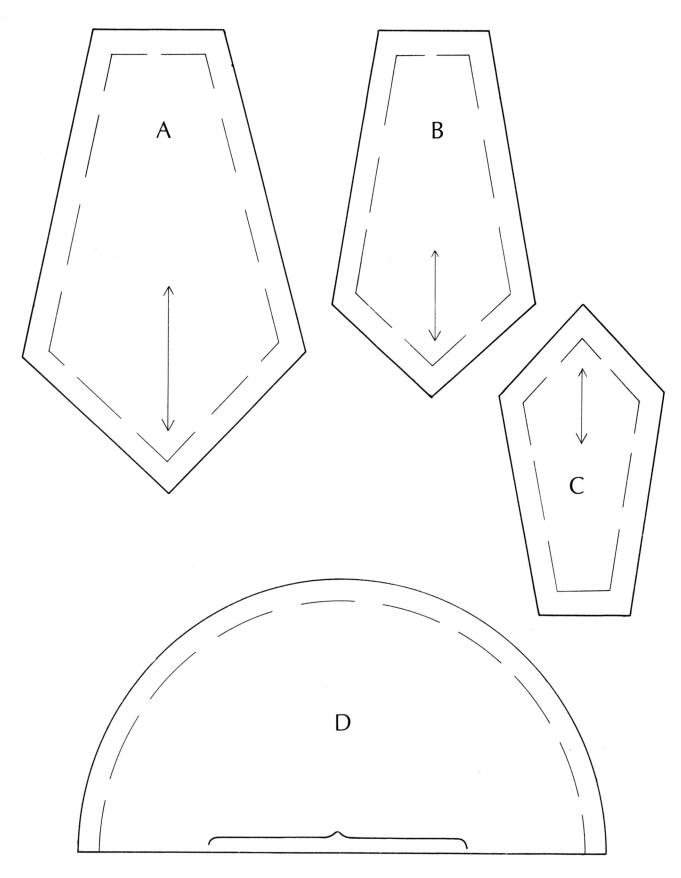

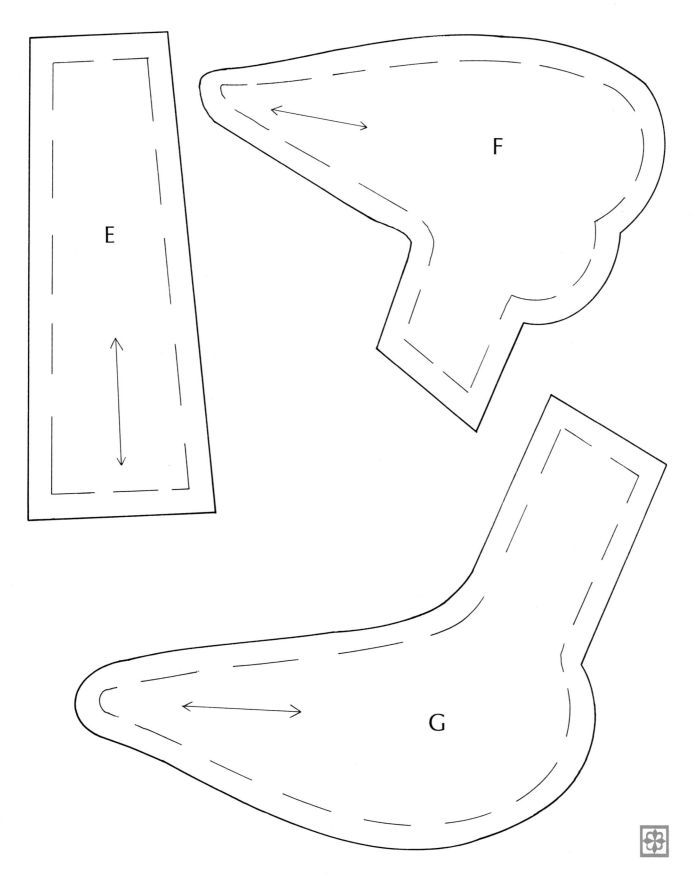

E

F

G

Proud Pine

Anna Lupkiewicz
Gainesville, Florida

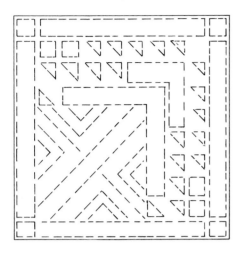

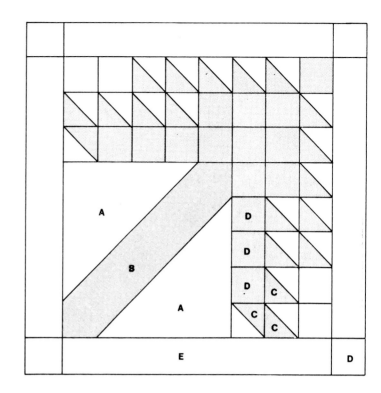

"An incident which happened almost 28 years ago inspired me to design a different pine tree quilt block. In the late '40s, my husband came to Florida alone in search of a home for his young family. We had 3 small children, and it was easier on all if a home was found before the real move began. After weeks of house hunting he wrote, simply elated over his find, 'A new home with 32 pine trees in the yard!' My mind was picturing Christmas trees, all shapes and sizes, filling up the small yard. When I finally saw the new home, I looked for the Christmas trees and instead saw the tall pines so typical of the South!

"Pine tree patterns have been popular since the earliest colonial days. I would like to add my design to those already in use; I feel the double feathering of the tree-shape is unique."

The pine tree is a favorite subject for patchwork patterns, and this particular pattern is easy to construct, with results you will be proud of!

Each block takes the following:
A—2 background triangles

B—1 tree trunk
C—40 triangles:
    20 for tree
    20 for background
D—23 squares:
    15 for tree
    8 for background and corner
    squares
E—4 rectangles for sashing
Finished size of block including sashing and corner squares is 12" x 12" (30.5cm x 30.5cm).

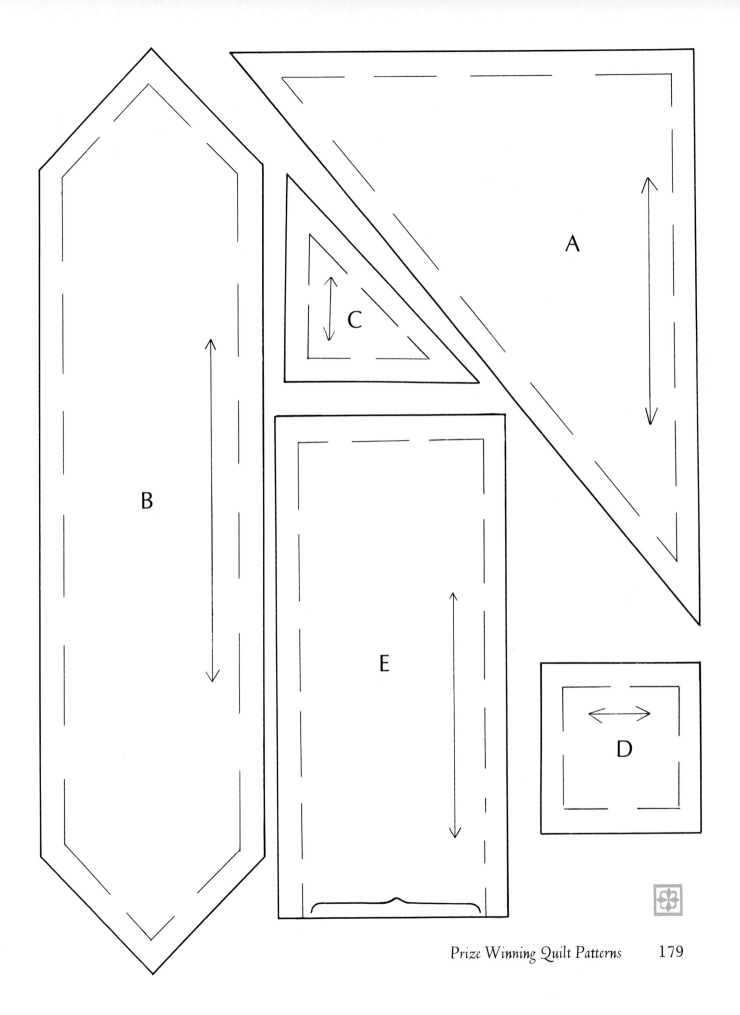

A

B

C

D

E

Red Barn*

Ann Weeks
Emmet, Arkansas

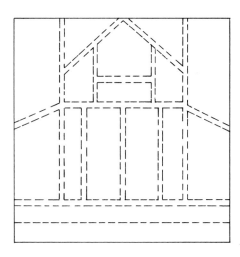

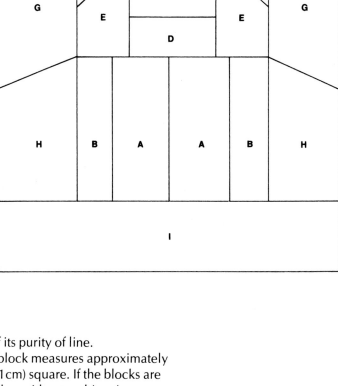

"I selected this design because this is the barn on our small farm. It has meant so much to our four sons. They have spent many happy hours playing with their friends in the barn. One boy was asked the highlight of his summer. He said, 'Playing in the Weeks' barn.'

"Now the grandchildren make it their place to play when they come for a visit. They take their sleeping bags and spend the night in the barn loft on the hay.

"This old barn has sheltered the cows as well as all the pets our boys collected, such as a goat, saddle horses, a Shetland pony, pigs, and a number of pigeons. Thousands of bales of hay have gone through this old barn, and at one time I milked a cow there.

"It holds a host of memories for the entire family. I think they are happy memories."

This nostalgic patchwork design was picked as a Judges' Choice be-

cause of its purity of line.

Each block measures approximately 15" (38.1 cm) square. If the blocks are set together without sashing, interesting negative spaces are formed by the roof of the barn. If the blocks are separated by sashing, choose a blue to match the windows.

One block takes the following:
A—2 red and white striped pieces
   (cut on the bias)
B—2 red pieces
C—1 red piece
D—1 blue piece
E—2 red pieces
F—2 white pieces
G—2 white pieces
H—2 red pieces
I—1 white piece

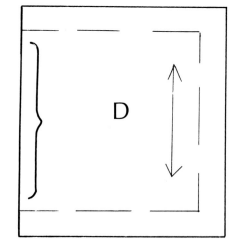

* Judges' Choice

180   *Prize Winning Quilt Patterns*

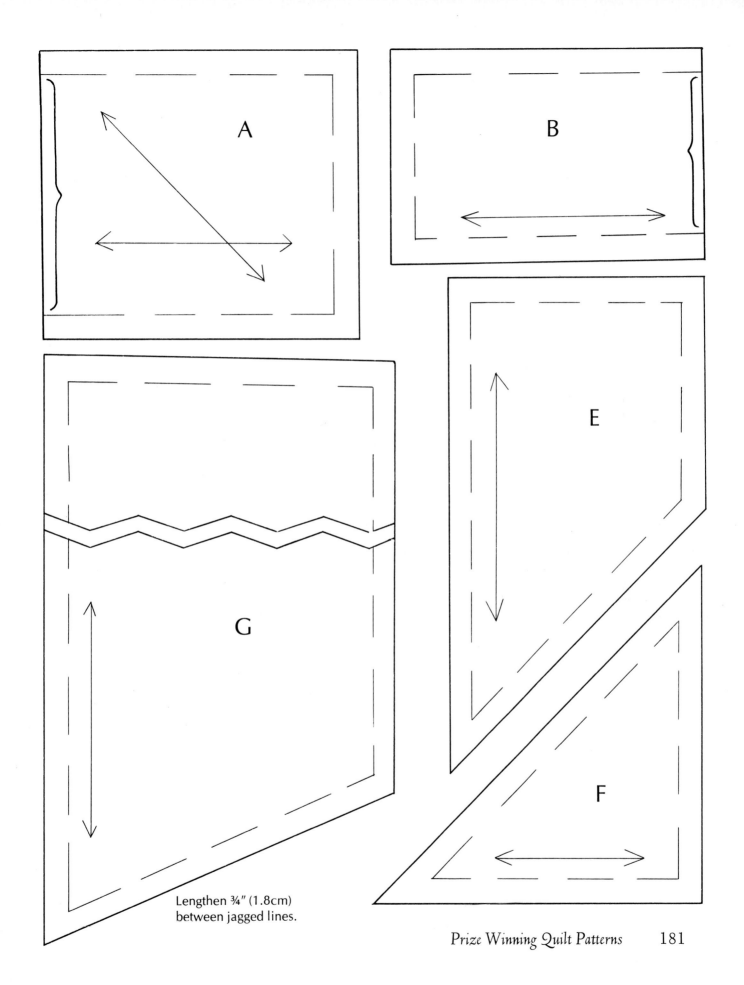

A

B

E

G

F

Lengthen ¾″ (1.8cm)
between jagged lines.

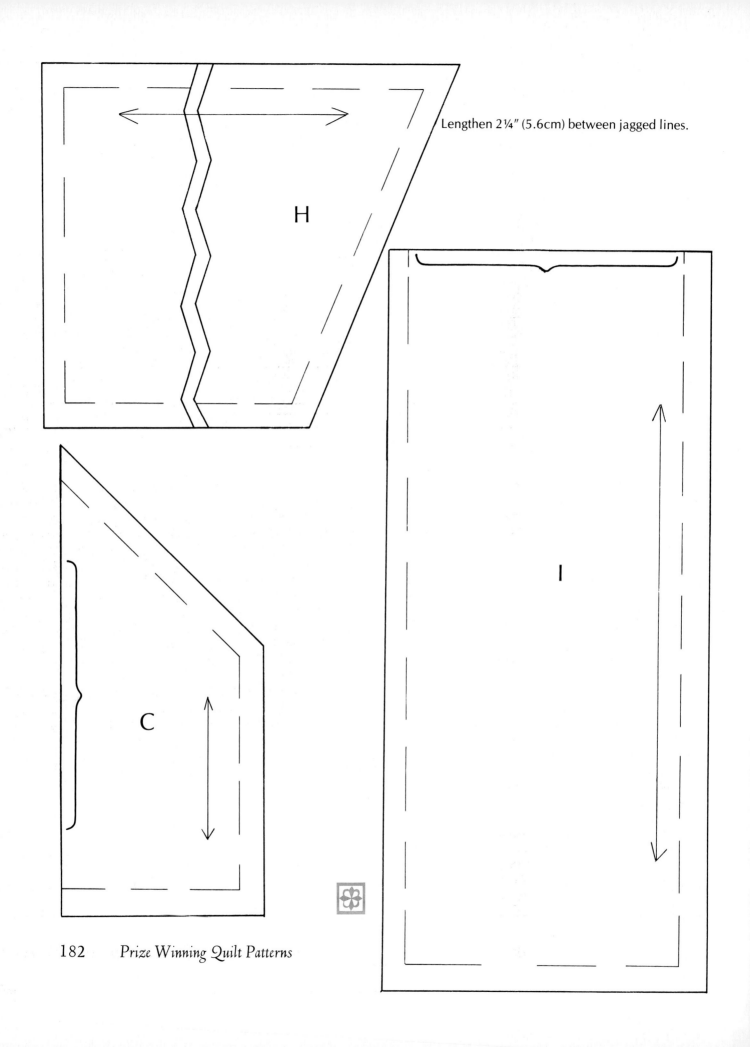

Lengthen 2¼″ (5.6cm) between jagged lines.

H

C

I

Rural Background*

Mrs. Ben F. Harris
Woodland, Alabama

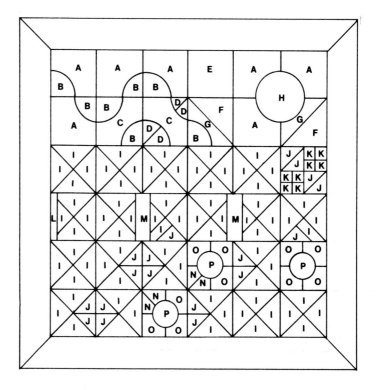

"I have been collecting pictures of quilt patterns for more than fifteen years and have folded 12" x 12" (30.5cm x 30.5cm) sheets of brown wrapping paper in the basic *Nine Patch* pattern and then have very easily drawn in and colored the different patterns that are popular. When you announced your contest, I started thinking about a scene. I knew it had to be about the soil and plants and the farmer's dependency on God to send the rain and sunshine. I thought that this type of scene could only be done with appliqué, and I had never sewed that type of quilt work. Finally I sat down, and as my daughter suggested ideas, I would fold and draw. I folded down to the smallest triangles I had ever used and by adding a form of the *Wonder of the World* pattern, I could see the clouds, the sun, the rocks, the grass, bushes, and trees with the clay soil in all the small triangles. I wanted to include God in the form of a dove and remembered a

pattern using squares and triangles to represent a bird. I found it in my scrapbook, and its name was *Game Cocks.*

"Since Cheaha Mountain was in the background of the land where I was raised and lived until I married, I had to have mountains in my picture and colored them purple. Recently we drove from Anniston to Lineville over the Cheaha Mountain range and to my surprise, the mountains were a dark blue, so I had to go home and change the color in my pattern . . . I have saved cotton scraps for years and had many color shades from which to choose. I stripped around my square because it should not be joined square on square."

Rural Background took top honor in the quilt contest. In the words of the judges, "Our first prize choice was based on the theme idea of the contest. We felt that this quilt block best interpreted country living heritage in a traditional quilt technique with a fine

---

* First Place Winner

display of originality and crafts-manship."

The most difficult part of this pattern is cutting the pieces.

One block takes the following:
A—7 total:
    6 skies
    1 cloud
B—7 total:
    3 skies
    4 clouds
C—2 clouds
D—4 total:
    2 skies
    2 mountains
E—1 sky
F—2 total:
    1 sky
    1 mountain
G—2 total:
    1 sky
    1 mountain
H—1 sun
I—74 total:
    5 skies
    5 mountains
    10 trees
    2 bushes
    22 fields
    18 grasses
    12 roadways
J—18 total:
    2 doves
    2 mountains
    6 grasses
    6 roadways
    2 bushes
K—8 total:
    5 mountains
    3 doves
L—1 tree trunk
M—2 tree trunks
N—4 grasses
O—10 total:
    8 grasses
    2 roadways
P—3 boulders

As you will see, each pattern piece is a portion of a basic square. Each of the 36 squares required should be pieced; then the squares should be set together into six rows of six squares each to make a block. (The exception is the 4 squares surrounding the sun in the upper right corner.)

After the row in which the tree trunks belong is pieced, the tree trunks are appliquéd in place.

Finished size of the block without sashing is 13½" x 13½" (34.3cm x 34.3cm). Blocks should not be set next to one another without sashing.

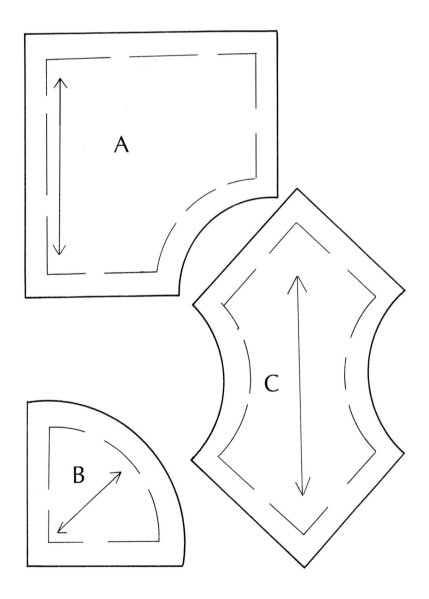

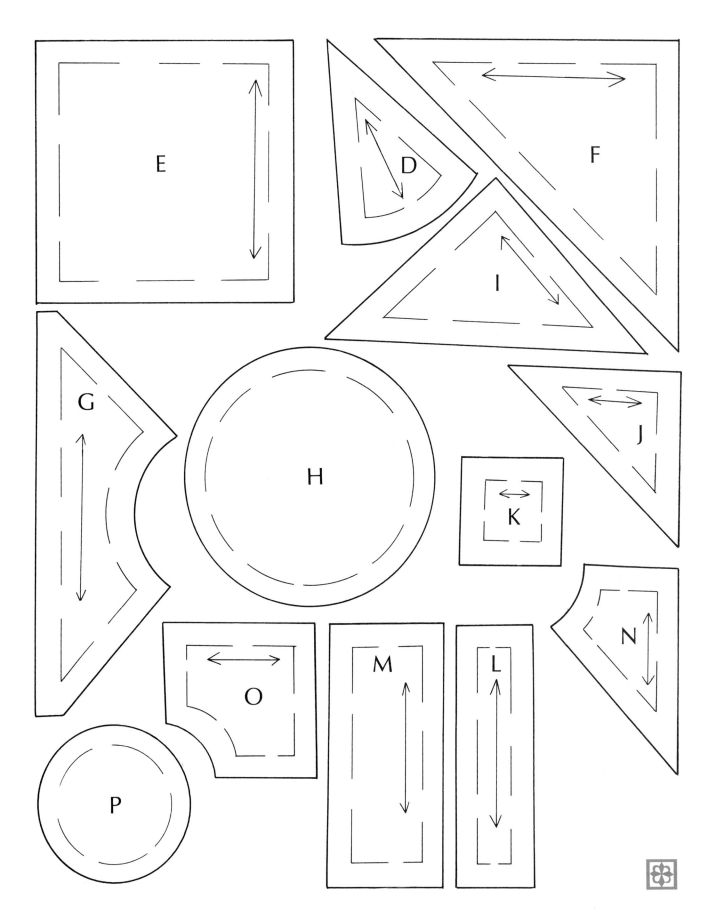

San José Rose

Mamie A. Callan
Cumby, Texas

"About 250 years ago the Spanish began building the San José Mission near San Antonio, Texas. A sculptor named Pedro Huizar was employed to carve a window in the south wall of the church. Pedro, who was hired by the missionaries, came to Texas from the Canary Islands and Mexico with other colonists. He fell in love with a girl named Rosa who sang in the choir of the church. Rosa became sick and died before they could get married.

"Pedro Huizar had only just begun to carve the window when Rosa died. Out of his grief, Pedro dedicated the window to his dead sweetheart. He carved it by hand and included in the carving of the limestone all of his love for her. The window is called the Rose Window for Rosa.

"Legend says that Pedro, soon after completing the window, died of a broken heart.

"This quilt pattern, the *San José Rose,* is designed in memory of the legend and the people in it.

"I designed the *San José Rose* quilt

pattern because I appreciate the Spanish element in our Southwestern heritage. Also I think the legend is one of deep human devotion and is likely true."

This easy-to-appliqué pattern can be seen on our swing cushions, page 57. Each piece in the design is padded as it is appliquéd to the design, so in addition to the fabric pieces listed below, you should cut fleece or batting for each shape. Each block takes the following:

　A—1 outer row of petals; requires a
　　　13″ (33cm) circle of fabric
　B—1 inner row of petals; requires
　　　an 8″ (20.3cm) circle of fabric
　Note: For both of the above pieces, fold circle of fabric down to one-eighth its original size; place pattern piece in position and trim outer edge only.
　C—1 center
　D—4 leaves
　Background square—18″ x 18″
　　　(45.7cm x 45.7cm)

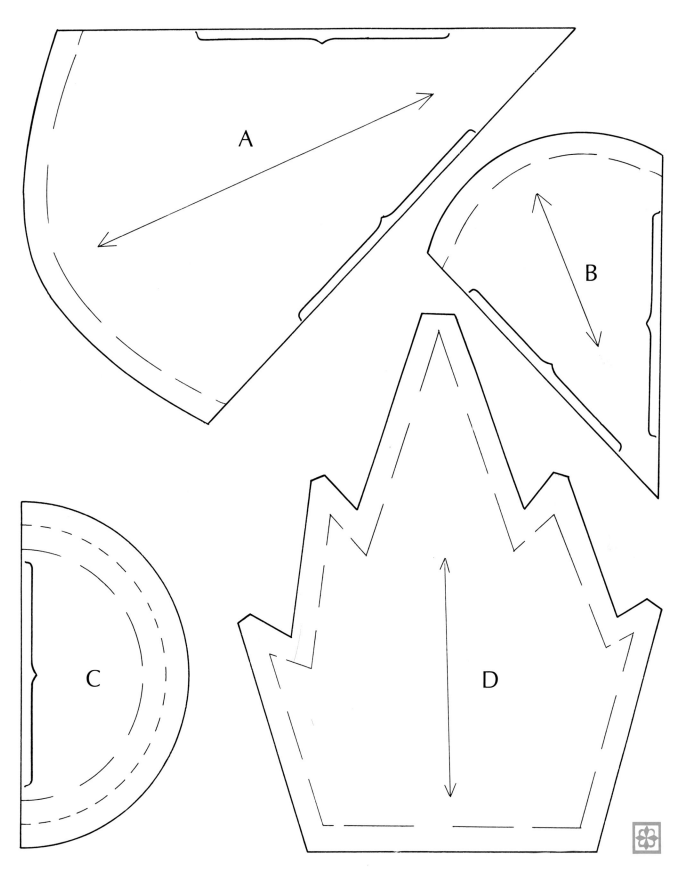

A

B

C

D

Southern Dogwood

Barbara Setzer
Huntersville, North Carolina

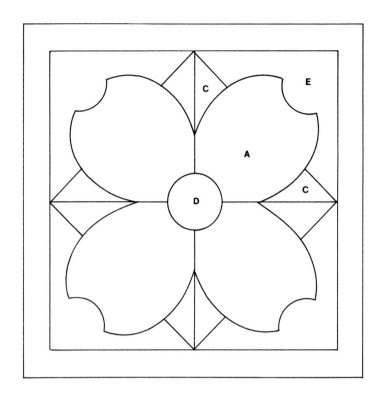

"For my original quilt square design, I selected the Southern dogwood. I was inspired to design it when I began to think of something to represent the rural South that was beautiful, well-known, and a part of the rural Southern heritage. Also, I love dogwood because it blooms for my birthday!

"The four petals remind us of four ways the dogwood represents our rural Southern heritage:

1) Historical heritage: it is North Carolina and Virginia's state flower.

2) Environmental heritage: it grows freely over much of the rural South.

3) Religious heritage: the legend of the dogwood reminds us of Christ's Resurrection, and the blooms coincide with Easter in many areas.

4) Cultural heritage: its beauty in spring and fall is one the joys of country living! It has been used in art, literature, needlework.

"The quilt can be made realistically with white, pink, or red flowers. It utilizes the three main types of quilting: the petals, leaves, and background are pieced; the center is

appliquéd; the petal edges are embroidered with a long blanket stitch. Each square is easily pieced by making four small squares of one petal each and assembling them into a full flower square.

"When flower squares are joined, leaves form a trellis pattern. By surrounding flower squares with solid ones, a beautiful quilt results with flowers in diagonal rows."

Each block takes the following:

A—4 petals

B—4 petal facings

C—8 half diamonds

D—1 center

E—4 background triangles

This design is a little tricky in that each of the four petals is faced on the end to stand up, away from the

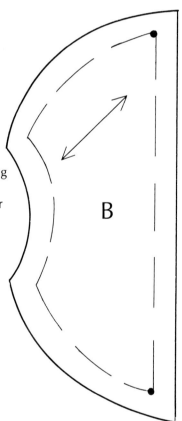

background. Make the dots on the petals and facing where the stitching begins and ends. Sew petal facing to petal, right side together, with a ¼" (6mm) seam. Clip seam, turn right side out, and press. Continue construction of block, sewing petal facing seam allowance only to E, background triangle.

Finished block without sashing measures 9" x 9" (22.9cm x 22.9cm).

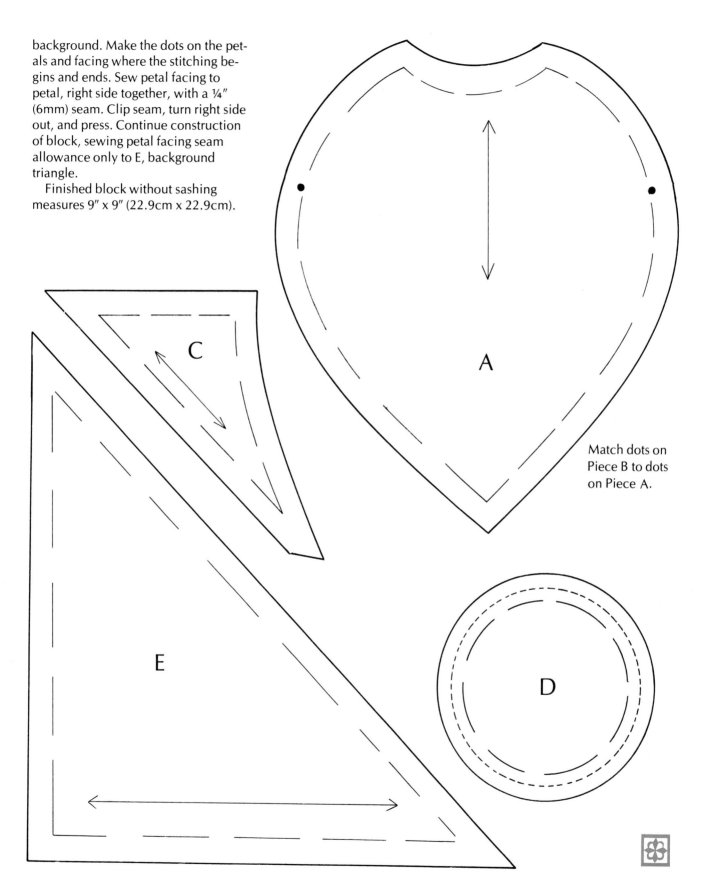

A

Match dots on Piece B to dots on Piece A.

C

E

D

Starflower

Janie Freeze
Jacksonville, Texas

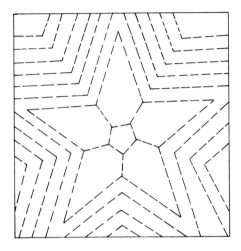

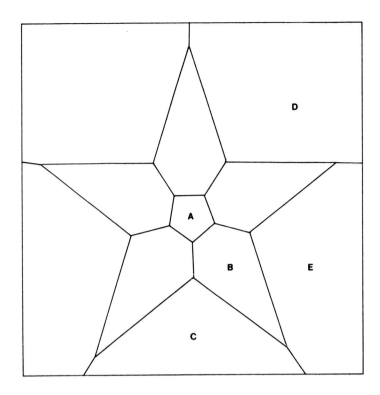

"A sky full of stars or a field of flowers is something to behold! I am awed by the sight of them.

"When I was about 12 years old, my grandma gave me a little star-shaped pincushion that was given to her as a child. It is now over a hundred years old. Being a native of the Lone Star State, I thought it seemed fitting to use a star pattern. Also, star phlox grow profusely along the roadside in this area, so I put a center in my star pattern to represent the flowers.

"The stars in this quilt can be all the same color or in a variety of colors and prints to represent a field of starflowers."

Starflower is so puffy and pretty it looks as though Mrs. Freeze used a trapunto technique with it. The finished block measures 11½" x 11½" (29.2cm x 29.2cm). This design would benefit from sashing if a large quilt is being made. Although the quilt block is pieced, the star could be pieced, then appliquéd onto a jacket, robe, or whatever.

One block takes the following:

A—1 center
B—5 star points
C—1 bottom center
D—2 top corners:
    one for right
    one for left
E—2 bottom corners:
    one for right
    one for left

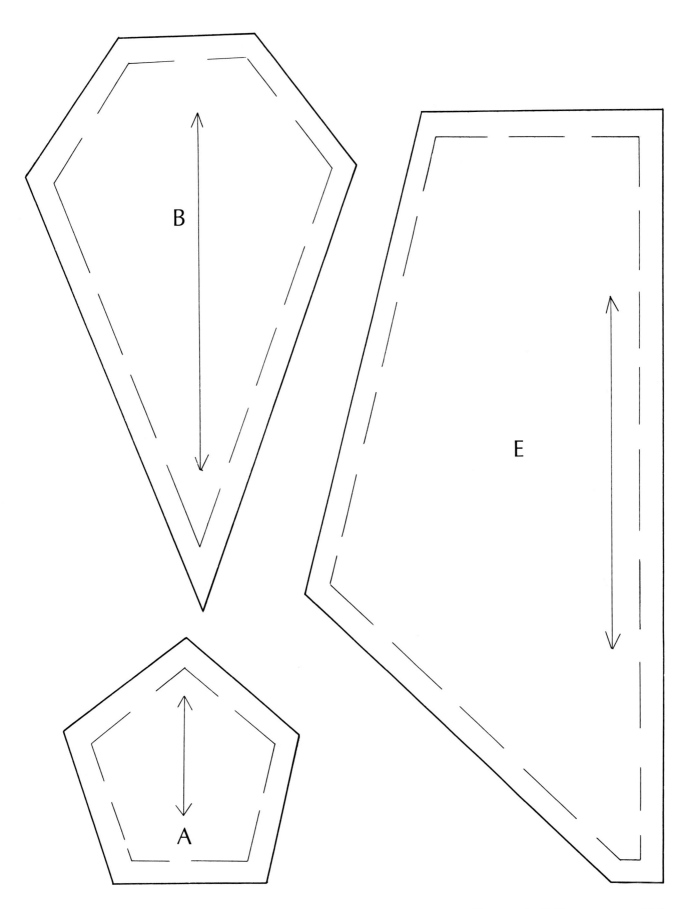

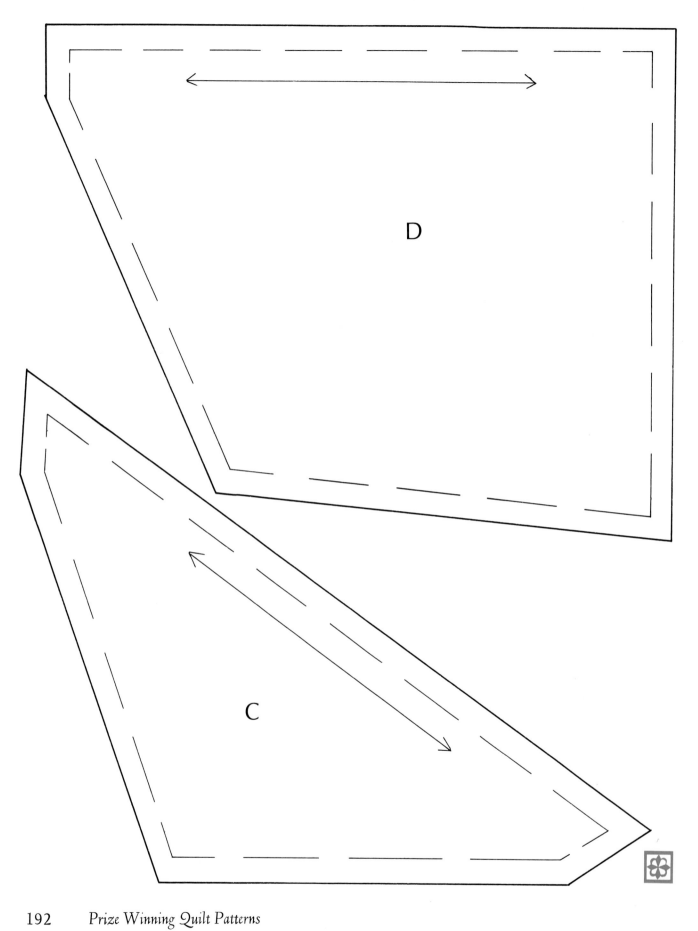

D

C

Summary Leaves

Effie R. Bell
Hampstead, North Carolina

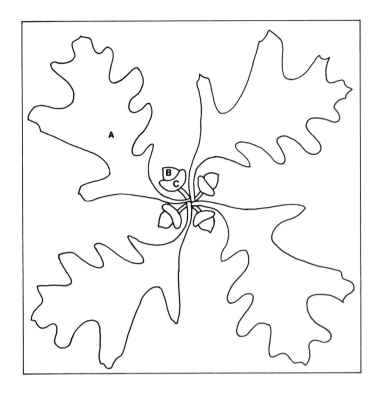

"My design is four oak leaves that join in the center with an acorn to each stem. The leaves are the actual size of the one I picked from the tree. I think that the trees never change; they are always there.

"I have made many quilts from patterns, but I like to make my own designs the best. My husband is 81; and I am 65. We have been married 44 years and lived most of the time in North Carolina. I have met some wonderful people whom I have quilted for, and I stay busy all the time. So here is my design. God gave the pattern. The stitches are mine."

Mrs. Bells's stitches are those of an extremely talented quilter. Her beautiful quilt block demonstrates a real talent for color and design as well as confidence in the techniques of appliqué and quilting. The four acorns are padded for added surface interest. This pattern is easy to make, as there are only three main pattern pieces.

One block takes the following:
A—4 leaves:
    2 of first color
    2 of second color
B—4 nuts of third color
C—4 caps of second color
Stems for acorns—four 1" x ¾"
    (2.5cm x 1.9cm) strips
Background square measures
20½" x 20½" (52.1cm x 52.1cm).

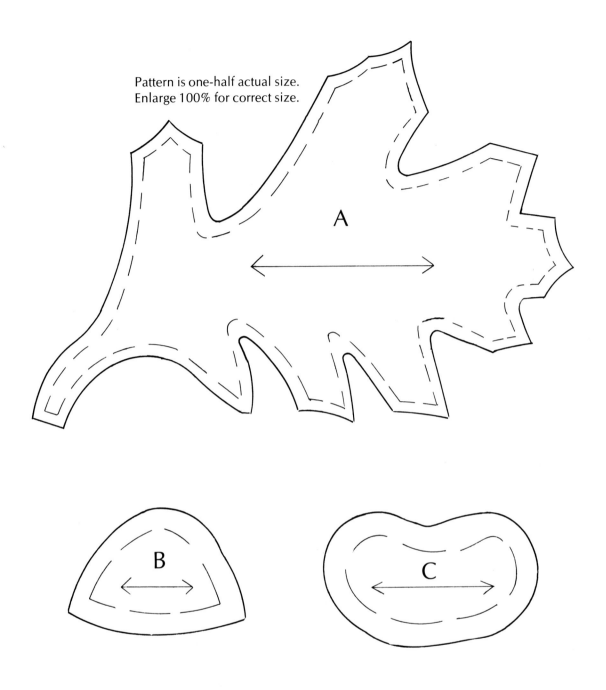

Pattern is one-half actual size.
Enlarge 100% for correct size.

A

B

C

Sunflower

Mrs. Hugh Eberhart
Fort Payne, Alabama

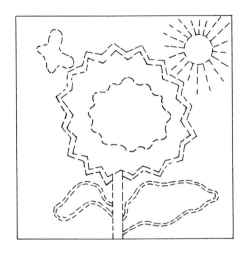

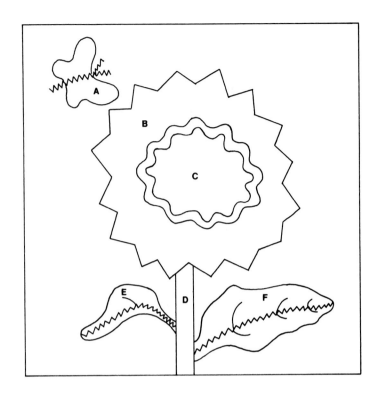

"I was inspired to design a quilt block of a sunflower after I received the issue of the *Progressive Farmer* with the huge sunflower on the cover. Sunflowers are somewhat like people—they lift their strong heads toward the heavens and seem to say 'thank you for the sunshine.' Then after a summer of proud stature, they begin to bow their heads toward the earth and say 'thank you for this good American soil that helps make me strong.' If we also would all lift our heads in reverence to God for our freedom and thank him for our country, we, like the sunflower, would be a light for all to see."

This appealing sunflower design incorporates rickrack for the body and antenna of the butterfly, for the veins of the leaves, and, in a larger size, for the perimeter of the center of the flower. Another charming detail is the sun quilted into the upper right corner. This 12" x 12" (30.5cm x 30.5cm) appliquéd block is easy and fun to do. We used this design for the bib of our apron, page 64.

Each block takes the following:
A—1 butterfly
B—1 sunflower
C—1 sunflower center
D—1 stem
E—1 small leaf
F—1 large leaf
Background square—12" x 12"
(30.5cm x 30.5cm)

Sashing is suggested if you plan to make a quilt. If you added 2" (5cm) wide sashing, it will take 5 squares across and 7 down to make a single bed quilt measuring approximately 70" x 98" (177.8cm x 248.9cm).

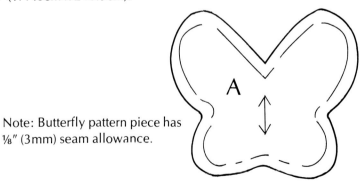

Note: Butterfly pattern piece has ⅛" (3mm) seam allowance.

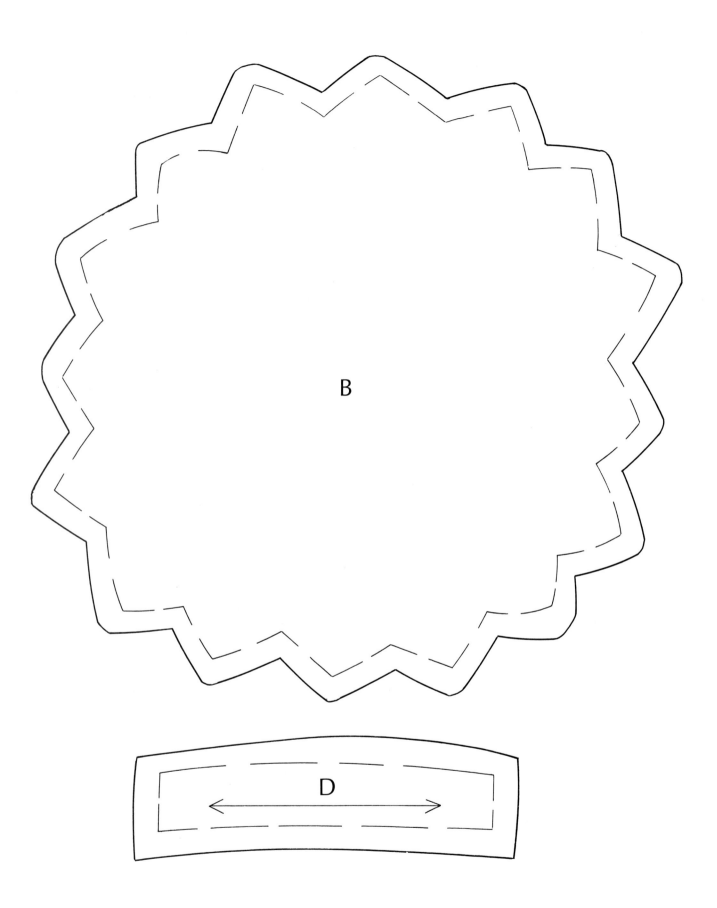

B

D

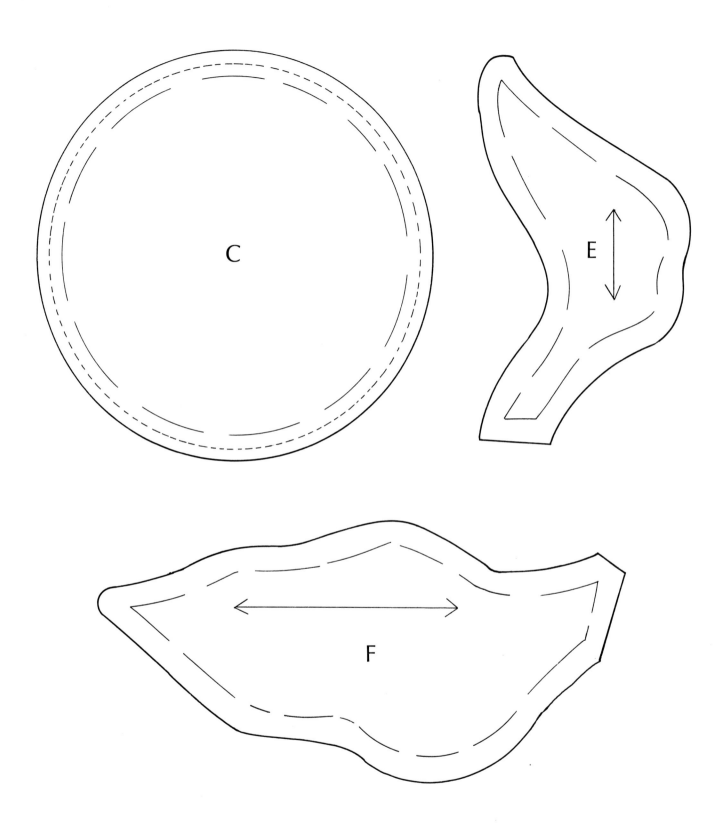

C

E

F

Sunshine and Stained Glass

Edith Hunter
Marrowbone, Kentucky

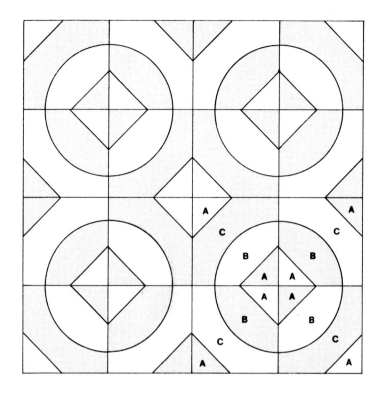

"I was inspired by the stained glass windows in the Marrowbone Presbyterian Church, which is a beautiful old church. It was built in 1878–1879. This church was moved to Marrowbone in 1898, taken to its present site in sections.

"The carpenter is unknown since the records do not give his name. He has long since passed from this world. He left a beautiful piece of architecture behind for generations to enjoy.

"At certain hours of the day, the sun strikes the stained windows at such an angle as to make sunbeams and shadows on the floor. The colors of the glass are rich and beautiful. I can imagine all kinds of patterns in the windows.

"Whoever set the windows in this church must have known that many eyes would gaze upon them and that someday people would wonder what he looked like and what was he thinking of as he went about building the church. He could never have dreamed that someone would design a quilt pattern from the windows."

Part of the merit of this fascinating patchwork design is that it is comprised of three shapes, set together into 4" (10.2cm) blocks, which are in turn set together to form circular patterns. The positioning of the print and the solid is opposite in adjoining blocks. You must count carefully the number of blocks you need for any project you plan so the overall design will be preserved.

One 8" x 8" (20.3cm x 20.3cm) block, incorporating 4 of the basic 4" (10.2cm) squares, takes the following:
> A—8 total:
> > 4 solid
> > 4 print
>
> B—4 total:
> > 2 solid
> > 2 print
>
> C—4 total:
> > 2 solid
> > 2 print

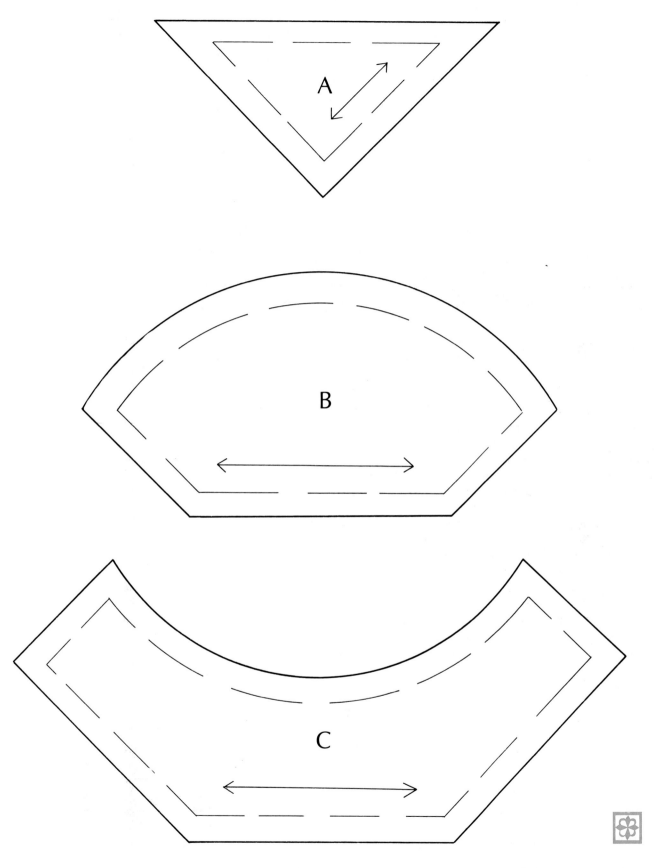

Texas Bicentennial Star

Mrs. W. H. Sultemeir
Lampasas, Texas

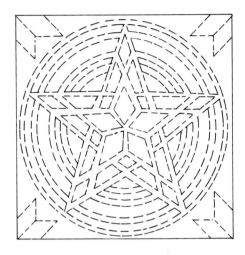

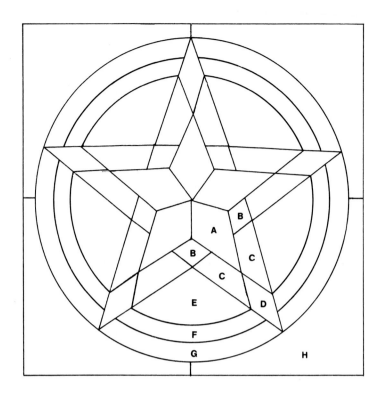

"Since this is our nation's 200th birthday, it seems that every design is for the Bicentennial. I'll admit I was no different from everyone else in my way of thinking.

"When I looked at the National Bicentennial Symbol, I thought that it sure would make a pretty quilt pattern. It wasn't long before I found out that there was already a pattern for that design.

"So I decided why couldn't Texas have a Bicentennial symbol, too? The official emblem for Texas is a five-point star, so by combining the two designs, I came up with this quilt pattern.

"Texas was the thirtieth state to join the United States, so there are thirty red stripes to designate its entry into the Union. The Texas flag is also red, white, and blue with only one five-point star. That is why I chose the colors I've used in my quilt block."

This strong graphic patchwork design is definitely a challenge to put together, but take heart—the outer striped edges of the star are made from a printed fabric—they are not pieced! Be extra careful when cutting the pieces; there are many curved and bias edges which must be cut accurately and handled as little as possible during construction. The finished block measures 17" x 17" (43.2cm x 43.2cm) and should not be sashed to take advantage of the eight-point stars which are quilted into the joined corners.

Each block takes the following:
A—5 long diamonds
B—5 short diamonds
C—10 trapezoids
D—5 diamonds
E—5 wedges
F—5 shorter curved strips
G—5 longer curved strips
H—4 corner pieces

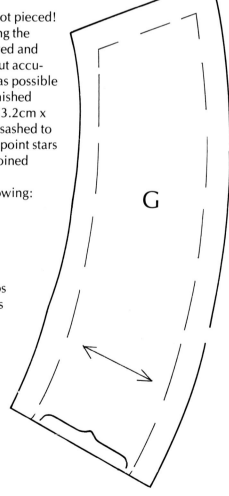

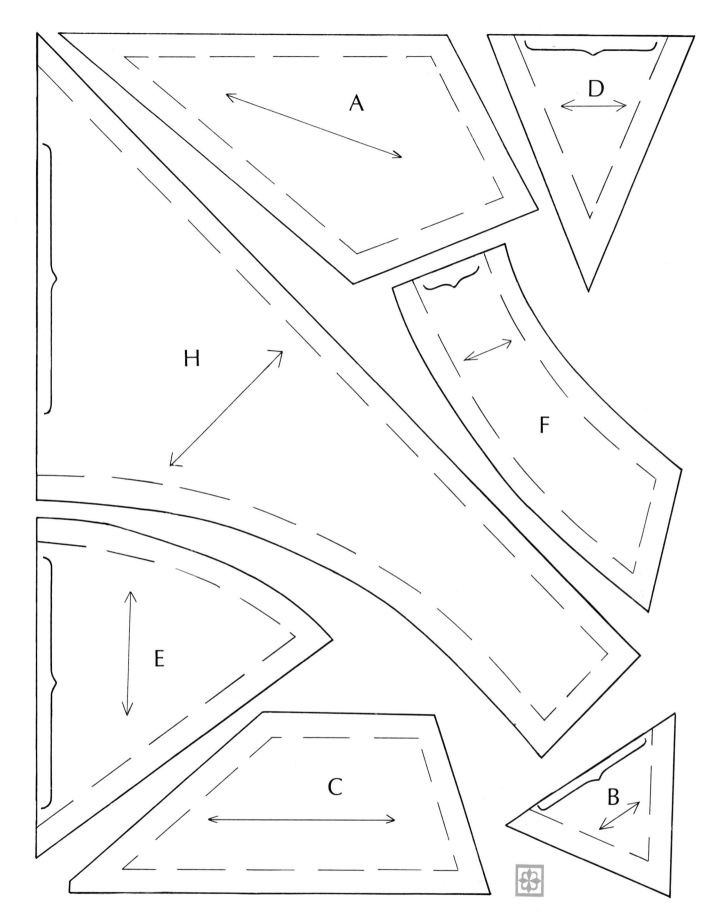

The Courthouse Square*

Mrs. Stella Davis
Silverton, Texas

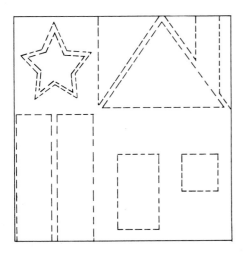

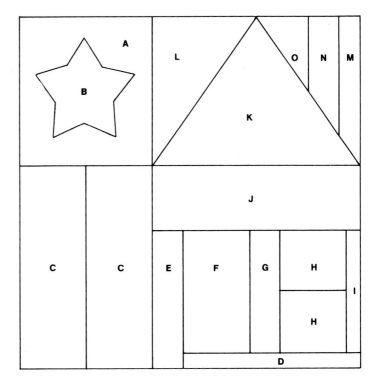

"The design for my quilt pattern consists of a courthouse and a replica of the Texas flag. The white star on a blue field and the red and white stripes are also symbolic of the American flag.

"This creation was inspired by the many historical writings concerning our nation's birth and growth that have recently been publicized. As our nation celebrates its Bicentennial, Briscoe County (where I live) celebrates its Centennial. This county was created by an act of the Texas Legislature in 1876, and was organized in 1892, 3 years before I was born.

"A contract was made to build the first courthouse at that time. Many of the activities of the people were centered around the courthouse—true not only in this county, but in other counties over the land.

"Disputes over location, changing of site, and type of building to be erected, and pride in the area are all a part of the history of the settling of our country.

———————————
*Second Place Winner

"The courthouse is a symbol of government, whether it be local, state, or national, where justice is dispensed and injustices are corrected. A banner, or flag, has long been a symbol of free men. Each courthouse, including the U. S. Supreme Court, proudly unfurls its flag to proclaim justice throughout the land.

"The Courthouse Square quilt pattern that I am submitting depicts justice as one important phase of the heritage of this great country."

Mrs. Davis' design took second place in the contest, because, as the judges said, "We agree this quilt block is a strong design graphically and that as a quilt block it would repeat well. Also, it has a versatility and use that would lend itself to an overall pattern."

The design is patchwork, except for the star, which is appliquéd in place. The block measures 13½" x 13½" (34.3cm x 34.3cm) and is easily sewed together.

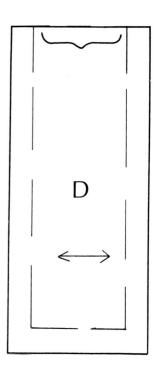

Each block takes the following:
A—1 flag field
B—1 star
C—2 stripes of different colors
D—1 bottom of door and window
E—1 left door facing
F—1 door
G—1 right door facing
H—1 window, 1 underwindow
I—1 right side of house
J—1 top of house
K—1 roof
L—1 left side of roof
M—1 right side of chimney
N—1 chimney
O—1 left side of chimney

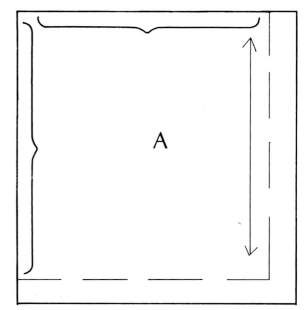

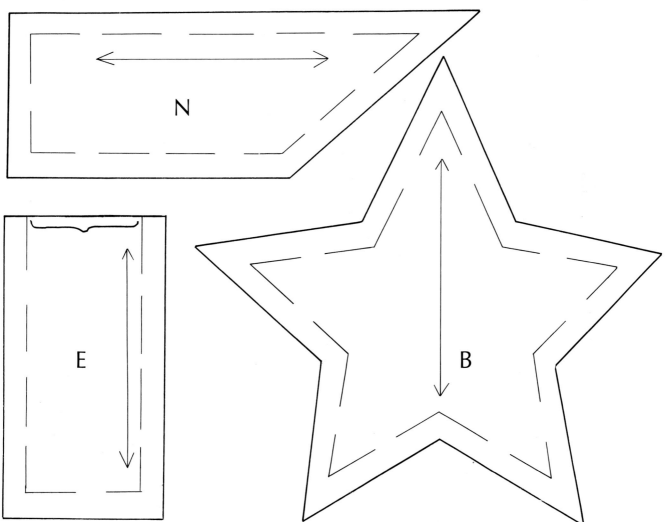

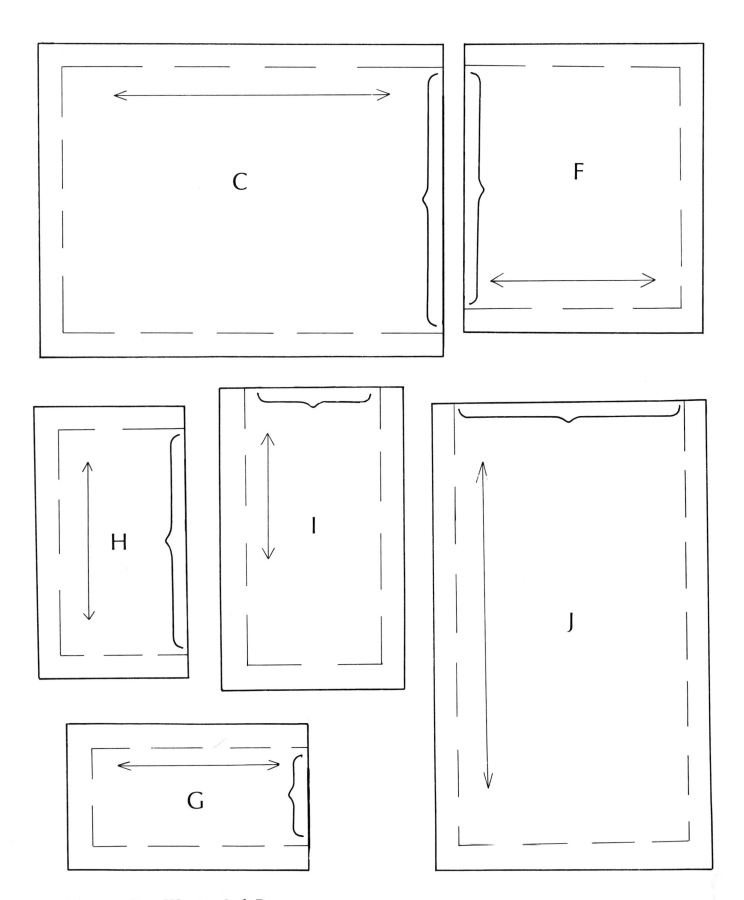

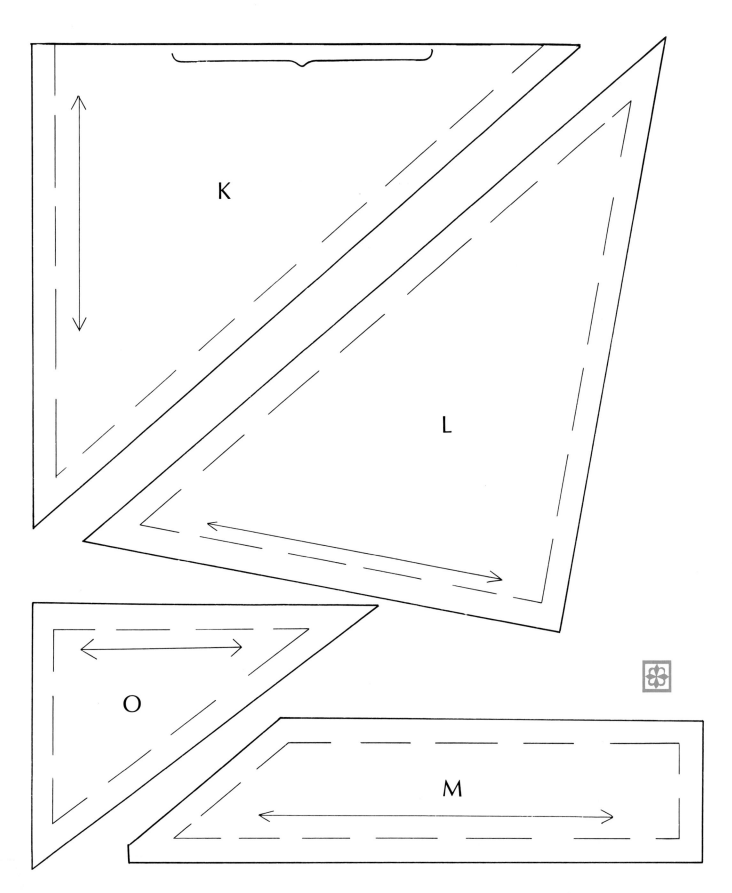

K

L

O

M

The Hay Wagon

Mary Jo Jackson
Estill Springs, Tennessee

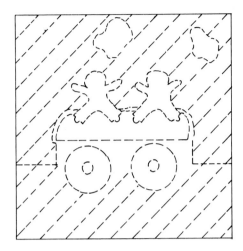

"Growing up on a farm in Moore County, Tennessee, was a delightful experience. I have seen five generations enjoying the many things that are to be found in country living. My mother and dad, my two sisters, myself, and my grandfather, who lived with us, all had a part in making a good life on the farm.

"We children had many ways to amuse ourselves. We had creeks to wade, hills to climb, and hay hauling by a horse-drawn wagon, which was more fun for us than work. We stood on the wagon and packed the loose hay as Daddy tossed it up. We hauled hay in the warm sun and sometimes by the moonlight if we expected rain before the next day. I have seen my own children having fun the way I did as a child, and now my grandchildren are enjoying many of the same things. We still haul hay, but now it is baled hay hauled in by trucks, and the work not nearly as much fun as I remember it being when I was young.

"In the summertime we sometimes pull a flat wagon under the shade trees in the yard and use the wagon as a table for a picnic lunch. The family all gathers together, and we enjoy the day and enjoy remembering the happy days of the past. Farm life is wonderful, and I am glad to be a part of it."

Mrs. Jackson's quilt block measures 15½" (39.4cm) square when finished. It combines three techniques— piecing, appliqué, and embroidery.

Special hint: The jagged edges of the hay, the wheels, and the hair on the children's heads may be glued in place with school glue before the blanket stitch is worked around the edges. This will keep the edges from shifting or raveling. After the quilt block is finished, this glue may be quite easily washed out of the fabric. Wash before quilting.

One block takes the following:
Grass—1 printed piece
Sky—1 blue piece
Wagon—1 green piece
Hay—1 brown and white check

Wheel spokes—2 tan pieces, embroider center of
spokes with a circle
of chain stitches
Wheel rim—2 tan pieces
Child—2 white or tan pieces
Hair—2 pieces (in different colors as
you desire)
Playsuits—2 pieces (as you
desire—Mrs. Jackson
used denim)
Clouds—2 white pieces
Sun—1 yellow piece
Note: Some pieces have the standard
¼″ (6mm) seam allowance and some
pieces do not.

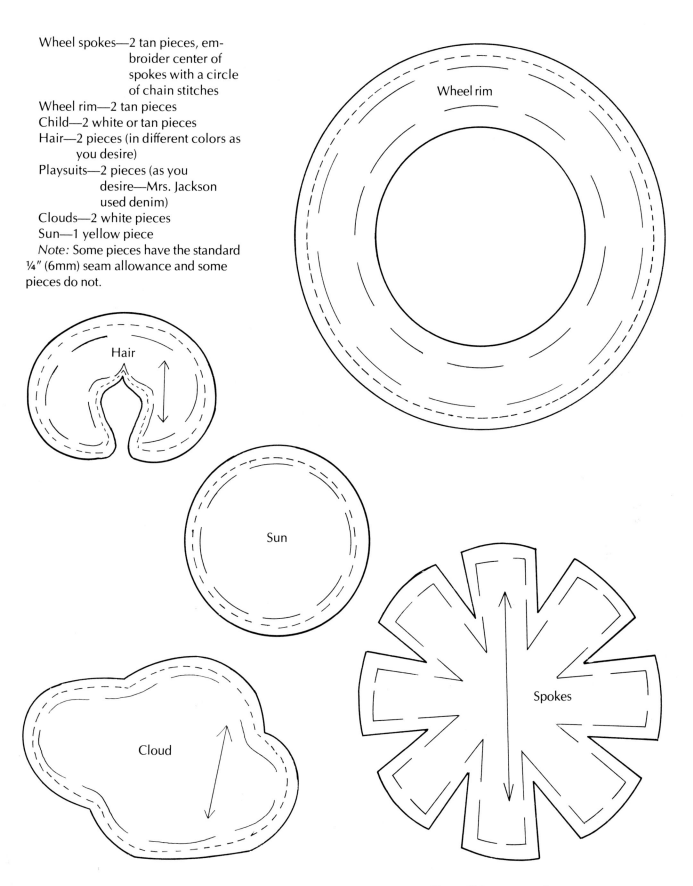

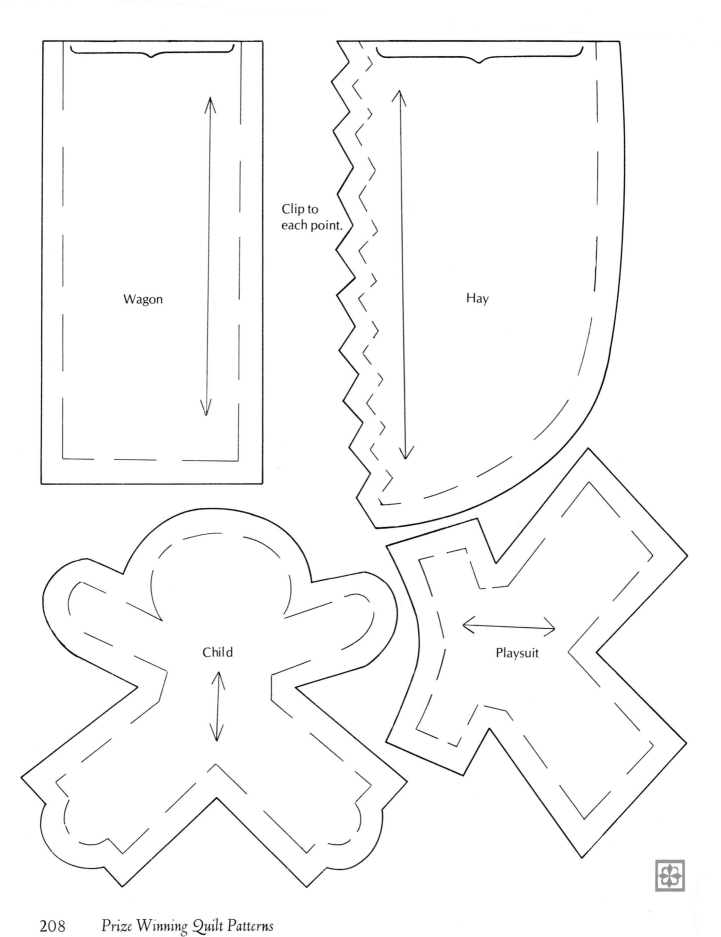

Wagon

Clip to each point.

Hay

Child

Playsuit

The Sunrise

Lena Gray Johnson
Cromwell, Kentucky

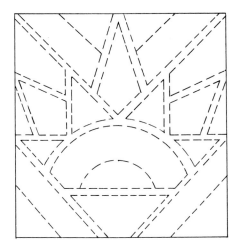

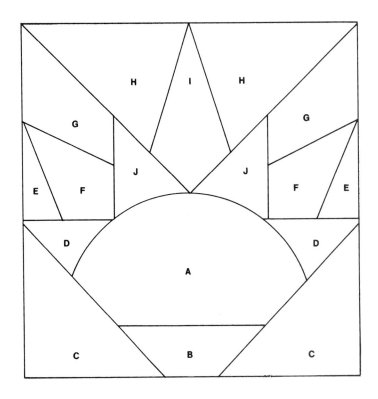

"The first thought I had when I read about the contest was that I would try to piece a quilt block about the sunrise. I loved the sunrise when I was a child growing up on a farm and had to get up early to do chores and walk to school. Now I am sixty years old and still love the sunrise and would enjoy a home with the sunrise shining through the kitchen window.

"I haven't pieced *The Sunrise* for a quilt, as I just got the pattern made; I plan to this spring. For variety, the sun rays could be made of different pastel colors instead of all yellow. The blocks can be stripped together with white or light blue or sewed together with other solid color blocks of the same size, or set directly next to one another to make a top large enough for a quilt."

This little 9½" (24.1cm) square block takes well to vivid colors. It surely sparks up the velour robe on page 64 where we used bath cloths to cut the pieces for this pattern. The easing of the pieces to fit requires some care and skill, and you want to be cer-

tain to get perfect points on your sun rays.

Each block takes the following:

A—1 sun
B—1 ground
C—2 grounds
D—2 rays
E—2 skies
F—2 rays
G—2 skies
H—2 skies
I—1 ray
J—2 rays

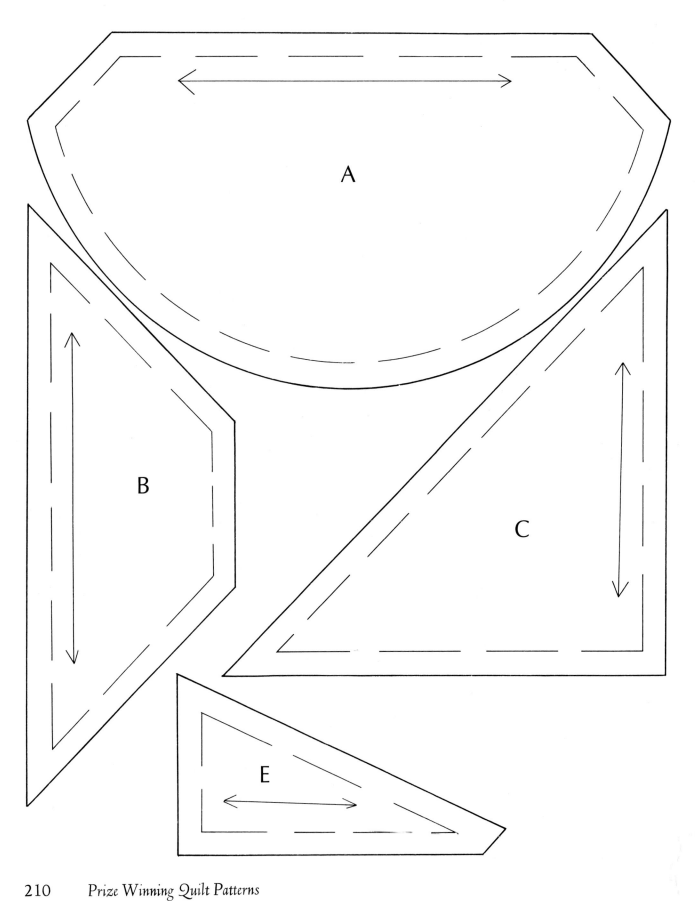

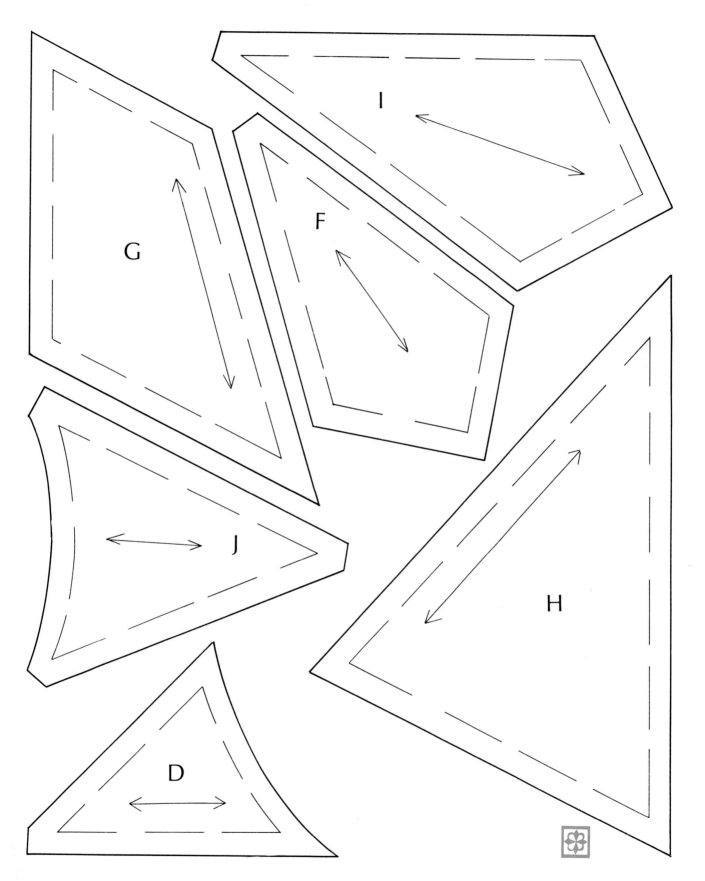

I

F

G

J

H

D

Tulip Bowl

Carrie Lou Huffaker
Strawberry Plains, Tennessee

"The reason for choosing this design is that it combines both tradition and modern styling to produce a very unusual quilt. My design has a traditional flavor taken from the tulip bloom but has an up-to-date look because the bloom has been stylized. Much of the interest in the design is shaped by the quilting itself.

"In East Tennessee, quilting has been a way of life for generations, and in days gone by, most designs used small bits of fabric left over from sewing necessities. I have been collecting quilt patterns and sewing quilts for 50 years—since I was 8 years old—and have about 1000 old patterns."

This gracious and lovely floral pattern is beautifully appliquéd and very closely quilted. It is not for a beginner because of the multiplicity of pieces and number of curved edges.

Each block takes the following:
A—1 bowl
B—1 bowl design
C—2 bowl designs
D—1 bowl base
E—8 circles:
    5 to match stem of flowers
    3 to match middle flower
F—6 ovals:
    4 to match bowl
    2 to match side flowers
G—2 stems for side flower
H—2 bases for side flowers
I—2 second layers for side flower
J—3 centers:
    2 for side flowers
    1 for middle flower
K—1 stem for middle flower
L—1 base for middle flower
Background square—21½" x 21½"
    (54.6cm x 54.6cm)

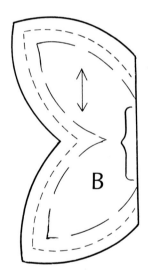

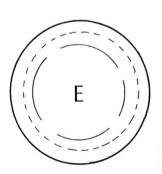

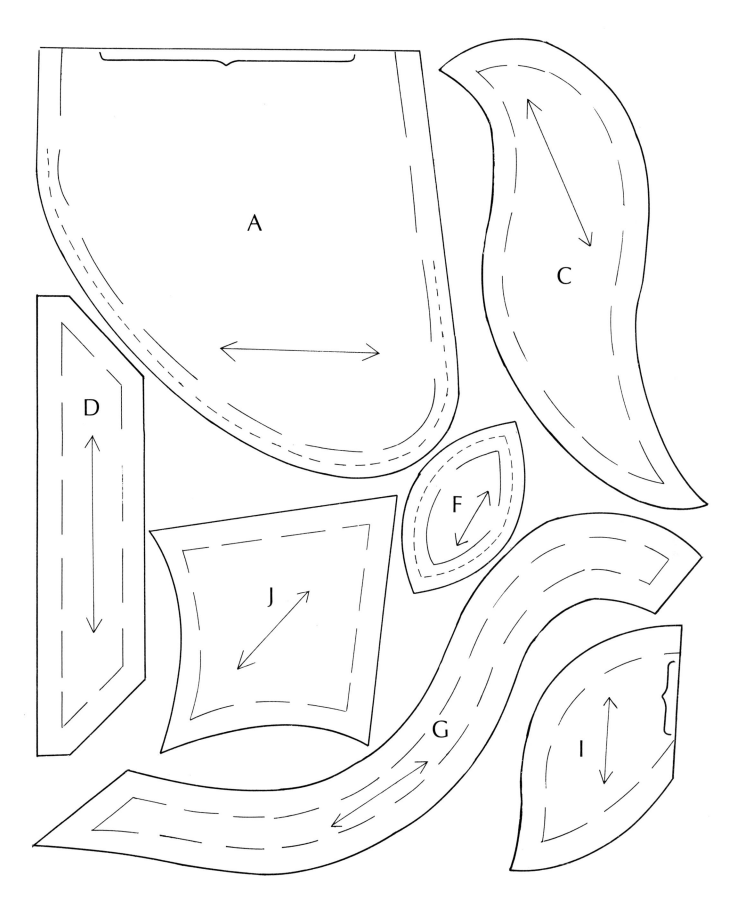

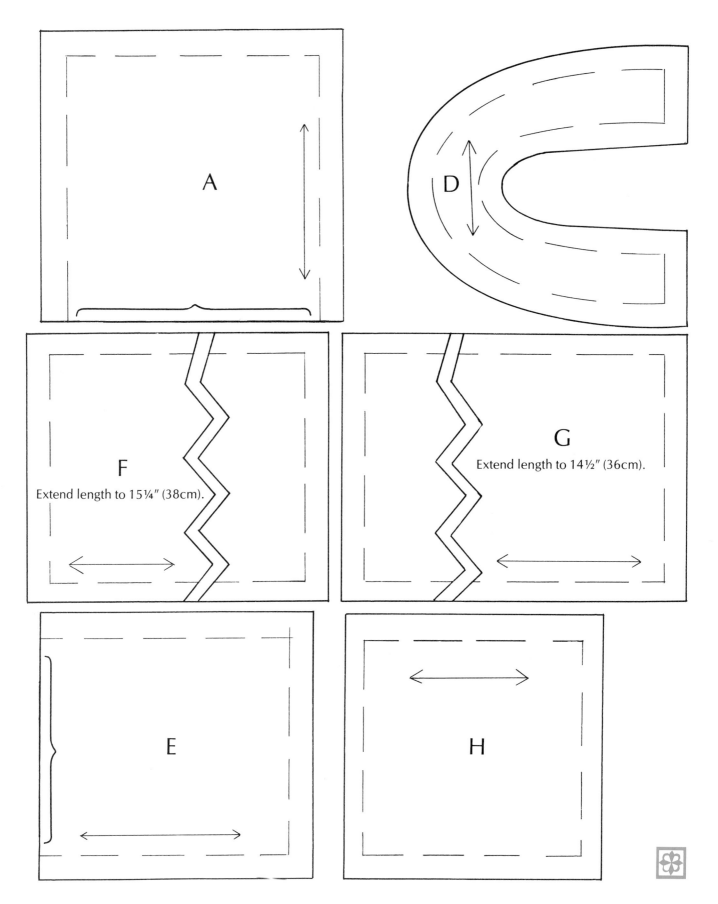

A

D

F
Extend length to 15¼″ (38cm).

G
Extend length to 14½″ (36cm).

E

H

Wheels

Katie Lee Edmunds
Thomson, Georgia

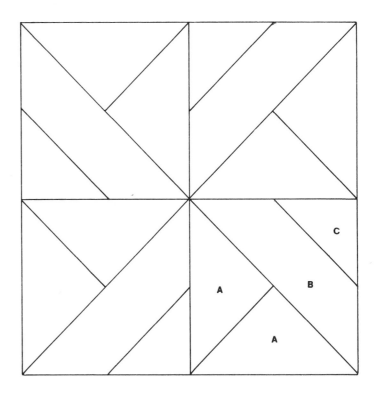

"I was reared on a farm in east central Georgia, and I realize the importance of wheels on a farm, especially in recent years of mechanized progressive farming. Wheels have always fascinated me. I was thinking along this line as I attempted to make my pattern. I accurately folded the paper and began shading portions for a wheel. Then I drew a picture of four blocks together and discovered that the light portions on the edges of the blocks form a light colored wheel which turns in the opposite direction. For this reason, the light portion for the entire quilt should be the same color."

Wheels is an easy patchwork pattern and when enlarged makes a bold and powerful statement. It is the pattern used for one of our floor pillows on page 12. The finished block using these pattern pieces measures 14" x 14" (35.6cm x 35.6cm).

Each block takes the following:
A—8 large triangles:
    4 solid
    4 print
B—4 long trapezoids, solid fabric
C—4 small triangles, print fabric

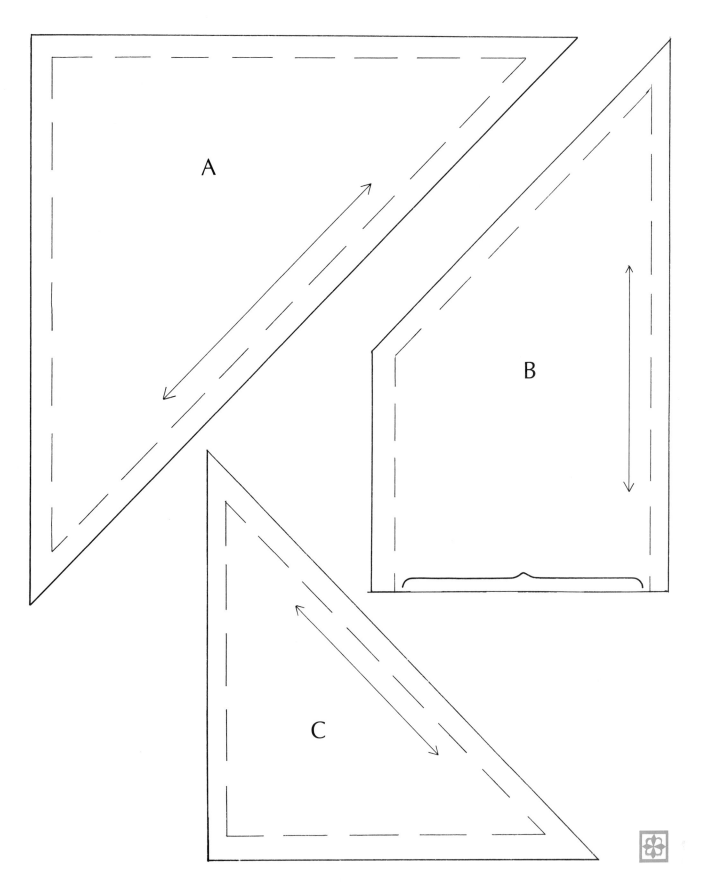

A

B

C

Wild Flower

Willie Cocanougher
Danville, Kentucky

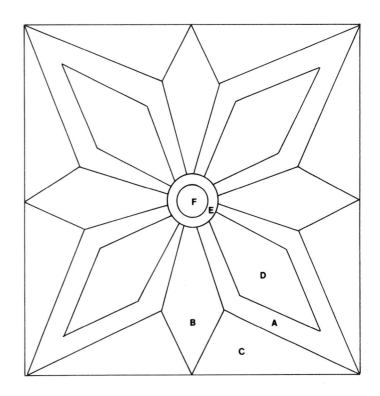

"Quilt making has been one of my favorite hobbies since I was a small girl. My mother lived to be ninety years old, and she pieced quilts until a few years before her death. My grandmothers also liked quilt making. This is my first try at making my own pattern. I chose this because I have always liked flowers. I grew up on a farm in the hills of Kentucky. Wild flowers grew in abundance in the pasture fields and along the fences.

"There is no living like country living, especially in summer when all the trees and flowers put forth their beauty. On our farm was a beautiful tulip poplar tree, as well as another kind of poplar which had lovely pink and white balls in the spring. Pink flowers are my favorite."

This really pretty pattern takes on two different looks, depending on where the lights and darks (or prints and solids) are placed. This is aptly illustrated on page 12 in the two square pillows on the loveseat, both of which are made from *Wild Flower*. You might want to follow this idea to make a quilt from this pattern, or you might want to alternate blocks of *Wild Flower* with plain blocks. Either choice would benefit from sashing.

One 10½" x 10½" (26.7cm x 26.7cm) block takes the following:
A—4 large petals of first fabric
B—4 small petals of second fabric
C—8 corner insets of background fabric
D—4 top petals of second fabric
E—1 bottom center of second fabric
F—1 top center of first fabric

Pieces A, B, and C, are sewed together for a patchwork background, and pieces D, E, and F are appliquéd in place over patchwork.

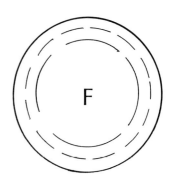

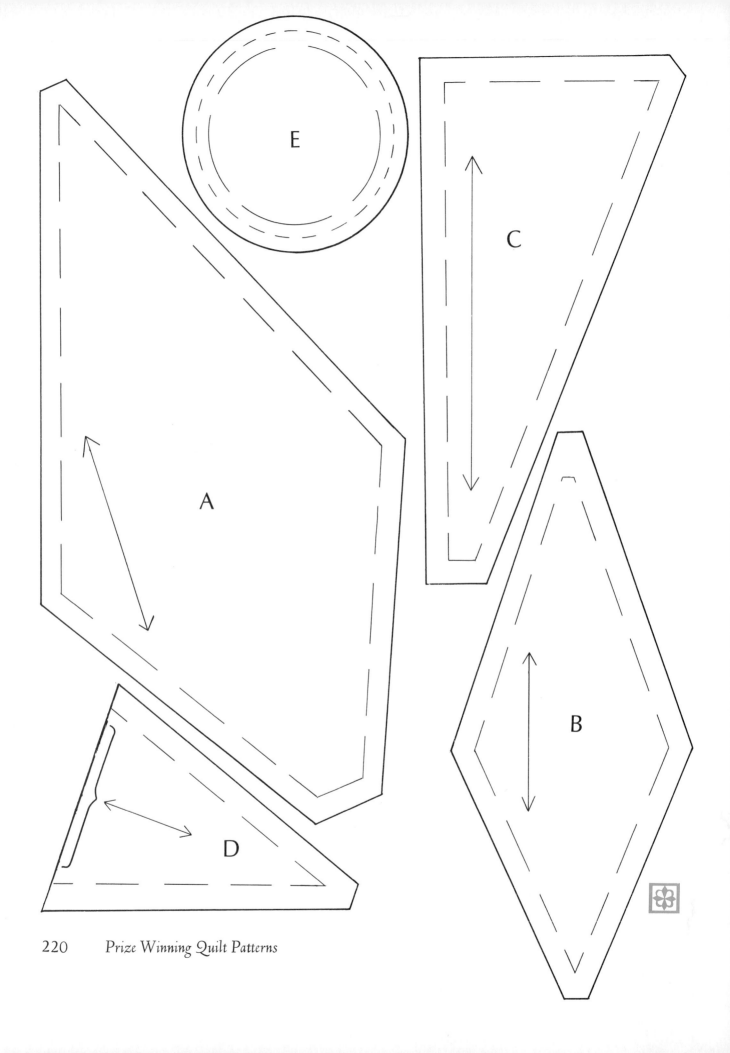

Windmill

Claire Vestal
College Station, Texas

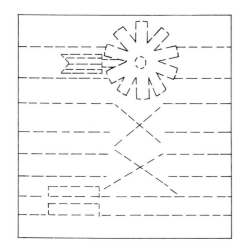

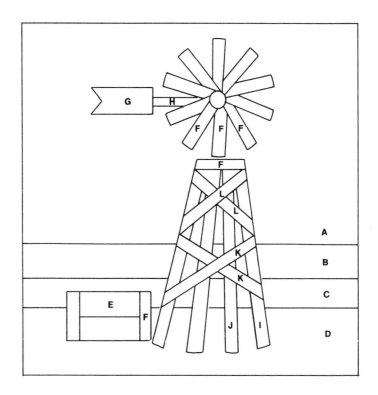

"I thought, wandered, and looked to discover the design to best depict my rich Southern and Southwestern rural heritage. Always the same idea returned—the *Windmill*. It is the most identifying mark of all the countryside. This includes the nostalgic past, the fast and furious present, and the uncertain future.

"To man and beast it gives comfort, security, and suggests dependability. Though weathered with age or youthful with the shine and glitter of new metal, the windmill strives to give its best performance. Whatever the weather, the time, or the place, the show must go on. It will work diligently or rest patiently, whichever its keepers desire.

"Its familiar silhouette is forever a sentinel on the horizon. The windmill sings out with lonely discord and the sweetest of harmonies to the unwritten music of the wind."

Mrs. Vestal used bias tape to make the appliquéd windmill and water tank. She cut the colorful strips for the background from larger fabric pieces and pieced them together. This design

is easily worked, especially if you use packaged bias tape, and it makes a 13¼" x 12½" (33.7cm x 31.8cm) finished quilt block. We have included pattern pieces in case you want to use fabric scraps.

One block takes the following:
A—1 yellow
B—1 orange
C—1 red
D—1 purple
E—1 tank (light blue)
F—13 total:
   2 tank sides (medium blue)
   10 blades for vane (medium blue)
   1 top brace (navy)
G—1 rudder (light blue)
H—1 rudder rod (navy)
I—2 outer braces (brown)
J—2 inner braces (brown)
K—2 lower cross braces (brown)
L—2 upper cross braces (brown)

Use pattern pieces to obtain correct lengths if using bias tape. Use single fold bias tape for everything except water tank, which uses two strips of wide bias tape.

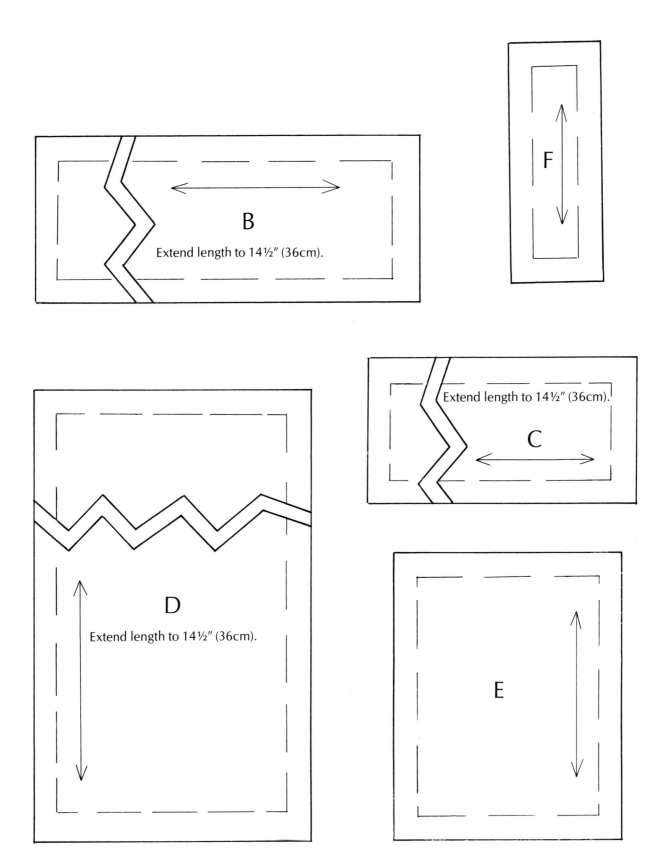

B

Extend length to 14½″ (36cm).

F

C

Extend length to 14½″ (36cm).

D

Extend length to 14½″ (36cm).

E

A

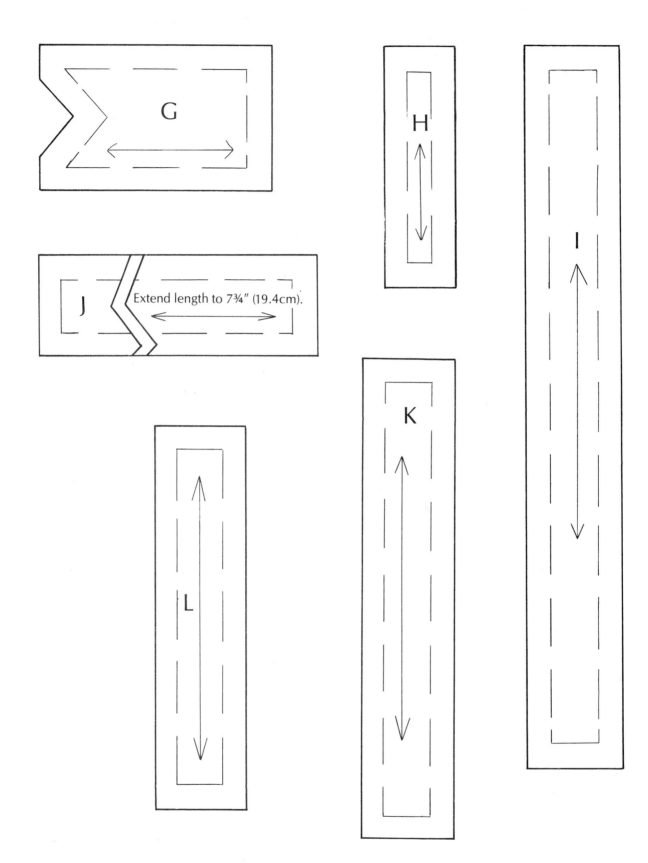

Extend length to 7¾″ (19.4cm).

Winners in the
Progressive Farmer Quilt Block Contest

The publishers acknowledge the award winners who helped make this book possible.

First Place

Mrs. Ben F. Harris
Woodland, Alabama
Rural Background

Second Place

Mrs. Stella Davis
Silverton, Texas
The Courthouse Square

Third Place

Mrs. Leon L. Lenderman
Raleigh, North Carolina
East Tennessee Farm

Honorable Mentions:

Minnie J. Abbott
Commerce, Texas
The Windmill

Myrtle Aldridge
Glen Allen, Alabama
Wild Rose

Elizabeth Alexander
Burnet, Texas
Blazing Star

Laura L. Allen
Jay, Oklahoma
Elkhorn

Myrtis Wood Allen
Fulton, Mississippi
Inspiration

Annie Lee Allison
Scottsboro, Alabama
Blocks and Stars

Mrs. Haven Amos
Cromwell, Kentucky
Bed of Peonies

Mrs. Wooster Atkinson
Bishopville, South Carolina
The Good Life

Mrs. Ruth Backus
Dimmitt, Texas
Windmill

Bessie Tucker Bagwell
Bankston, Alabama
Pioneer Apple

Mata J. G. Banks
New Tazewell, Tennessee
South's Pride Daisy

Della L. Beach
Greeneville, Tennessee
Heritage '76

Effie R. Bell
Hampstead, North Carolina
Summer Leaves

Mildred Lowry Berryman
Town Creek, Alabama
Community Circle

Bertha Bingham
Tyner, Kentucky
Trillium

Barbara Bogard
Clarksville, Tennessee
Holly Haven

Miss Carolyn Bogard
Clarksville, Tennessee
Memory Box

Mariena Bordelon
Bordelonville, Louisiana
Grandma's Fan

Ethel J. Bowman
Looneyville, West Virginia
Jack-in-the-Pulpit

Miss Sergie Bowman
Butler, Tennessee
No Name

Fannie Boyd
Town Creek, Alabama
Liberty Pride

Ruby Amanda Braddy
Council, North Carolina
Coming Back

Mrs. Charles Brady
Temple, Texas
Wagons Westward

Violet Brake
Mulberry, Arkansas
America's Heritage

Elizabeth Brawner
Lafayette, Tennessee
Maple Leaf

Mauvine Brown
Pikeville, Tennessee
American Family Star

Lois Bruner
Coeburn, Virginia
Old Country Church

Dorothy Burnette
Amelia, Virginia
Amelia's Gem-Stone

Lydia Burns
Walnut Grove, Mississippi
Street Lights

Mamie A. Callan
Cumby, Texas
San José Rose

Olive Campbell
Vienna, Virginia
The Falls Church

Kittie Carter
Marion, Kentucky
Cherry Quilt

Alice Clay
Enfield, North Carolina
Checker Board

Willie Cocanougher
Danville, Kentucky
Wild Flower

Bessie Corpier
Gainesville, Texas
Landmark in Autumn

Mrs. T. C. Couch
Jersey, Arkansas
Morning Glory

Mrs. D. S. Creasy
Disputanta, Virginia
Merchants Hope Church

Claudia B. Croy
Sarasota, Florida
Dairy Receptacles

Velma Culbert
Beggs, Oklahoma
USA

Mrs. Kenneth Davies
Slaton, Texas
Today

Mrs. C. E. Dodson
Odessa, Texas
Points of Beauty

Eula Dodson
Bryan, Texas
Mississippi Paddlewheel

Gladys S. Dodson
Halifax, Virginia
The Wheel or Wagon Wheel

Mrs. Doug Dorhauer
Denham Springs, Louisiana
The Tractor Pull

Mrs. A. S. Dorminy
Pavo, Georgia
Sweet Gum Leaf

Mrs. Shirley Doyle
Macomb, Missouri
Be it Ever so Humble

Mrs. Frances Driggs
Cushing, Oklahoma
Sooner Wagon

Anna May Duke
Black Springs, Arkansas
Mountain Homestead

Margaret Eason
Williamston, North Carolina
Aunt Fanny's Flower Basket

Mrs. Hugh Eberhart
Ft. Payne, Alabama
Sunflower

Katie Lee Edmunds
Thomson, Georgia
Wheels

Lula Emfinger
Vidor, Texas
Tulip

Laura N. Estes
Franklin, North Carolina
Mountain Morning Glory

Hazel Ferrell
Middlebourne, West Virginia
Snow Ball

Mrs. Clarice Fields
Bonnieville, Kentucky
Field's Lost Acre

Mrs. R. H. Fields
Ashville, Alabama
Flower Bed

Mrs. Zola Fish
Sonora, Texas
The Windmill

Imogene Foshee
West Memphis, Arkansas
Cotton Bale

Mary Franklin
Temple, Texas
Texas Heritage

Janie Freeze
Jacksonville, Texas
Starflower

Shirley Fulton
Mayslick, Kentucky
United We Stand

Hazel Geveden
Arlington, Kentucky
Mail Box

Mrs. M. L. Gibbs
Cheriton, Virginia
Country Echoes

Helen Gibson
Masontown, West Virginia
Bicentennial Star '76

Bess Gover
Nancy, Kentucky
Farm Sho

Mrs. Donnell Gowey
Seattle, Washington
*Cotton Patch Treasures

Mrs. Louis Graben
Oxford, Alabama
Flowers from Mother

Alta Green
Brownwood, Texas
*Homestead

Edith Hanna
Chico, Texas
Chico Centennial Flag Design

Gayla Harber
Nacogdoches, Texas
Dog-trot House

Stella Hardin
Pontotoc, Mississippi
The Country Church

Irene Harper
Evergreen, Alabama
Evergreens

Mrs. Gus Harrell
Cairo, Georgia
Grady Country

Laura Harris
Grantsboro, North Carolina
Tiny Stars and Squares

Lorene Harrold
North Wilkesboro, North Carolina
Wild Flower of Stone Mountain

Mrs. W. O. Havens
Perkinston, Mississippi
The Spirit of '76

Ruth Hawkins
Warne, North Carolina
Wheel of Progress

Glenna Hayes
Roanoke, Virginia
Abundance

Mamie Heasley
Little Rock, Arkansas
Calico Bokay

Virginia Heath
Cartersville, Virginia
Rose Garden

Mabel Henkins
Pentress, West Virginia
West Virginia Scrappalachia

Mary Hensley
Gravette, Arkansas
*Jay, Oklahoma, Huckleberry
Capital of the World*

Virginia Herndon
Witter, Arkansas
National Anthem

Doris Hill
Chocowinity, North Carolina
Sun Flower

Mrs. P. M. Holland
Kenly, North Carolina
Sunflower

Jane Howard
Pineville, Kentucky
No Name

Carrie Lou Huffaker
Strawberry Plains, Tennessee
Tulip Bowl

Helen Hughey
Heber Springs, Arkansas
Arrows Goal

Georgia Humphrey
Cynthiana, Kentucky
Little Red School House

Edith Hunter
Marrow Bone, Kentucky
Sunshine and Stained Glass

Evelyn Infinger
Lexington, North Carolina
The Dairy Barn

Mrs. Elbert Jackson
Oliver Springs, Tennessee
Golden Wheat

Lola Jackson
Gassaway, West Virginia
Bay Rose

Marie Jackson
Talcott, West Virginia
Heritage Bells

Mary Jo Jackson
Estill Springs, Tennessee
The Hay Wagon

Lena Gray Johnson
Cromwell, Kentucky
The Sunrise

Mrs. Aron Jones
Dumas, Mississippi
King Cotton

Marceil Jones
Quitman, Arkansas
Magnolia Blossom

Mrs. F. F. Keating
Reform, Alabama
Bicentennial Fan

Mrs. Cleo Kelley
Bardwell, Kentucky
Bicentennial Wheel

Mrs. A. V. Kennedy
Shelby, North Carolina
Space Age

Blanche Ketron
Kingsport, Tennessee
Victory Bicentennial Quilt Square

Erma Keyes
Crossville, Tennessee
Little Country Church

Mrs. Ray Kimbrell
Warren, Arkansas
Mrs. Feathersome

Helen Knott
Stillwater, Oklahoma
Little House on the Prairie

Dortha Lauderdale
Maysville, Oklahoma
Stars and Stripes

Lellie Lee
Cumberland Furnace, Tennessee
Dogwood and Butterfly

Nova Lee
Brownwood, Texas
The Old Wind Mill

Esther Leiber
Anderson, Texas
Freedom Train Wheel

Alta Leonhardt
Vale, North Carolina
Uncle Sam's Crutch

Ruth Davis Lesseig
Grove, Oklahoma
Green Country Oklahoma

Karen Owens Lilley
New Waverly, Texas
Hill's Heritage House

Annie Linder
Eastview, Kentucky
Mystery Block

Lydia Livingston
Hamilton, Texas
The Wild Sunflower

Anna Lupkiewicz
Gainesville, Florida
Proud Pine

Eunice McAlexander
Meadows of Dan, Virginia
Morning Glory

Ruth McLoud
Amherst, Virginia
Blue Ridge View

Mrs. J. J. McDaniel
Memphis, Texas
Windmill of the Prairie

Mary McElrath
Centre, Alabama
Sunflower

Edith McGlothlin
Siloam Springs, Arkansas
*Log Cabin

Norma McGlove
Carter, Kentucky
Emblem of Honor

Annie McGukin
Starr, South Carolina
Grandma's Favorite

Edna McMurtrey
Emmet, Arkansas
Hope Watermelon

Erlby McPherson (Mrs.)
Henderson, Tennessee
Tulip Rose

Myrtle McRorey
Blackwell, Texas
Precious Memories

Mrs. C. B. Madden
Ruston, Louisiana
Mrs. Mae's Flowers

Mrs. E. E. Maddux
Daisy, Tennessee
Apple Blossom Time

Ruby Magness
Jennie, Arkansas
Night Flight

Izola B. Marple
Buckhannow, West Virginia
State of the Nation

Dorothy Marshall
Colorado Springs, Colorado
Choctaw Star

Reba Marshall
Williford, Arkansas
Stars and Tulip

Annie Bell Matthews
Flackler, Alabama
The Country Garden Trail

Alice May
Ashland, Mississippi
Bicentennial

Mrs. Leonard M. Meredith
Seguin, Texas
Country Barn

Florence Mims
Columbia, South Carolina
A Page from Farming History

Gertrude Mitchell
Russell Springs, Kentucky
1776 to 1976

Hazel Moore
Milton, North Carolina
Old Place

Lois Moore
Buffalo, Texas
The Old Rugged Cross

Bessie Mullens
Avondale, West Virginia
Paw

Mrs. W. H. Myers
Mosheine, Tennessee
Butterflies are Free

Violet D. Nemky
Pittsville, Virginia
The Fruit Jar

Mrs. Clio Niebauer
Pittsburg, Pennsylvania
Tranquility

Thalia Nimmo
Lake Creek, Texas
Six Stars Over Texas

Susan Oncal
Port Allen, Louisiana
Louisiana's Pride

Edna Penson
Alma, Arkansas
Star and Crescent

Velma Perry
Winfield, Alabama
Pride of the South

Anita Raddatz
Salt Lake City, Utah
Dancing Stars

Mrs. T. W. Redding
Asheboro, North Carolina
Cotton Boll

Suzie Rhodes
Conway, Arkansas
Four Seasons

Nancy Richardson
Zephyrhills, Florida
Sweet Heart

Mrs. Rick Russell
Red Boiling Springs, Tennessee
Dogwood Limb

Mrs. Paul Sauer
Doss, Texas
Community Church

Mrs. Theo Scrudder
Subiaco, Arkansas
The Well

Mrs. Clarence Scruggs
Fairfield, Texas
Bicentennial Star

Lucille Seed
Blanket, Texas
Rural Heritage

Barbara Setzer
Huntersville, North Carolina
Southern Dogwood

Mable Shankles
Henegar, Alabama
Ice Cream Cone

Sharon Shelley
East Ridge, Tennessee
God's Bounty

Jewell Shores
Plant City, Florida
George Washington's Cherry Tree

Teresa Shultz
Calhoun, Kentucky
Making Maple Syrup

Mrs. M. C. Sides
Lawrenceburg, Kentucky
200 Years of Progress

Martha Skelton
Vicksburg, Mississippi
Glory of Spring

Mrs. Frank Skrla
El Campo, Texas
Windmill

Mrs. Gladys Smith
Moorefield, West Virginia
Lily Garden

Lloyd R. Smith, Jr.
Lebanon, Virginia
Blue Bars, Gray Bars, No Stars

Maudy Myrtle South
Fulton, Mississippi
Burr or Sunflower

Mrs. L. B. Southerland
Mt. Olive, North Carolina
Country Memories

Pauline Staerkel
Covington, Oklahoma
My Memory Heritage

Jamie Stephenson
Lafayette, Georgia
Birds and Flowers

Mabel Stewart
Campbell, Missouri
Mirandy

Mrs. E. L. Sturm
Holland, Texas
The Out House

Mrs. Hubert Suchadoll
New Ulm, Texas
Shades of '76

Mrs. W. H. Sultemeir
Lampasas, Texas
Texas Bicentennial Star

Delma Summers
Russellville, Alabama
Summers' Family Farm

Mrs. W. A. Summers
Monroe, Louisiana
The Christmas Wreath

Mrs. G. W. Taylor
Maryville, Tennessee
Liberty

Mrs. Melvin Taylor
Lawrenceville, Virginia
Christmas Wreath

Jullia Mae Trammell
Cedar Bluff, Alabama
Christmas Poinsettia

Leila Traylor
Blackstock, South Carolina
Chiquepen Arrowhead

Ira Belle Trucks
Tarrant, Alabama
Red Rose

Edna Underwood
Piggott, Arkansas
Bicentennial Quilt

Claire Vestel
College Station, Texas
Windmill

Thelma Waller
Glasgow, Kentucky
Bicentennial

Reta Ward
McDade, Texas
My Grandmother's Rose

Ann Weeks
Emmet, Arkansas
Red Barn

R. O. Welborn
Lefors, Texas
Gray County, Texas

Mrs. Clifford Westerfield
Athens, Georgia
Cherokee Rose

Edna Williams
Paducah, Kentucky
Dr. Thomas Walker

Mary Williams
Timberville, Virginia
Old Rail Fence

Ruth Williams
Tallapoosa, Georgia
Cherokee Rose

Lillian Willis
Taylors, South Carolina
The Four Seasons

Alma Willmon
Alma, Arkansas
Basket of Flowers

Mrs. David Wilson
Etowah, Tennessee
Turkey Tracks

Laura Wilson
Clover, South Carolina
Fan

Caroline Winslow
Newbury, Pennsylvania
Pride of the South

Mable Wolford
Lake City, Florida
Florida Forest

Eugenia Youens
Saraland, Alabama
Mobile Bay

Margaret Yount
Hickory, North Carolina
Old St. Paul's Church

Nora Yount
Lenoir, North Carolina
Our Heritage, the Church

---

* These were honorable mentions selected
especially by the quilt judges Jean Ray Laury,
Lloyd Herman, and John Meigs.

Bibliography

Anderson, Donald M. *Elements of Design*. New York: Holt, Rinehart, and Winston, 1961.

Bates, Kenneth Francis. *Basic Design*. Cleveland: World Publishing Co., 1960.

Belvin, Marjorie Elliott. *Design through Discovery*. New York: Holt, Rinehart, and Winston, 1970.

Birren, Faber. *Principles of Color*. New York: Van Nostrand Reinhold Co., 1969.

Brightbill, Dorothy. *Quilting As a Hobby*. New York: Bonanza Books, 1963.

Creative Patchwork. New York: Crown Publishers, Crescent Books, 1971.

Dittrick, Mark, and Morrow, Susan. *Patchwork Plain & Fancy*. New York: Lancer Books, 1973.

Fabre, Ralph. *Artist's Guide to Composition*. New York: Watson-Guptill, 1970.

Finley, Ruth E. *Old Patchwork Quilts and the Women Who Made Them*. Newton Center, MA: Charles I. Bradford Co., 1957.

Gammell, Alice I. *Polly Prindle's Book of American Patchwork Quilts*. New York: Grosset & Dunlap, 1973.

Giberson, Gail, and Puckett, Marjorie. *Primarily Patchwork*. Redlands, CA: Cabin Craft, 1975.

Gonin, Eileen, and Newton, Jill. *Quiltmaking for Your Home*. London: Octopus Books, Ltd., 1974.

Grafton, Carol Belanger. *Traditional Patchwork Patterns*. New York: Dover Publications, Inc., 1974.

Gutcheon, Beth. *The Perfect Patchwork Primer*. New York: David McKay Co., Inc., 1973.

Heirloom Quilts to Treasure. Birmingham, AL: Oxmoor House, Inc., 1971.

Holt, Verna W. *Yarn Stitchery on the Sewing Machine*. Las Vegas NV: AMI Printing Co., 1973.

Houck, Carter, and Miller, Myron. *American Quilts and How to Make Them*. New York: Charles Scribner's Sons, 1975.

Johnson, Pauline; Loenig, Hazel; and Mosley, Spencer. *Crafts Design: An Illustrated Guide*. Belmont, CA: Wadsworth Publishing Co., Inc., 1962.

Lee Wards Illustrated Library of Arts and Crafts. Vol. 2. Montgomery, AL: Fuller and Dees, n.d.

Lewis, Alfred Allan. *The Mountain Artisans Quilting Book*. New York: Macmillan Publishing Co., Inc., 1973.

Lithgow, Marilyn. *Quiltmaking & Quiltmakers*. New York: Funk & Wagnalls, 1974.

McKain, Sharon. *The Great Noank Quilt Factory*. New York: Random House, Pequot Press, 1974.

McKim, Ruby. *101 Patchwork Patterns*. New York: Dover Publications, Inc., 1962.

Mahler, Celine Blanchard. *Once Upon a Quilt—Patchwork Design Technique*. New York: Van Nostrand Reinhold Co., 1973.

Palmer, Dennis. *Introducing Pattern: Its Development and Application*. New York: Watson-Guptill Publishing, 1970.

Pforr, Effie Chalmers. *Award Winning Quilts*. Birmingham, AL: Oxmoor House, Inc., 1974.

Sargent-Wooster, Ann. *Quiltmaking—The Modern Approach to a Traditional Craft*. New York: Drake Publishing, 1972.

Webster, Marie D. *Quilts: Their Stories and How to Make Them*. New York: Doubleday, 1928.

Index